D1286202

THE
SLIDE

THE
SLIDE

LEYLAND, BONDS, AND THE STAR-CROSSED PITTSBURGH PIRATES

RICHARD PETERSON AND STEPHEN PETERSON

UNIVERSITY OF PITTSBURGH PRESS

Published by the University of Pittsburgh Press, Pittsburgh, Pa., 15260
Copyright © 2017, University of Pittsburgh Press
All rights reserved
Manufactured in the United States of America
Printed on acid-free paper
10 9 8 7 6 5 4 3 2 1

Cataloging-in-Publication data is available from the Library of Congress

ISBN 13: 978-0-8229-6444-5
ISBN 10: 0-8229-6444-9

Jacket photograph: Copyright © *Pittsburgh Post-Gazette*, 2017, all rights
reserved. Reprinted with permission.
Jacket design: Joel W. Coggins

To Everett and Adeline

CONTENTS

Photographs follow page 101

PREFACE

FATHERS

Even before I saw my first baseball game, I fell in love with the Pittsburgh Pirates. My father was a sandlot pitcher in his day and played catch with me in the alley on the working-class South Side where we lived. With each toss, he talked about the legendary Pirates, like Pie Traynor and the Waner brothers, he had watched at old Forbes Field.

On May 2, 1948, at the age of nine, I finally saw my first Pirates game. I had no doubt the Pirates would win that day and that some Pirate would match the heroics of those greats who had thrilled my father when he was a boy. That Sunday afternoon, the Pirates did not disappoint. They defeated the Cincinnati Reds, and slugger Ralph Kiner hit two home runs off an intimidating sidewinder, Ewell Blackwell.

On the streetcar ride back to the South Side, I thought I had just spent a few hours in Baseball Heaven, where the Pirates would always win and Ralph Kiner would always hit at least two home runs. The following Sunday, however, I sat in the left-field bleachers with my father and watched the Pirates as they turned my baseball heaven into a baseball hell by losing a lopsided game in which no Pirate, not even Kiner, hit a home run.

It is a good thing my father taught me to love my Pirates before I saw them play baseball, because for the next decade, until 1958, they were terrible. In 1952, when I was playing in the Little League, Branch Rickey's "Rickey Dinks" also played like Little Leaguers and set a modern Pirates record by losing 112 games in a 154-game season. It wasn't until 1960, when I was twenty-one, that the Pirates, with one swing of Bill Mazeroski's bat, gave me the miracle I had dreamed of since that first game at Forbes Field.

In 1969 my wife, Anita, and I—with our two young daughters, Anne and Amy—moved to Carbondale, Illinois, where I had accepted a teaching position at Southern Illinois University. When the Pirates won the 1971 World Series, Anita was pregnant with our son, Stephen, who was born that November. Stephen was a bit too young to share my joy in the World Series victory, but I thought his birth was a good omen for his future life as a Pirates fan. By the time he approached the age when I saw my first Pirates game, the Pirates had won the 1979 World Series and confirmed my belief that Stephen was born under a lucky baseball star.

During much of the 1980s, as Stephen entered his teenage years, that lucky star seemed to vanish from the heavens. The Pirates lost their best players, fired a popular manager, and almost left Pittsburgh to play bad baseball in another city. But at the beginning of the 1990s that star seemed to reappear as new Pirate heroes, like Barry Bonds, Bobby Bonilla, and Andy Van Slyke, and another popular manager, Jim Leyland, led the Pirates to the postseason.

The Pirates struggled in the 1990 and 1991 playoffs, but in 1992, as Stephen approached his twenty-first birthday, they were only one out away from defeating the Atlanta Braves and winning their first National League pennant since 1979. We sat anxiously in front of our television set, praying for that last out, but in one heart-breaking moment, our dream of watching the Pirates play in the World Series was gone. With two outs and the bases loaded, little-used Braves pinch-hitter Francisco Cabrera singled home the tying run, and when former Pirate Sid Bream, carrying the winning run on his surgically repaired knees, slid home safely just ahead of Mike LaValliere's lunging tag, the Pirates suffered one of the most devastating defeats in team history.

I was stunned by the loss, but before I could say anything, Stephen burst into tears and threw his plastic foam hook at the television screen. I tried to comfort my son by telling him that pain was part of being a fan, but he was inconsolable. I even brought up my remembered joy of watching Mazeroski's miracle home run and Franco Harris's immaculate reception, but Stephen was so upset that nothing I said could ease his pain.

Former baseball commissioner and Yale president A. Bartlett Giamatti once wrote that baseball is a game that "breaks your heart. It's designed to break your heart." Giamatti could have been writing about what Stephen and I and so many Pirate fans experienced that night. At the end of three remarkable seasons the Pirates, even after two disappointing playoffs losses, raised our hopes of a World Series, once again, until a heart-breaking slide by a former Pirate who did not want to leave Pittsburgh turned our hope into hopelessness.

SONS

The Pirates won the World Series in 1971, the year I was born. I've always felt that was more than a coincidence. My own son, Everett, was born in 2013, the year the Pirates finally ended the streak of twenty losing seasons. That was also more than a coincidence in my eyes. My life has always been connected to the Pirates in some way, partially by fate, mainly because my dad didn't give me a choice. He was born and raised in downtown Pittsburgh and my mother was born and raised in nearby Coraopolis. I was not actually born in Pittsburgh, however. I've never even lived in Pittsburgh. My roots to the city consist of the two weeks every summer that I spent there visiting my grandmothers (my favorite two weeks of the year) in the 1970s and 1980s. But my father made sure that none of this mattered when it came to my sports loyalties. I was born into a world of black and gold, outfitted with Pirates hats and T-shirts, regaled with heroic stories of Clemente and Mazeroski since the day I was born, all while growing up in the middle of southern Illinois. As a result, I've been a devoted Pirates fan for forty-three years.

I was seven years old when the Pirates won the World Series in 1979. My memories of that championship run are fuzzy at best. They have less to do with the actual games than with the fun and celebration that followed. I have no memory of Willie Stargell's home run in Game 7, but I can still see the fire hydrants painted to look like Stargell on the streets of downtown Pittsburgh in the summer of 1980. That summer I also saw my first Pirates game (my first professional baseball game anywhere) at Three Rivers Stadium, a rainy night game against the Mets that would barely register as an official game. It was my first win, though, and I was instantly hooked. It was less than a year since the Pirates had won the World Series and the place was electric. I attended the game with my whole family, my mom, my dad, and my two sisters. My dad bought me a

Dave Parker button and the notorious pillbox hat, both of which I wore every day for the rest of the summer. The game went into a rain delay in the fifth inning and we spent most our time playing along with games posted on the jumbotron. But I had also seen Stargell, Parker, and some of the great Pirates of the 1970s play that night. I had also unknowingly fallen in love with the entire experience and this baseball team. My love, although severely tested through the years, would never waiver.

Like most kids, my rooting for the Pirates may have started when they were winning, but it solidified while they were losing. I was born and raised in Carbondale, Illinois, a small college town located about two hours southeast of St. Louis and six hours south of Chicago. Most of the kids I grew up with were devoted Cardinals fans; the rest rooted for the Cubs. But in my younger days, in the late 1970s and early 1980s, I was rarely teased because the Pirates were good. In the 1980s, when my baseball memories finally had to do with baseball, the Pirates were really bad. All those Cardinals and Cubs fans reminded me just how bad throughout my adolescence. My pillbox hat became less cool every year. It would have been much easier just to become a Cardinals fan, but my loyalty to the Pirates was too deep already.

In the late 1980s that loyalty finally paid off. When the Bucs finally returned to the National League Championship Series (NLCS) in the fall of 1990, I was a directionless high school graduate, working at a fast food fish place. Nothing much was going right for me, but after years of bad teams, the Pirates came through when I needed them the most. The Pirates finally had a winner, and I finally had my own greats to worship, like Bonds, Bonilla, and Van Slyke. My dad and I—who weren't seeing eye-to-eye on much at that time—had something to share.

The Pirates would stay good for the next few years, returning to the NLCS in 1991 and 1992. During that time my dad and I watched every Pirate game we could together. When the Pirates lost in 1990 and 1991, we shared the losses together. He got me through both of them, reminding me that it was just a game and there was always next year. But nothing prepared us for what was then to come. When Sid Bream slid into home plate in Game 7 of the 1992 NLCS, I was sitting next to my dad once again. It was the only time in my life I cried after a sporting event of any kind. I was devastated. And unlike Stargell's home run, I remember it all—Lind's error, Bream chugging around the bases—like it happened yesterday. My grandmother had mailed me a foam Pirates hook from Pittsburgh that I wore on my hand throughout the entire series. I threw it down afterward, inconsolable. I can still see it lying on the floor the next morning. My dad knew nothing would make things better. It was the worst Pirates loss in their history, and he knew it. At least we went through it together.

After that loss and the two decades of hell that followed, it again would have been easy to jump ship. People still ask me how I stayed loyal to this team all this time, and I tell them it is not a choice. I'm a Pirates fan until I die, like my dad and as my son will be too.

ACKNOWLEDGMENTS

We have many present and past members of the Pirates organization to thank for their cooperation and support, but we'd like to begin with Jim Leyland, who was generous and gracious with his time. We'd also like to thank Sid Bream, Darnell Coles, Doug Drabek, Bob Kipper, Bill Landrum, Mike LaValliere, Roger Mason, Bob Patterson, Chris Peters, Don Slaught, Zane Smith, Paul Wagner, Bob Walk, and John Wehner for sharing stories of their ball-playing days with the Pirates.

Besides Walk and Wehner, we'd like to thank other members of the Pirates broadcasting team, including Steve Blass, Greg Brown, Lanny Frattare, and Rob King for sharing their memories. We appreciate the help of Dan Hart, Neal Huntington, Patti Mistick, and Jim Trdinich for their help when we visited the archives at PNC Park.

Our deepest gratitude to a member of the Pirates family goes to the late Sally O'Leary, long-time Alumni Liaison with the Pirates and the editor of the Pirates alumni newsletter, for her invaluable close reading of the manuscript and for the many interviews that she arranged for us. Sally was recently given the first Woman of the Year Award presented at the Rotary Club's annual Chuck Tanner Awards banquet. The award is now named in her honor.

During the preparation of our book, we had the good fortune of talking with writers of numerous baseball columns, articles, personal essays, and books, including Gene Collier, Paul Meyers, John Mehno, Laurie Graham, and Erik Sherman. We are especially grateful to Jeff Pearlman, author of *Love Me, Hate Me: Barry Bonds and the Making of an Antihero*, for sharing his challenging experiences in writing his book on Bonds. Special thanks also go to Joe Shuta, the talk show host for *Leading Off* out of Altoona, for his insights and for his help in setting up interviews for our book.

Those helping with the research include Jim Gates of the Baseball Hall of Fame, Brian Butko of the Heinz History Center, Gil Pietrzak of the Pennsylvania Room in the Carnegie Library, and George Skornickel, president of the Forbes Field chapter of the Society for American Baseball Research. We'd like to thank Mario Moccia, current athletic director at New Mexico State, for sharing his experiences playing college baseball with Barry Bonds, and we offer special thanks to Sam Reich for his many insights into Pirates history, especially the Pittsburgh cocaine trials.

Our thanks to the editors of the University of Pittsburgh Press begin with Maria Sticco, chief publicist, who encouraged us to submit our proposal and was its earliest supporter. We thank Josh Shanholtzer, senior acquisition editor, for his enthusiasm throughout the project and his insights and guidance from the early stages to the completion of the manuscript, and Alex Wolfe, editorial and production manager, for his preparation of the manuscript.

Our last expression of gratitude goes to our wives, Anita and Anna, for their encouragement, understanding, and patience. While it often isn't easy being a baseball fan, it's much more challenging and difficult being the wife of a baseball fan. No matter what our frustrations and anxieties, Anita and Anna never wavered in rooting for us.

THE
SLIDE

CHAPTER ONE

THE DECLINE AND FALL OF THE PIRATES FAMILY

The 1980–1985 Seasons

As over forty-four thousand Pirates fans headed to Three Rivers Stadium for the home opener of the 1980 season, they had every reason to feel optimistic about the Pirates and Pittsburgh sports in general. In the 1970s, their Pirates had captured six divisional titles, two National League pennants, and two World Series championships. Their Steelers, after decades of futility, had won four Super Bowls in the 1970s, while the University of Pittsburgh Panthers led by Heisman Trophy winner Tony Dorsett added to the excitement by winning a collegiate national championship in football. There was no reason for Pittsburgh sports fans to doubt that the 1980s would bring even more titles to the City of Champions.

After the "We Are Family" Pirates, led by Willie Stargell, won the 1979 World Series, the ballclub's goals for 1980 were "Two in a Row and Two Million Fans."[1] If the Pirates repeated as World Series champions, it would mark the first time that a Pirates team had accomplished that feat in franchise history. If two million fans came out to Three Rivers Stadium to see the Pirates win back-to-back World Series titles, it would break the attendance record of 1,705,828, set at Forbes Field during the improbable championship season of 1960. The offseason after the 1979 World Series victory was a whirlwind of awards and honors, highlighted by World Series Most Valuable Player (MVP) Willie Stargell and Super Bowl MVP Terry Bradshaw of the Steelers appearing on the cover of the December 24, 1979, *Sports Illustrated* as corecipients of the magazine's Sportsman of the Year Award.

The Pirates had lost veteran pitcher Bruce Kison to free agency during the off season, but manager Chuck Tanner replaced Kison by moving 1978 *Sporting News* Rookie Pitcher of the Year Don Robinson into the starting rotation. Utility infielder Rennie Stennett also opted for free agency, but the Pirates already had a strong infield with Bill Madlock, Tim Foli, and Phil Garner, all acquired in brilliant trades in 1979 by General Manager (GM) Harding "Pete" Peterson. With "Pops" Stargell at first base, Dave Parker in the outfield, and a veteran bullpen led by Kent Tekulve, the 1980 Pirates were considered by many to be heavy favorites to defend their World Series title. During spring training, there was a brief walkout and threatened player strike, but the Pirates had almost their entire starting lineup returning and were a confident team when they opened the season in St. Louis. After taking three out of four games from the Cardinals, they headed to Three Rivers Stadium in Pittsburgh for their home opener against the Cubs.

Rain threatened throughout the pregame festivities, which included Sister Sledge delighting the sellout crowd with a rendition of the team's 1979 theme song. Pirates players received several awards and honors during the pregame ceremony, but the moment that drew the greatest roar from the crowd came when the team received its World Series rings. Outfielder Bill Robinson said, "This was a special day in my life. . . . Getting the ring. It meant so much to me."[2] Once the game started, there were four rain delays totaling more than two hours, but the fans who stayed to the end saw a dramatic victory they hoped was a harbinger of things to come in the 1980 season. Leading 4–2 in the top of the ninth, the Pirates brought in the usually reliable Tekulve, but he yielded the tying runs that sent the game into extra innings. In the bottom of the tenth, Robinson gave fans a reminder of the heroics of the 1979 World Series in which the Pirates rallied from a 3-games-to-1 deficit when he homered to give the Pirates a 5–4 victory and their fourth win in a row.

After a fast start in April, however, the Pirates dealt with a variety of injuries, slumps, and clubhouse distractions and struggled to stay above .500 in May and June. Though several players were having sub-par years, discontented Pirates fans vented their unhappiness on Parker, who had signed a five-year seven-million-dollar contract going into the 1979 season, the largest in the major leagues at that time. On July 20, 1979, the frustration grew ugly when a fan threw a battery at Parker from the upper deck of the right-field stands at Three Rivers in the eighth inning of the first game of a double-header between the Pirates and the Los Angeles Dodgers.[3] The timing of the incident was unfortunate for the Pirates because they had scheduled a Willie Stargell Day celebration between games of the doubleheader. More than forty thousand fans watched the Pirates shower Stargell with gifts ranging from a mink cowboy hat to a solid gold star, while Parker, who removed himself from the first game after the battery barely missed his head, stood in anger and tears at the ceremony.[4] Afterward, Parker told reporters that racism was behind the incident and asked the Pirates to trade him. Years later, in his autobiography, Stargell claimed that, after the battery incident, Parker "played the game out of hate and revenge instead of love."[5]

Despite their early struggles, the Pirates bounced back in July and moved into first place. As late as August 24, they were on top of their division, two games ahead of the Expos. Unfortunately, the Pirates lost thirteen of their next fifteen games, and they never recovered. When they went on a seven-game losing streak in late September, their pursuit of a division title and National League pennant and their dream of becoming the first Pirates team to repeat as World Series champions were over.

Throughout the 1970s, the Pirates had developed a reputation for late-season surges that carried them to the top of their division and into the postseason. The problem in 1980 was that an experienced championship team became an aging, often injured team. The Pirates began the season by losing pitcher Jim Rooker to a career-ending arm injury and finished the season with Stargell on the disabled list. Every regular failed to match the production of his 1979 season, and veteran starting pitchers, including Bert Blyleven and John Candelaria, as well as bullpen ace Tekulve, finished with a losing record.

During the 1980–1981 offseason, GM Peterson's biggest move was to acquire hard-hitting first baseman Jason Thompson from the California Angels. An optimistic Stargell had signed a two-year contract at the end of the 1980 season, but Peterson wanted insurance in case the forty-one-year-old Stargell could not come back after his season-ending injury. Peterson also traded away Blyleven, who was unhappy pitching in Tanner's five-man rotation, but the Pirates' GM felt that younger pitchers like Rick Rhoden and Eddie Solomon were ready to step up. He also believed that several players from the farm system, including catcher Tony Peña and infielders Dale Berra and Vance Law, would strengthen the Pirates' regular lineup.

The hope that 1981 would mark an easy transition proved mistaken, but it was something beyond the Pirates' performance on the field that turned the 1981 season into a disaster. Three months into the season, after acrimonious negotiations between the Major League Baseball Players Association (MLBPA) and team owners over a new contract and free agency compensation reached a stalemate, Players Association president Marvin Miller declared, "We have accomplished nothing. The strike is on."[6] The long and bitter players' strike began on June 12, 1981, and lasted until July 31, though games did not resume until August 10. With more than one-third of the 1981 season lost to the strike, Major League Baseball commissioner Bowie Kuhn decided to divide the season into two halves, with the division winners of each half meeting in a playoff. At the time of the walkout the Pirates stood at 25–23 and were in fourth place. When the season resumed, the Pirates went into a tailspin, never recovered, and ended the second half with a record of 21–33 and a last-place finish.

After just two seasons, the Pirates had gone from favorites to repeat as World Series champions to a team expected to finish last in its division. A franchise that had hoped to attract two million fans in 1980 now hoped that one million would show up in 1982 (only 541,789 paid their way into Three Rivers in the strike-shortened 1981 season). When the Pirates opened the 1982 season, only three starters from the 1979 World Series champions were in the lineup: Omar Moreno, Parker, and Madlock. Moreno would be a free agent at the end of the season, and an overweight, unhappy Parker would follow a year later. Stargell was still on the team, but injuries reduced him to pinch-hitting in what would be his last season.

Other than the optimistic manager Tanner, no one was surprised when the Pirates were nine games under .500 at the end of May 1982, but thanks to the hot hitting of Thompson and Madlock and excellent starting and relief pitching, the Pirates surged in July and August to six games over. They went back to the future to pick up Richie Hebner, who played on the 1971 World Series championship team, at midseason, but they also got help from youngsters Johnny Ray and Peña. Ray was named the *Sporting News* 1982 National League Rookie of the Year. For the first time since 1979, the Pirates had a winning record in September, and they finished the 1982 season at 84–78, good for fourth place in their division.

The Pirates did manage to reach their modest goal of attracting one million fans, but the final figure was only 1,024,106 for the 1982 season, which was 622,651 less than their last full-season attendance in 1980, and an average home attendance of only 12,643, second lowest in the major leagues ahead of only Minnesota. Moreover, the Pirates would have finished the 1982 season with attendance under one million if more than 38,000 fans had not come to Three Rivers for a second Willie Stargell Day. The Pirates held the ceremony honoring Stargell's retirement on Labor Day, because Pittsburgh was in the midst of a Rust Belt depression. Stargell asked the Pirates to turn the event into a fundraiser for unemployed steelworkers. Fans attending the game were asked to bring cans of food to the stadium. In thanking the crowd, Stargell told them, "During these trying times economically, there are a lot of people who would like to work and can't."[7]

While a dark economic cloud hung over the city, the Pirates had reason for optimism going into the 1983 season. After defying predictions of a losing record and possible last-place finish in 1982, the Pirates were once again regarded as contenders by sportswriters and fans. Stargell was gone, but Parker, knowing he was headed for free agency, came into camp in great shape, as did Madlock, who went on to win the National League batting title, as he had in 1975, 1976, and 1981. With a strong starting rotation headed by Rhoden, Candelaria, and newly acquired Larry McWilliams, and a durable Tekulve heading the bullpen, the Pirates looked poised to oust the St. Louis Cardinals as division champions.

Despite their talent and optimism, the Pirates played inconsistent baseball and struggled in the first half of the 1983 season. By mid-June, they were thirteen games under .500. They received a boost after the All-Star break, however, with the July call-up of rookie pitching sensation José DeLeón and went on a tear that took them over .500 and within a few games of first place. On September 17, they were in a first-place tie with the Philadelphia Phillies, but with Madlock out with a torn calf muscle, the Pirates' bats cooled off, and the pitching could not carry them past the division-leading Phillies. They lost eight of their last fourteen games and finished the season in second place at 84–78, an improvement in the standings but with the same record they had in 1982.

As a parting "gift" for Parker, a fan threw another battery at him from the upper deck on September 10, 1983. With the season nearly over, Parker stayed in the game and dismissed the incident. In the clubhouse he told reporters, "I have 19, 20 more days on my contract here and no one is going to intimidate me out there."[8] During the offseason, Parker signed a multiyear contract with his hometown Cincinnati Reds. With Parker lost to free agency, the consensus going into the 1984 season was that, for the Pirates to remain contenders they would need to trade a veteran pitcher to strengthen the offense. To the astonishment of sportswriters, fans, and even some of the players, Peterson did just the opposite when he traded Mike Easler, the Pirates' most consistent hitter for the past few seasons, to the Red Sox for pitching ace John Tudor.

With Tudor added to an already strong starting rotation, Pirates pitchers would go on to lead the National League in 1984 with a 3.11 earned run average, but they had little support from the team's offense. Accustomed to watching sluggers like Roberto Clemente, Stargell, and Parker in the 1970s, Pirates fans now looked out at a mix of no-names and has-beens, ranging from newcomers Marvell Wynne, Joe Orsulak, and Doug Frobel to veterans Lee Mazzilli, Amos Otis, and Milt May, a rookie in the 1971 World Series, who hit just one home run and batted only .177 in 1984. The only remaining regular from the 1979 World Series champions was Madlock. As team captain he questioned, even before the season started, how the Pirates offense would score without Parker and Easler. When GM Peterson failed to trade for more offense, Candelaria, who had won the critical sixth game in the 1979 World Series, called Peterson "a bozo" and an "idiot."[9] To make matters worse, outstanding relief pitcher Rod Scurry revealed that he had a drug problem and headed into rehab.

Predictably, the Pirates got off to a poor start in 1984 and finished April in last place, where they stayed for the rest of the season. With disgusted fans staying away from Three Rivers, attendance dropped from 1,225,916 in 1983 to 773,500, the lowest figure for a full season of play in the stadium's history. The Pirates did play better in September, but they finished the season in last place in their division with a record of 75–87. Going into the 1985 season, the Pirates were a team in turmoil, but the worst was yet to come, including the threat of a move to another city.

If ever the Pirates experienced a complete disaster in franchise history, it was the during the 1985 season. It actually began during the offseason when the Galbreath family decided to sell the franchise. John W. Galbreath, who built a fortune in real estate and horse breeding, bought into ownership in 1946 and became majority owner in 1950. But the Galbreaths had become increasingly frustrated with the team's poor play, falling attendance, and financial losses, and they decided it was time to step aside. The family, who lived in Columbus, Ohio, were also upset with fan perceptions that they were absentee landlords and unwilling to spend money to improve the ballclub. Dan Galbreath, John's son and the team president at the time, complained that, even though the family had put time, effort, and money into the franchise for twenty-nine years and had given Pittsburgh three World Series championships, fans were constantly comparing his family unfavorably with the Rooneys: "Hey, the Steelers went nearly forty years without winning a damned thing. But did Art Rooney catch hell here? Of course not. Why? Because he's Irish, and he's Catholic and he's lovable. In this city, he can do no wrong."[10] They hoped to sell the franchise to local ownership, but if that failed, they would listen to offers from those interested in moving the franchise to another city.

Realizing his own future in Pittsburgh was in a precarious position after the Tudor-Easler trade, Peterson tried to improve the Pirates' poor offense by turning around and trading Tudor, a potential twenty-game winner, to the St. Louis Cardinals for outfielder George Hendrick. He also sent a package of players, including Berra, and outstanding prospect, Jay Buhner, to the Yankees for outfielder Steve Kemp and Foli, the shortstop for the 1979 World Series champions. Peterson thought that he was getting players capable of hitting twenty-five home runs and driving in one hundred runs in Kemp and Hendrick and a solid defensive player in Foli, but he soon found out that Kemp and Hendrick were damaged goods and that Foli no longer had the range to play shortstop. Now thirty-five years old, Hendrick was coming off an unproductive and injury-prone season with the Cardinals in which he hit only nine home runs and had sixty-nine runs batted in. He was unhappy about being traded from a contender to a struggling ballclub with an uncertain future. He expressed his dissatisfaction by refusing to talk with the press and merely going through the motions on the playing field. When he failed to run out groundballs, he quickly replaced the departed Parker as the most hated ballplayer in the hearts of Pirates fans, who dubbed Hendrick "Joggin' George."

While there was no questioning Kemp's heart—he was so aggressive at bat that when he swung and missed a pitch, his body corkscrewed like a character out of a Looney Tunes cartoon. He had a bad shoulder that limited him to ninety-four games for the Yankees in 1984 with seven home runs and only forty-one runs batted in (RBIs). When he arrived at the Pirates' spring training camp in 1985, he was sporting a lengthy scar from offseason surgery that Peterson knew nothing about. Kemp swung with the gusto of Babe Ruth, but with no power left in his shoulder he went well into the 1985 season before he hit his first home run and finished the season with only two, the same number hit by Hendrick before he was traded in late season to the California Angels.

The problem with having a bad ballclub in Pittsburgh in 1985 was that it coincided with the city's deepening Rust Belt depression. During its Smoky City days as the country's leading producer of steel, Pittsburgh developed a strong reputation as a working-class town. For the Pirates, that meant that ever since Barney Dreyfuss took over ownership of the franchise at the beginning of the twentieth century, the team identified with and relied upon a working-class fan base. Dreyfuss's proudest boast was that "We are a first-division town, and I am a first-division club owner."[11]

During the early 1980s, 130,000 jobs were lost in Pittsburgh as the steel industry eliminated 90 percent of its workers. U.S. Steel on its own eliminated 30,000 jobs. The city also experienced a drop of 176,000 in population, including 14 percent of its young people.[12] With the steel mills closing, the unemployment rate double the national average, and the city's population in decline, the Pirates faced a diminishing fan base.

The Decline and Fall of the Pirates Family

Instead of fathers taking their sons to a Pirates game, they were taking their families to another city in search of a job.

With the team playing poor baseball, the fans who were still willing to spend money to come to Three Rivers came in a surly mood. Thompson, who had signed a multiyear contract after the 1982 season, complained, "If I had known the team would go the way it has, I wouldn't have signed. Everything has been so negative for two years. Opening day this year they booed us." When 14,029 showed up in mid-April for Buck Night, a promotion that offered fans a general admission seat for one dollar as well as a coupon for a hot dog and a drink, Pittsburgh sportswriter Bob Smizik saw the attendance as a rare positive sign. On the night of the same promotion a year prior, the Pirates had drawn only 2,752 fans. He pointed out that Peterson had called 1985 a crisis year for the Pirates, "the most important season in the history of the franchise."[13] Peterson believed that if the Pirates could play well, reconnect with the community, and draw a million fans to Three Rivers that would be a sign to new owners to keep the team in Pittsburgh.

The Pirates started out 1985 with a record of 14–28, and the desperately hopeful Peterson did not have a chance to see the season through to the end. Growing increasingly frustrated with the poor play of the Pirates and the lack of interest by potential buyers, the Galbreath family fired Peterson and asked Joe L. Brown to return as general manager. Brown was the architect of the Pirates' 1960 and 1971 World Series championship teams. When he retired in 1976, Peterson had been the man who replaced him. Now Brown took over for Peterson.

What Brown discovered was a ballclub lacking in leadership in the clubhouse and on the field: "The retirement of Willie Stargell left us without a dominant personality. There's no one to capture the imagination." Thompson believed that when the Pirates lost Parker and Easler they lost more than their bats in the lineup: "Both guys were upbeat. They were leaders. When we lost them we lost a lot." Adding to the problem was the negative atmosphere in Pittsburgh. Brown continued, "It's tough to play where almost everything you read and hear is negative—possible sale of the club, possible move of the franchise. . . . Baseball generally is drawing well, but not here. Crowds help players. Players like to have their accomplishments recognized and applauded." Earlier in the season, the outspoken Candelaria had claimed, "There's a lot of guys who'd like to get out. . . . If you asked, I'll bet half the people here would say they want out." Even the optimistic Tanner admitted that he never had seen a season with so many distractions. "It's been a very difficult year for everything, as if there was a black cloud hanging over us."[14]

The Pirates management tried to attract fans to Three Rivers, but every move seemed to fail. On May 3, 1985, the Pirates brought back the legendary Bob Prince to the broadcasting booth, ten years after firing Prince and his partner Nellie King in one of the most unpopular decisions ever made by the franchise. When he was introduced to Pirates fans, Prince received a standing ovation. Incredibly, when Prince starting broadcasting the game, the weak Pirates offense came to life and scored nine runs in the first inning. When Thompson came to bat, Prince told Pirates fans, "We've had everything else. Jason might as well ding one." As if on cue, Thompson hit a home run. The Pirates went on to a lopsided 16–2 victory over the Dodgers. Sadly, Prince was in failing health and died a few weeks after his broadcast.

In another attempt to revive fan interest, on June 30, with rumors swirling that the Pirates would be leaving the city, the Pirates held a Ballot by Ballpark Day to save the franchise. Fans were encouraged to "vote" their support of the team by coming to the game. An impressive crowd of 31,384 showed up, the largest crowd at Three Rivers Stadium since Opening Day, but unfortunately the Pirates failed to show up on the field and lost to the Cubs, 9–2. Fans were so disgusted with the team's poor play that many began rooting for the Cubs and booing the Pirates. Calling Pirates fans "miserable people," infielder Jim Morrison told a sportswriter, "This is a miserable environment to play baseball. There were 31,000 here today, and 26,000 were rooting for the Cubs and 5,000 were cheering for us. My opinion is that it's time for the team to move."[15]

That season, pitcher Bob Walk was trying to resurrect his career with the Pirates after being released from Atlanta, but he recognized that the 1985 Pirates "were a sinking ship." Players were openly expressing their desire to get out of Pittsburgh, and attendance was poor. The pitcher remembered walking from the dugout to the bullpen before the start of games, looking up, and seeing row after row and deck after deck of empty seats. There were more fans coming to games in Buffalo, where Walk had started the 1985 season in the minor leagues, than there were coming to Three Rivers to watch a Pirates team that "was going down hill fast."[16]

◆◇◆

As if poor play and fan disgust were not bad enough, a Pittsburgh grand jury began deliberations in May in what would become known as the "Pittsburgh Drug Trials." What emerged from grand jury testimony was a clear indication that the use of drugs, including cocaine, was common at Three Rivers Stadium. The names of current Pirates Rod Scurry and Lee Mazzilli, as well as former players Dave Parker, John Milner, Lee Lacy, and Dale Berra turned up in the testimony, as well as that of Kenneth Koch. Employed as the Pirate Parrot team mascot, Koch was accused of being a go-between for dealers and Pirates players.

On May 30 and 31, 1985, the grand jury came back with indictments for seven dealers but no customers, which meant that no ballplayers were indicted. Even Koch escaped an indictment because he cooperated with FBI agents during the investigation. Players, including current and former Pirates, would have to testify at the upcoming trials, but under immunity from prosecution. As for the indicted dealers, Aaron Skirboll described them in The Pittsburgh Cocaine Seven "as a ragtag group of seven local men. The Pittsburgh cocaine seven consisted of a pair of heating repairmen, an accountant, a bartender, a caterer, a land surveyor, and an out-of-work photographer. . . . nothing more than an assortment of sports groupies."[17]

The first to go to trial was Curtis Strong, a part-time caterer who was from Philadelphia. The most shocking testimony during the trial came from Berra. When questioned by Strong's defense attorney about amphetamines, or "greenies," Berra claimed they were easily available in the Pirates clubhouse. When asked, "From whom did you get amphetamines in Pittsburgh?" he responded, "From Bill Madlock." When asked, "Who else, if anyone, did you get them from?" he shocked those at the trial by responding, "From Willie Stargell."[18] Madlock, who was still on the Pirates team, and the retired Stargell, who had returned to the team in 1985 as a first-base coach to help with player morale, vehemently denied the accusation. Stargell would later be cleared of Berra's accusation by baseball commissioner Peter Ueberroth, but the stain of the drug trials would convince many fans that the money they spent at the ballpark was being used to support players' drug habits.

While Berra's testimony was the most sensational during the trial, former Pirate and current Cincinnati Red Parker was the main attraction among the witnesses and drew a crowd. During his examination by federal attorney Alan Johnson, Parker described cocaine as a recreational drug, "sort of the in-thing to do. . . . Cocaine was becoming vastly popular in society and was constantly available because of who I was."[19] Sam Reich, the Pittsburgh attorney who represented Parker, recalled in an interview the circus atmosphere as Parker arrived at the courthouse. Reporters and photographers hounded Parker when he entered and left the building, and at one point a reporter yelled out, "What about the kids?" Parker's response was that it was "my mistake" and has "nothing to do with kids."[20] Reich also remembered that Pete Rose, the manager of the Reds, wanted Parker in the lineup even on the days he was testifying, so the unhappy Parker had to fly back and forth between Pittsburgh and Cincinnati during the trials.

When Strong's defense attorney, Adam Renfroe, who confronted every government witness about the money he was making as a ballplayer, cross-examined Parker, he first drew attention to Parker's "twenty-five thousand dollar Rolex watch" and his "twenty-thousand dollar diamond rings." He then challenged Parker's testimony that he just "having fun" by accusing him of destroying the careers of younger players like Scurry and Berra by introducing them to drugs. He then asked, "How do you carry that burden, knowing because of you the Pirates went from the world championship to being the worst in the National League?" Parker's response was that he did not carry "that burden because I don't take responsibility for what adults do."[21]

On September 20, 1985, after nine hours of deliberation, the jury convicted Strong on eleven counts of selling cocaine. On November 5, Federal District Judge Gustave Diamond, after sentencing Strong to twelve years in prison, criticized the players who testified under a cloak of immunity and the gullible fans who still supported and applauded them. Days later, Robert McCue, the only other accused dealer to stand trial, was also convicted and sentenced to ten years. The remaining five worked out plea deals and received lighter prison terms.

Looking back on the trials, Reich believed that the defendants were poorly represented by Renfroe who used the trials as a platform for his own theatrics and was eventually cited for contempt of court. He said that the cases against the "Cocaine Seven" should have ended in plea bargains, and that the trials should never have taken place. But they did, and as a result, drug use among ballplayers, which was common on teams around the major leagues, was perceived as a "Pittsburgh problem" and became an embarrassment to the city.[22]

After the trials, Parker was sued by the Pirates, who still owed him millions of dollars in deferred salary, for breach of contract. The Pirates claimed, among other things, that Parker was responsible for "the poisoning of the team's relationship with the fans and the sports press."[23] The team and Parker eventually settled out of court. Berra and Scurry continued their struggles with cocaine addiction. In 1989 Berra was arrested for possession of cocaine and agreed to a three-year intervention program, which he completed in 1992. In late October of the same year, Scurry, who still struggled with his addiction, collapsed into a coma after a drug overdose. He died a few days later, on November 5, at the age of thirty-six.

As the 1985 season deteriorated, Brown managed to get rid of malcontents like Madlock, Candelaria, and Hendrick and those associated with the growing drug scandal, like Scurry, who was shipped to the Yankees, where he joined Berra. Brown's moves, however, had little effect on the team's performance. Even the Pirates' younger players, probably demoralized by the ballclub's misfortunes and threatened move, suffered through off years. Peña's average dipped from .286 to .249, while former rookie sensation Ray dropped from .312 to .274. The only exception was Sid Bream, a young first baseman acquired from the Los Angeles Dodgers in midseason, who was destined to play a key role in Pirates history, but this was several years later, and for the wrong team.

Perhaps no player exemplified the Pirates collapse more than pitcher DeLeón, who just two seasons before was considered a rising star. Toward the end of the 1985 season, when DeLeón's record sank to an abysmal 2–19, Tanner sat his young pitcher on the bench so he would not suffer the ignominy of losing twenty games, a fate not suffered by a Pirates pitcher since Murry Dickson in 1952. Tanner may have spared DeLeón, but he could not prevent the Pirates from losing 104 games, the franchise's most losses since 1953—tied for the third most losses in Pittsburgh baseball history, better only than the 1952 Pirates, who lost 112 games, and the 1890 Alleghenies, who lost 113.

Tanner also could not prevent getting fired himself. At the end of the season, he told his coaching staff, which included Bob Skinner, Grant

Jackson, and Stargell, all veterans of World Series championship teams, that new ownership probably would want a fresh start next season and that he would not be returning as manager. It was another dark moment for fans who remembered that Tanner, who grew up in New Castle, just forty-five miles from Pittsburgh, had inspired the Pirates in the 1979 World Series by continuing to manage the team after his mother died just before Game 5. With the Pirates trailing 3–1 in games, he told his team, "My mother is a great Pirates fan. She knows we're in trouble, so she went upstairs to get some help."[24] At the end of the 1985 season, there appeared to be no help, divine or otherwise, for the Pirates. After hoping that an attendance of more than one million fans might convince new owners to keep the team in Pittsburgh, the Pirates finished the season with a home attendance of 735,900, down slightly from the previous year. After their remarkable record in the 1970s, which culminated in a dramatic victory in the 1979 World Series, the Pirates, just six seasons later, had finished the season with one of the worst records in team history and had drawn national attention as the most dysfunctional franchise in baseball.

The September 9, 1985, issue of the *Sporting News* appeared on newsstands around the country with a cover photograph of empty seats at Three Rivers Stadium. The banner across the photograph read, "Empty Hopes, Empty Seats." Inside was a feature article by senior correspondent David Nightingale, detailing the reasons for what he perceived as the death of baseball in Pittsburgh. As far as Nightingale was concerned, the 1979 Pirates' theme song, "We Are Family," had become a "dirge," and Three Rivers Stadium "a funeral parlor."[25] One of the harshest indictments of Pittsburgh fans in Nightingale's article was that the Pirates, the first franchise in MLB history to field an all-black line-up back in 1971, had "too many black players for their own good" in a city of "first-, second- and third-generation European immigrants" not known for their "color blindness."[26] Garner, a member of the 1979 World Series–winning team, told Nightingale that when he played his "first game for Pittsburgh, after coming over from Oakland, the plate umpire asked how it felt to break the color barrier."[27]

Interim GM Brown admitted that "Pittsburgh is a difficult town for blacks." He believed that Pittsburgh's white ethnic population felt threatened by the passage of the Fair Employment Practices Act, which opened unions to minorities, especially once the Rust Belt depression led to so many job losses: "So it was hard for many of them to accept a black idol on the baseball field despite the fact that Roberto Clemente, Willie Stargell and Parker were our most popular players at their respective times." Echoing Brown's judgment, Garner told Nightingale that "Pittsburgh is blue-collar, Middle America, and the current baseball product just doesn't fit that market." Selling the current product, "well, it's like trying to sell swimsuits in Alaska."[28]

The first Pittsburgh team in the National League to sell its product to baseball fans took the field in 1887. During its long history, the franchise had become one of the most fabled in baseball history. The Pirates played in the first World Series in 1903 and went on to win five World Series, each in a seventh and deciding game. Over the years, Pittsburgh fans watched baseball legends like Honus Wagner, Pie Traynor, Bill Mazeroski, Clemente, and Stargell lead the Pirates to world championships. As the 1985 season came to an end, the Pittsburgh Pirates franchise should have been starting preparations for the celebration of its centennial year in the National League. Instead, it faced the likelihood that the Pirates, after ninety-nine years in Pittsburgh, would be selling their product the next season in another city. The city of Pittsburgh desperately needed a hero to save it from an approaching sports calamity, and it would find one in a Pittsburgh kid who grew up to become mayor.

CHAPTER TWO

THE UNKNOWNS SYD THRIFT AND JIM LEYLAND

The 1986–1989 Seasons

On October 19, 1990, a statue honoring former Pittsburgh mayor Richard Caliguiri was unveiled at the entrance to the City-County Building. Caliguiri had served as mayor from 1977 until his death in 1988 at the age of fifty-six. He was, in many ways, the architect of the city's recovery after its Rust Belt depression, a recovery that became known as Renaissance II, in recognition of the city's first renaissance begun by Mayor David L. Lawrence in the 1950s to rid Pittsburgh of its "smoky city" reputation. Caliguiri's greatest strengths as mayor were his optimism about Pittsburgh's future and his ability to form partnerships with community, corporate, and academic leaders. Under his leadership, Pittsburgh transformed itself from a dying industrial giant into a vibrant home for technology and the arts.

The nine-foot bronze statue has Caliguiri, hands in pockets, staring down at a street map of Pittsburgh's Downtown area. He grew up in the Greenfield neighborhood and graduated from Allderdice High School in 1950. He first learned his way around the city's streets when, as a young boy, he kept his father company on early morning milk deliveries. He began his career in city government in the parks and recreation department, which he eventually headed. He was elected to Pittsburgh's city council in 1971 and, six years later, as city council president replaced Mayor Pete Flaherty when Flaherty joined the Jimmy Carter administration. Caliguiri's legacy included the development of riverfront projects, like the Station Square mall on Pittsburgh's South Side, and the revival of the Golden Triangle, including the construction of Mellon Center, Oxford Centre, and PPG Place. Recognizing that Renaissance I had done little for the arts, he also led the renovation of the old Downtown movie district as the city's cultural center. One of Caliguiri's greatest challenges, however, and one of his finest moments as mayor came in the same year that Pittsburgh was named America's most livable city by Rand McNally and one of the country's top twenty-one major cities by the *U.S. News and World Report*.[1] In 1985 Caliguiri, an avid Pirates fan, faced the likelihood that his city was going to lose its Major League Baseball franchise.

At the October 19, 1990, unveiling no one could have blamed a Pittsburgh sports fan if he had placed a Pirates cap on the head of Mayor Caliguiri's statue. Just one week earlier, the Pirates had lost the National League Championship Series to the Cincinnati Reds, but it was their first postseason appearance since 1979. Led by the hitting of Barry Bonds and the pitching of Doug Drabek, the Pirates had finished the season in first place in their division with a record of 95–67, a twenty-one-game improvement over 1989. During the offseason, Bonds would be named the National League Most Valuable Player, Doug Drabek, the NL Cy Young Award winner, and Jim Leyland the NL Manager of the Year. Also important, the Pirates had reached the two million attendance goal they originally set after the 1979 World Series championship season. In 1990, a record-breaking 2,049,908 fans came out to Three Rivers Stadium to watch their Pirates play baseball.

Things were far different and darker in Pittsburgh at the end of the 1985 season. The Pirates were up for sale and, with no serious local interest, were on the verge of moving to another city. At that point Caliguiri stepped forward and announced that he was not going to let his hometown team become the New Orleans or Carolina Pirates. His strategy began with a strong-arm approach to prevent the Galbreath family from selling the team to outside interests. Pointing out that the Pirates' lease at Three Rivers ran through the 2011 season, he threatened lawsuits against the Galbreaths and any potential buyer interested in moving the team to another city.

At one point, when Caliguiri found out that the Indianapolis mayor, William Hudnutt, was sending a representative to Pittsburgh to talk with the Galbreath family about acquiring the Pirates, Caliguiri warned that he would be arrested as soon as he entered Pittsburgh's city limits. The threat was obviously a bluff, but with Indianapolis already accused of stealing the NFL Colts from Baltimore, Hudnutt decided to cancel the trip. The Galbreath family's reaction to Caliguiri's threat was to declare that they were not bluffing: "We are out. We just can't pull it off any more. We can't afford it."[2]

Recognizing that his threats of legal action were no more than a delay tactic, Caliguiri knew he had to find local buyers to keep the Pirates in Pittsburgh. David Roderick, former USX chairman, recalled that Caliguiri invited several corporate and civic leaders into his office and told them, "Let's not let this happen."[3] The group included Douglas Danforth, chairman of Westinghouse Electric, Malcolm Prine, president and CEO of Ryan Homes, and Carl Barger, a senior partner at the law firm Eckert, Seamans, Cherin, and Mellott. Together they formed an association of thirteen members that eventually included two Fortune 500 firms, Alcoa and PPG; the city's two largest banks, Mellon and PNC; steel conglomerate National Intergroup; and engineering firm Schneider Inc. Heinz was unwilling to commit itself publicly to the group, but it did participate financially by using Carnegie Mellon University as its surrogate. Each member agreed to contribute $2 million toward the purchase of the Pirates franchise from the Galbreaths. For its part, the city agreed to help with operating costs by lending the association $20 million through its Urban Redevelopment Authority and promising to ease the financial burden of the stadium lease.[4]

Calling itself the Pittsburgh Associates, the group made an offer of $22 million to the Galbreath family. The rest of the $50 million raised by the group would be set aside to cover anticipated future financial losses. The offer was far short of the $35 million the Galbreaths believed they could get from an outside buyer, but they eventually decided it was the best they could do under the strained circumstances. After some hesitation, they agreed to sell the franchise to Caliguiri's coalition. The deal kept the Pirates in Pittsburgh, but after thirty-nine years of ownership, it was a bitter ending for the Galbreath family. Colorful owner Bill Veeck, who sold several franchises in his Hall-of-Fame career, once said that the only time an owner makes any real money is when he sells his team. After paying off minority owners and the Pirates' existing debts, the Galbreaths were barely able to break even.[5]

The initial problem with the Pittsburgh Associates ownership was that few of its members, with the exception of Prine, Barger, and Danforth, had any real interest in baseball beyond helping keep the team in Pittsburgh. To make matters worse, those who were interested, although they were successful CEOs, had no experience running a baseball organization. That did not prevent Prine from offering to become the ballclub's new president, an offer that the other members eagerly accepted.

Prine's first task as president was to find someone to run the Pirates' baseball operations. His choice for the new general manager seemed to confirm fears that the worst franchise in baseball was now in the hands of amateurs. Instead of offering the position to someone with experience as a major-league general manager or to a promising assistant GM, Prine announced on November 7, 1985, that he had hired Syd Thrift, who for the previous several years had been running a real estate business.

This choice came as a shock to Pirates fans. Since 1946—when Galbreath had hired an experienced and respected baseball man in Roy Hamey to run the team's operations—the Pirates had had only four general managers, including the legendary Branch Rickey, the popular Joe L. Brown, who produced championship teams in 1960 and 1971, and the recently fired Harding Peterson, whose trades were key to the 1979 championship season. Fans knew nothing about Thrift and could not take much encouragement from his answer to a reporter's question about his plans for the Pirates: "It ain't easy resurrecting the dead."[6]

While few doubted that the dead-last Pirates needed resurrecting, most found it hard to believe that the widely unknown Thrift was a baseball savior. A closer look at his background, however, indicated that he just might be capable of performing a miracle. Since the end of his brief playing career in the Yankees organization, he had been involved with player evaluation and development. He had spent eleven years scouting with the Pirates from 1957 to 1967, where Brown eventually named him scouting supervisor. After leaving the Pirates, Thrift became the founding director of the Kansas City Royals' baseball academy, where talented athletes with little baseball experience were taught the skills needed to play baseball. He served there from 1969 to 1972, then spent two years as farm director for innovative owner Charlie Finley's Oakland As, where, Thrift claimed, he earned his "Ph.D. in baseball." Thrift became involved in the Pirates' search for a new general manager when Brown called his old scouting director and asked for a recommendation. Thrift seemed to be offering himself for the position when he told Brown that the Pirates, with little money to sign free agents, needed to hire someone who knew something about player development. When Brown wondered if Thrift would be interested in the position, Thrift first said that he would have to be crazy to take the position. Then he jumped at the chance to return to baseball.[7]

The reaction of Pittsburgh sportswriters to Thrift's hiring ranged from outrage to mockery. Smizik of the *Pittsburgh Press* wrote that it was obvious that to qualify for the job of Pirates GM you "must have no experience." After attending the press conference introducing Thrift, he pleaded with the Pirates, "Say it isn't so. . . . You're kidding. Please say you're kidding."[8] Phil Musick's column, written in the form of a letter to Thrift, assured the new GM that Pirates fans, after watching the team lose 104 games the previous season, would be very patient—"it will be two weeks, maybe a month, before the fans get out the rope." Musick added, "All you really have to do is hire a manager with a strong stomach, turn the Pirate farm system into a phoenix, and, in a matter of about 150 days, put on the field a baseball team that can, ah, keep its nose clean and doesn't make the fans retch. If you can manage that, an entire city will be at your feet, Syd. Pittsburgh? No, Lourdes."[9]

Thrift understood the hostile reaction to his hiring, but he felt that his years in scouting and player development more than qualified him for the job. He also believed that the most negative criticism—that he had spent the past several years in real estate—was misplaced. He told the noted writer and editor William Zinsser during spring training in 1988 that, in the real estate business, "I learned much that I needed to know about finance, and I also learned about human nature. Real estate and baseball are very much alike. You're making judgments about people and gambling on how well you evaluate them."[10]

Once Thrift was in place, his first job was to find a manager to replace the popular Chuck Tanner, who was fired at the end of the 1985 season. There were several candidates with big-league experience, including former Mets and Braves manager Joe Torre, but the obvious fan favorite was Willie Stargell, who had come back to Pittsburgh as a coach during the 1985 season to help with waning player morale and fan support. Stargell had first expressed a desire to manage as early as 1979, after leading the Pirates to a World Series victory. Three years after his retirement in 1982, he now felt he was ready emotionally and mentally to take on the responsibilities of running a team. He even offered to manage in Puerto Rico during the winter so as to prepare himself for managing the team.

Thrift claimed that an essential part of his mission as GM was to restore the trust of the Pirates fans who had been treated so shabbily during the club's recent collapse. No move would do more to restore that trust than the hiring of the popular Stargell, affectionately known as "Pops," as the new Pirates manager. The move would also be a challenge to those who argued that one of the team's major problems was it had too many black players to suit the fan base. Stargell, who was in left field when the Pirates made history fielding an all-black lineup in 1971, would have been the first black manager in Pirates history.

On November 21, 1985, just two weeks after Thrift became the GM, he announced his selection of the new manager, and his choice was as stunning as the earlier announcement of his own hiring. Instead of reaching into the Pirates family, Thrift decided to offer the position to forty-year-old Jim Leyland, the third-base coach for the Chicago White Sox. Few in Pittsburgh had heard of Thrift at the time of his hiring, and fewer had heard of Leyland. Even Leyland was surprised by his selection, because he had been an also-ran for so many major league managerial positions in recent years he thought he would never receive an offer.

A native of Perrysburg in northwestern Ohio, Leyland had family in Butler and Kane Counties in Pennsylvania, but he had "never stepped foot in Pittsburgh."[11] When Thrift called him, Leyland, who had just lost out to Hal Lanier for the Houston Astros managerial job, was "on the couch half asleep." When the caller identified himself as the new Pirates GM, Leyland thought that one of his brothers was playing a prank. So he replied in jest, "And I'm [Hall-of-Fame manager] John McGraw." When Thrift finally convinced Leyland that he really was the Pirates general manager, he invited Leyland to Pittsburgh for an interview. Leyland told him, "I didn't want to be just another newspaper article or a token interview. I told him if he was serious, OK. He said if he wasn't serious, he wouldn't have called."[12]

Leyland remembered being picked up for his interview by Branch Rickey III, head of player development. Rickey was the grandson of the legendary Branch Rickey—the general manager who played an instrumental role in integrating the major leagues by signing Jackie Robinson for the Brooklyn Dodgers organization in 1945 and who later became GM for the Pirates. On the way to Three Rivers Stadium, Rickey told Leyland that if he got the job he should name the Pirates' best player, Tony Peña, as team captain. Leyland's own thought was that the Pirates, who were so strapped for talent, would do well to trade Peña for several prospects. Once at Three Rivers, the interview went well. Leyland thought Thrift liked him, but he did not think he had impressed club president Prine. Worried he was not going to get the job, he received a phone call a few days later from Brown, who told Leyland he was looking forward to seeing him at the winter meetings. Shortly after Brown had tipped the Pirates' hand, Thrift called and asked Leyland, "Are you ready to manage?"[13] He then offered a one-year contract for one hundred thousand dollars to manage the Pirates, an offer quickly accepted by a much relieved and exuberant Leyland.

Leyland did not have big-league experience in running a team, but he had the strong background in player development that Thrift was looking for in a manager. He had spent the previous four seasons coaching for the highly regarded Tony La Russa, whose White Sox team had won its division in 1983. Leyland and La Russa had played against each other in AA ball but did not get to know each other until they were opposing managers in AAA, where "they talked about baseball all the time." It was La Russa, remembering their conversations in the minor leagues, who put Leyland "on the map in the major leagues" by hiring him as his third-base coach with the White Sox.[14] Before taking a coaching job with the White Sox in 1982, Leyland had been a successful manager in the minor leagues for eleven years and had won league championships at three different levels, including AAA Evansville in 1979. He was known as a communicator, a "players' manager," and for his no-nonsense approach to the public and the press. Thrift believed he was a perfect fit, because "the manager of the Pirates should be someone who reflected the work ethic of the Pittsburgh area—someone who you knew was a hardworking guy. With Jim that comes across real quick."[15]

At his first press conference, in response to a question about his failure to land a big league job before the Pirates' offer, Leyland responded, "I'm the marathon man. I've been in the running for a lot of positions, but this is the first time I've finished first. But I feel I've paid my dues and that I'm supposed to be a Pittsburgh Pirate."[16] After admitting that he was not completely familiar with the Pirates' personnel, he said, "I'm no miracle worker; I'm a hard worker."[17] He also admitted that, in the dugout, he was no Danny Murtaugh, the laid-back manager who had four stints leading the Pirates, including the 1960 and 1971 World Series champions: "I'm a little nervous. Some managers can sit back and fold their arms. . . . I find I'm a little more effective if I move around." As for his one-year contract, Leyland said, "if these people are not satisfied with the job I've done at the end of the year, I have no future here anyway. I don't want to hold anyone up for a few bucks."[18]

Leyland may have been an unknown in Pittsburgh, but he was coming to Pittsburgh with a strong recommendation from La Russa, the manager featured by Pulitzer-Prize-winning columnist George Will in his acclaimed *Men at Work: The Craft of Baseball* as the perfect example of intelligent baseball thinking.[19] La Russa told Jerome Holtzman of the *Chicago Tribune*: "He'll have big shoes to fill. Chuck Tanner is a tough act to follow. But Jim Leyland's ready. And I'll say something else: Give him a few years and he'll be the best manager in the big leagues."[20] La Russa would soon see his prediction fulfilled.

Unfortunately for Thrift and Leyland, they had little to work with in 1986, other than the remnants of the disastrous 1985 team. The starting lineup for an Opening Day loss to Dwight Gooden and the New York Mets had a few new faces in it, but mostly it was a mixture of the disappointing, the disgruntled, and the inept. The Pirates still had Steve Kemp in the lineup, but he was released after batting .188 in thirteen games. After using six shortstops in 1985, the team settled on Sam Khalifa to start the season, but he was benched after he hit an anemic .185, fifteen points below baseball's Mendoza line, a measure of basic hitting competence named after Mario Mendoza, a Pirates shortstop from the 1970s. Mendoza, notorious for his poor hitting, hit under .200 in three of his five years with the Pirates.

While the Pirates team that took the field in 1986 was bad, it was not, however, completely hopeless. The talented Johnny Ray and Peña, carryovers from 1985, were joined in the 1986 Opening Day lineup by promising newcomers R.J. Reynolds and Sid Bream, both acquired by Brown from the Dodgers in a 1985 midseason trade for Madlock, the disgruntled 1979 World Series veteran. Bream remembered that he and Reynolds were not bothered by the trade and welcomed the opportunity "to make the major leagues."[21] Veteran Jim Morrison, however, was not so thrilled and probably could not believe he was still wearing a Pirates uniform as the 1986 season opened or that the team was still playing in Pittsburgh. In one of the darkest moments of the 1985 season, Morrison called Pirates fans "miserable people" and Pittsburgh "a miserable environment to play baseball."[22]

After losing their first two games of the 1986 season, the Pirates went on a six-game winning streak, thanks to the excellent pitching of veterans Rick Reuschel and Rick Rhoden and to an early schedule that had them playing six of their first eight games against the equally hapless Chicago Cubs. Once they stopped playing the Cubs, however, they lost their next five games and finished April at 7–10. With prolonged losing streaks becoming a pattern, the Pirates had a losing record in every month of the 1986 season and finished in last place in their division with a record of 64–98. The New York Mets, on the other hand, were a powerhouse in 1986, winning 108 games and going on to defeat the Boston Red Sox in the World Series. During the regular season, they bullied their way to a 17–1 record against the lowly Pirates, who barely avoided losing one hundred games. A feisty and determined Leyland was unwilling to back down against the Mets or any other team, however. When questioned by a reporter about the Mets' dominance of his Pirates, he shot back, "If they were that good then how did they lose that one game to us?"[23]

While Leyland bristled and the Pirates floundered in 1986, GM Thrift was not content to wait until the offseason to improve the team. One of the few good moves the Pirates made in 1985 was drafting Arizona State University outfielder Barry Bonds with the sixth pick in baseball's amateur draft that June. The son of former major leaguer Bobby Bonds, the cousin of Reggie Jackson, and the honorary godson of Willie Mays, Bonds had baseball in his DNA. In his last year at Arizona State he hit twenty-three home runs and batted .368. After drafting Bonds in the first round, the Pirates sent him to their Class A Prince William, Virginia, farm club in the Carolina League, where he was named Player of the Month for July and excelled at bat and on the field for the rest of the season.

At the beginning of the 1986 season, the Pirates had moved the twenty-one-year-old Bonds up to their Hawaii Islanders farm club in the AAA Pacific Coast League. When Bonds batted .311 with seven home runs, thirty-seven RBIs, and sixteen stolen bases in just forty-four games, Thrift decided to fly to Phoenix, where Hawaii was playing, to take a look at the Pirates prospect. Thrift was so impressed that when he flew back to Pittsburgh, he brought Bonds with him. The only question, besides Bonds's readiness to play in the major leagues after such a short stint in the minors, was whether he could handle the pressure of being expected to live up to the reputations of his famous father and godfather.

Bonds made his major league debut on May 30, 1986, in a game played at Three Rivers Stadium against the Los Angeles Dodgers. Playing center field and batting leadoff, he faced Orel Hershiser in his first big-league at-bat and popped out to short. For the evening, he went 0-for-5 and struck out three times in a 6–4 Pirates loss to the Dodgers. He would get his first hit, a double against Rick Honeycutt, the next night in a 3–0 Pirates win and his first home run on June 4 against the Atlanta Braves' Craig McMurtry.

Bonds's first season with the Pirates was rocky at best. On June 30, Bonds had what Ron Cook, writing in the *Pittsburgh Press*, called Bonds's "first taste of failure" in a loss to the Montreal Expos. Mired in a deep slump, Bonds performed so poorly in the outfield and at-bat that he refused (in what would become a pattern) to talk with reporters after the game. Jim Leyland, in between expletives, summed up the game by saying, "We stunk. Period."[24] On September 23, after experiencing the thrill of hitting his first game-winning home run against the Philadelphia Phillies, a jubilant Bonds told reporters, "This is what I dreamed of all my life." He added, "We're going to be better. A lot of us are rookies and we've done some stupid things this year. But we're going to work to correct our mistakes and we're going to make the city proud of us."[25]

Another of the new players, Bobby Bonilla, was in the on-deck circle when Bonds hit his dramatic home run. After promoting Bonds to the major leagues, Thrift worked out a deal to reacquire Bonilla, a player Thrift had scouted and signed for the Pirates in 1981. After Bonilla was hurt at the Pirates' spring training camp in 1985 and spent most of that season on the disabled list, the Pirates left Bonilla unprotected in the Rule 5 winter draft by not listing him on their major-league roster.

This meant that he could be claimed by another team. On July 23, 1986, Thrift sent pitcher DeLeón to the Chicago White Sox to bring Bonilla back to Pittsburgh. Neither Bonds nor Bonilla had outstanding starts with the Pirates in 1986 (Bonds batted only .223, while Bonilla hit only one home run), but both were highly talented and gave Pirates fans some reason to hope that a moribund franchise was beginning to show signs of life again.

With about a month remaining in the 1986 season, the *Post-Gazette*'s Charley Feeney wrote an analysis of the Pirates' challenges at season's end. At the top of his list of concerns was the question "Who will lead the Pirates next year?"[26] A few days after Feeney's article appeared, Thrift announced that Leyland would be retained for the following season. Thrift also reiterated that the Pirates would not waver from their commitment to "build with youth." Pointing out that no other team in baseball had as many first-year players in its everyday lineup, he singled out Bonds, Bonilla, and Bream as the team's building blocks.

Once Leyland signed his second one-year contract with the Pirates, he decided to buy a home in Pittsburgh. He told Bob Hertzel of the *Pittsburgh Press* that, "contrary to popular belief, it is not a mobile home." In looking to the future, Leyland thought that the Pirates, besides facing the challenge of putting a winning team on the field, had to overcome the deep wounds suffered by Pirates fans: "We had to not only manage the team, but the press and the city."[27] But he agreed with Thrift that the Pirates were improving in talent and had given Pittsburgh fans a reason to feel optimistic about their baseball team.

During the offseason, however, Thrift had Pittsburgh sportswriters and baseball fans questioning his competence all over again when he traded away three veteran pitchers, including staff leader Rhoden, to the Yankees for three young and unproven pitchers, Doug Drabek, Brian Fisher, and Logan Easley. Just before the start of the 1987 season, he had sportswriters and fans questioning his sanity when he traded the Pirates' best player, catcher Peña, to the Cardinals for outfielder Andy Van Slyke, catcher Mike LaValliere, and minor league pitcher Mike Dunne. That Thrift had made the trade on April 1 convinced sportswriters and fans all over again that the Pirates had a fool for a general manager. Despite the public outrage, Leyland was happy with the influx of young talent and understood Thrift's philosophy of always "getting a pitcher back" in a trade.[28]

Pittsburgh fans and media were not the only ones to question Thrift's trades. A wary Drabek, who grew up in Texas, "didn't know what to expect" after hearing about the city's "mills, soot," and "drug scandals." That began to change when the Pirates took him to Mount Washington to dine at a restaurant overlooking the city. Impressed by the city's beauty, he also learned about the "great history" of the Pirates franchise and the "blue-collar" nature of its fans. Drabek, who saw himself as a "grinder" in his approach to the game, soon felt that the city and its fans were a perfect fit for his own character.[29] While Drabek was growing more comfortable with the city and its baseball fans, LaValliere and Van Slyke were miserable about leaving St. Louis, which they considered "a fabulous baseball town," for Pittsburgh, a city with the "stigma of drug trials" and a losing baseball team in complete "disarray." The Cardinals, who finished second to the Mets in the National League East Division in 1986, were stacked with talent, so LaValliere and Van Slyke had suspected that they might be traded. They just hoped it would not be to Montreal—"it was like playing in Europe"—or to Pittsburgh.[30] The trade was particularly hard on Van Slyke, who recently had purchased a home in Chesterfield, an exclusive St. Louis suburb. The Cardinals, however, already had an all-star center fielder in Willie McGee and were willing to part with young talent to add an all-star catcher such as Peña to their lineup.

For all of Thrift's moves before the start of the season, both he and Leyland were convinced that the key to the Pirates' success in 1987 was Bonds. Thrift told reporters, "There are a lot of things we don't know about this club, but one thing we know is that we have a center fielder." Thrift was particularly impressed when Bonds showed up for a media news luncheon in January and promised the Pirates would "tip Pittsburgh upside down by the time I'm 25. . . . We all want to do well not only for ourselves but for Pittsburgh, because we don't want people calling us losers anymore." Leyland believed Bonds could "be a real leader on this team, a real catalyst. He's got the talent and he's got the tools."[31]

When the Pirates took the field for their 1987 season opener in New York against the Mets, Ray, Morrison, and Bream were the only players back from the previous year's Opening Day lineup, and Ray and Morrison would be gone before the end of the 1987 season. The Pirates had finished in last place in 1986 with a record of 64–98, but when the Pirates played their home opener against the Cardinals on April 10, Pirates fans, perhaps sensing or at least hoping for the beginning of a turnaround, came out in record numbers. When 52,119 fans attended the 1987 season opener, it was the largest crowd in the history of Three Rivers Stadium and the first time the Pirates had opened the season at Three Rivers with a sellout.

For all the early optimism, the Pirates, with so many new players on the team, struggled during a good part of the season. They had a losing record in every month from April through July, and by late August, were eighteen games under .500 with a record of 53–71. Then, to the delight of Pirates fans, they started playing winning baseball. After trading Ray and Morrison to make room for rookie José Lind to play second base and for Bonilla to move from the outfield to third base, the Pirates went on a surge that included two seven-game winning streaks. After winning their last four games of the season, they just missed reaching .500, finishing with a record of 80–82, but the eighty wins were a sixteen-game improvement over 1986.

There were a number of success stories in the 1987 season, including improved performances from rising stars Bonds, who led the team with twenty-five home runs, and Bonilla who batted an even .300, but it was the players acquired in trades by Thrift who led the way. Van Slyke, LaValliere, and Dunne each had an outstanding year. Van Slyke hit with power and for average, and he was so strong defensively that Leyland moved him into center field and shifted Bonds, with his weaker throwing arm, to left. Tutored in St. Louis by coach Dave Ricketts, who played fourteen games for the Pirates in 1970, LaValliere won a Gold Glove award, while the *Sporting News* named Dunne the National League Rookie of the Year after he finished with a 13–6 record.

Thrift's trade with the Yankees also paid dividends when Drabek (after a slow start) and Fisher won eleven games each as starters. The bullpen received a late-season boost when Thrift picked up Jeff Robinson and Jim Gott in a deal with the San Francisco Giants for veteran pitcher Reuschel. When Gott took over the closer's role from Don Robinson, the last player still on the roster from the 1979 World Series champions, he saved thirteen games with a 1.45 earned run average. Bob Walk, a castoff from the Atlanta Braves, also pitched well when Leyland inserted him into the starting rotation and finished the season with an 8–2 record.

The Pirates generated so much optimism and enthusiasm in 1987 that *Pittsburgh Magazine* named the team its "Pittsburghers of the Year" in recognition of the franchise's dramatic recovery after the disastrous 1985 season.[32] Just two years after nearly moving to another city, they had gone from a team of underachieving malcontents to a young, talented ballclub on the verge of becoming playoff contenders. They had Gold Glove winners on defense, power and speed on offense, and solid pitching in their starting rotation and bullpen. Fans were ready to come out to Three Rivers Stadium in record numbers to watch the most exciting Pirates team in years.

Once the 1987 season was over, however, the Pirates had to secure their manager and general manager to new contracts. At a press conference in late October, the Pirates announced that Leyland had signed a new one-year contract. Leyland told reporters, "I was proud to be named manager of the Pittsburgh Pirates two years ago, and I'm even prouder to be the manager of the Pittsburgh Pirates now." Leyland, who was to marry the Pirates' events coordinator, Latrobe native Katie O'Connor, in November, added, "The Pirates have treated me fairly both financially and emotionally—plus, I got a wife out of it, too."[33]

The *Post-Gazette*'s Meyer reported that the Pirates also had announced the retention of Thrift. "Thrift hasn't signed his contract yet, but he anticipates signing a two-year deal in the near future."[34] But this announcement proved premature. Two weeks later, *Post-Gazette* writer Bruce Keidan reported, "Healthy and serene though they appear from a distance, the Pirates are a troubled franchise, beset by internal strife at the highest levels of management."[35]

The nature of the internal strife became clear in the two-year contract offered to Thrift by Pirates president Prine. The proposed contract called for Thrift to make a two-hundred-thousand-dollar salary, an increase of seventy-five thousand dollars, but it also stipulated that Thrift had to seek Prine's approval for all personnel and financial decisions, including player trades, free agent signings, and the hiring and firing of scouts. Keidan reported that, "Thrift is disturbed over his loss of autonomy and will not accept it. Nor will Prine budge. The relationship between the two is sulfurous."[36] The power struggle was particularly difficult for the newly re-signed Leyland, who had developed a close working relationship and friendship with both men.

Reportedly, Prine explained his position by telling Thrift that the "primary goal for the 1988 season was to break even. . . . to keep a lid on the player payroll."[37] Realizing that, to become a contender, the Pirates needed to increase their payroll, the lowest in the major leagues, Thrift rejected the contract and asked permission from the board of directors to look at other jobs. Three days later, on October 24, 1987, the board signed Thrift to a two-year contract that met all of his demands. The board also announced they had accepted Prine's resignation as president, replaced him with Barger as president, and named Danforth to replace Barger as chairman of the board. When reporters asked Thrift about his threat to leave Pittsburgh, apparently he responded, "They talk about me leaving Pittsburgh. That would be like Wayne Gretzky leaving Canada."[38] For all his foresight in judging player development, Thrift would prove a poor prophet on Gretzky's fate in Canada (he was traded to the Los Angeles Kings in 1988) and on his own fate in Pittsburgh.

In early January 1988 Thrift received the Sportsman of the Year Award at the annual banquet of the Dapper Dan Club, a charitable organization founded by *Post-Gazette* editor Al Abrams in 1936. In his acceptance speech, Thrift proudly announced, "We passed through the excuse-making age. We do not have to apologize for this team." He then boldly predicted, "Pittsburgh should draw 2 million people in 1988." He also told those in attendance, "I have found that the spirit here is something special and have known that for a long time."[39]

As the Pirates prepared for the 1988 season, William Zinsser visited their camp in Bradenton, Florida, gathering research for a book he was preparing to write on spring training, which he described as "baseball's annual season of renewal." During his visit, he was particularly impressed by Leyland, who, he said, "had brought discipline to a club that was in disarray and had won the respect of his players for his fairness." Zinsser noted that Leyland's reputation, since his "Jim who?" moment at his hiring, had grown throughout the league: "In early 1988 *Sports Illustrated* called him 'the best young manager in the game,' and every article written about him used the same word: 'respect.'"[40]

When the season opened, the Pirates surged to the front of the division, as Thrift and Leyland had expected. By late April they were solidly in first place and finished the month with a record of 16–6. Dampening the excitement for Pittsburgh fans, however, was the failing health of the man who had kept the Pirates from moving to another city. At the height of his political success and popularity, Mayor Caliguiri became ill and was diagnosed with amyloidosis, an incurable disease that attacks the body's tissues and organs. Caliguiri refused to step down from office and fought valiantly against his illness, but in the early hours of Friday, May 6, 1988, his heart gave out. He was only fifty-six at the time of his death. That evening, the Pirates hosted the San Diego Padres. The game that night went into the twelfth inning before Bream hit a dramatic three-run homer to give the Pirates a 4–1 victory. It was a fitting farewell to Caliguiri, the kid who grew up loving the Pirates and the man who saved baseball for future generations of Pirates fans in Pittsburgh.

After their impressive start in April, the Pirates went 14–14 in May and 13–14 in June before going on a five-game winning streak just before the All-Star break in early July. Walk, who finished the first half of the season with a 10–4 record, joined his teammates Van Slyke and Bonds on the National League All-Star team. Once the season resumed, the Pirates extended their streak to ten games behind the hot hitting of Bonds and Bonilla, who were tied for the National League lead in home runs. They also had more home runs than their American League counterparts, the Oakland As' "bash brothers," José Canseco and Mark McGwire.

The Pirates finished 15–11 for the month of July and then struggled in August, going 13–17 before bouncing back in September with a 14–11 record. In October they lost their last two games of the season but finished in second place, with a record of 85–75. It was their first winning season since 1983. Pirates fans rewarded the team by setting a new home attendance record. Although they fell short of Thrift's predicted two million, the 1,866,713 fans who watched the Pirates at Three Rivers in 1988 eclipsed the record set by the 1,705,828 fans who came out to Forbes Field to watch the 1960 World Series champions.

There were plenty of heroes in 1988, including Bonds and Bonilla, but the Pirates' most valuable player at the end of the season, and the clear fan favorite, was Van Slyke. After leading the Pirates in hits, home runs, runs scored, runs batted in, and stolen bases, he was named the *Sporting News* National League Player of the Year. Along with Bonilla, who played most of the season at third base, Van Slyke received the Silver Slugger Award as the best offensive player at his position and, after an outstanding season in center field, joined LaValliere as a Gold Glove winner. His teammate Darnell Coles regarded Van Slyke as a "tremendous center fielder" and a clutch hitter, but he also admired him for the way he played "with a chip on his shoulder" and wasn't afraid "to get on players."[41]

Most of the starting pitchers had solid years. They were led by Drabek, who had fifteen wins. Only Dunne and Fisher, who both finished with losing records, disappointed. John Smiley, who had pitched out of the bullpen since making the remarkable jump from minor-league A ball to the major leagues in September 1986, won thirteen games as a starter in 1988. Used as a spot starter since being acquired from Atlanta, Walk responded after becoming a regular part of the starting rotation by winning twelve games.

The 1988 Pirates were a team of rising stars, but no player attracted more media attention than bullpen ace Gott, who finished the season with a team-record thirty-four saves, good for second most in the National League. In *Men at Work*, George Will, who saw his first major-league game at Forbes Field in 1950, commented that "you do not have to be a bit touched in the head to want to earn a living as a reliever, but many relievers seem to be. There is a tendency for relief pitchers to seem mad—mad meaning angry (Goose Gossage), mad meaning crazed (Sparky Lyle) or both angry and crazed (Al Hrabosky)."[42] In Gott's case, his personality "tend[ed] toward the manic."[43] Catcher LaValliere said that when Gott came in from the bullpen to save a game, "I just try to stop him from snorting. He comes in like a horse. . . . He's huffing and puffing, so the first thing I want to do before I go back to warm him up is let him catch his breath a little bit." LaValliere also pointed out that the emotional Gott, once he started pitching, had to throw from the stretch even with no one on base. "He gets so excited he really couldn't keep all the body parts going in the same direction enough to throw strikes." Gott's response—"We're little kids playing a little kid's game. Why shouldn't we show emotion?"[44]

There was plenty of improvement on the field during the 1988 season, but unfortunately, the front office was still in turmoil. At the beginning of the 1988 season, Hertzel wrote a piece in the *Pittsburgh Press*, titled "Second Banana: That's the Way Leyland Likes It." Hertzel pointed out that, while Leyland maintains he does not care, "There has been . . . a 'Syd Thrift Show' on radio and no 'Jim Leyland Show.' Thrift was Dapper Dan Man of the Year, not Leyland. *Sport Magazine*, *The Sporting News*, *Inside Sports*, even the *PITTSBURGH Magazine* . . . did Pirates stories centered on Thrift with Leyland little more than a footnote."[45] Leyland may have said he did not care, but he told management at the end of the season that after three seasons of one-year contracts and being one of the lowest-paid managers in baseball, he wanted a two-year contract worth $250,000 a year, an increase of $100,000 per year. "They've seen me manage here for three years. Why give me a one-year deal? If they want me and think I can do the job they must think I can do it for two years."[46] A few days later, Thrift announced that Leyland had signed a two-year contract to continue managing the Pirates through the 1990 season. It was the last official act in Thrift's tenure as Pirates GM.

The relationship between Thrift and Pirates ownership continued to deteriorate, and by season's end, Danforth and the board members had had enough of what they perceived as Thrift's egotism and arrogance in taking credit for the Pirates' success. On October 4, they fired Thrift and replaced him with his assistant, Larry Doughty. The decision to fire Thrift was unpopular with both players and fans, but Leyland, who had to deny reports of Thrift's meddling in the dugout, said, "The strain was evident in the entire organization the last month of the season. It did not take a rocket scientist to know something was not right."[47] Perhaps Smizik, in a *Pittsburgh Press* column, summed up management's position best when he wrote that Thrift "had an ego that was unsurpassed in a profession of large egos. He would have had everyone believe he solely was responsible for the Pirates rise." But Smizik, while writing that Thrift was "no saint, no perfect general manager," added, "when they write the history of the salvaging of the Pirates there will be many heroes, but none who should be more acclaimed than Syd Thrift."[48]

Doughty had a background similar to Thrift's. Before leaving the Cincinnati Reds, where he was the director of scouting, to become the Pirates' assistant GM, Doughty had been a scout and a scouting supervisor. Unlike the aggressive and flamboyant Thrift, however, Doughty was cautious and conservative in making personnel moves. He seemed the perfect choice for a team that had finished in second place in 1988 and appeared to have the players to challenge for the division title in 1989.

In his poem *The Waste Land*, T. S. Eliot proclaimed, "April is the cruellest month." The line could well serve as an epitaph for the Pirates' 1989 season. Trouble began in spring training when ace reliever Gott began experiencing pain in his elbow. Concerned about Gott, who underwent shoulder surgery in 1986, Leyland kept him out of a bottom-of-the-ninth loss to the Expos in the season opener. Drabek pitched a shutout in the next game, and the Pirates took a 2–0 lead into the bottom of the eighth of the final game of the series. When starting pitcher Smiley faltered and gave up the tying runs, Leyland brought Gott into the game. He managed to strike out one batter before giving up the winning run. He left the game with throbbing pain in his elbow and did not pitch in another game for the rest of the season. Just ten days after Gott's injury, the Pirates lost his battery mate when LaValliere tore ligaments in his knee trying to block home plate. He would not play in another game until after July 4. The Pirates also lost Bream in April when he injured his knee and had season-ending surgery. Even the team's most valuable player, Van Slyke, had to go on the disabled list in April with a torn muscle in his rib cage, and he would miss a month of the season. Bonds was one of the few players to escape an early injury, but in June he injured his left knee making a diving catch. He played the rest of the season with a noticeable limp and had arthroscopic surgery at the end of the season.

While the injuries were piling up, the players who were still healthy made matters worse by having poor seasons. Acquired in one of the few moves Doughty made during the offseason, shortstop Jay Bell, a former first-round draft pick of the Minnesota Twins, played so badly that he was sent to the minor leagues to get his confidence back. Third baseman Jeff King, the overall number one pick in the 1986 draft, replaced the injured Bream on the roster so that error-prone Bonilla could move to the outfield, but King struggled at the plate and batted below .200 for the season. Drabek, Smiley, and Walk had decent starts to the season, but Dunne struggled early and was traded to the Seattle Mariners. Jeff Robinson flopped as a replacement for Dunne in the starting rotation after pitching exclusively and effectively in relief in 1988.

The undermanned Pirates finished the month with a 10–14 record. They had an 11–14 May and were well on their way to another losing month in June when they experienced the highlight and the lowlight of the season in the same game. On June 8 in Philadelphia, the Pirates scored ten runs in the top of the first inning against the Phillies. Jim Rooker, who had become a color analyst for Pirates games after his retirement from baseball, said, "If the Pirates lose this game, I'm walking home."[49] The Pirates went on to blow the lead and lost the game 15–11.

Rooker flew back from Philadelphia with the team, but when fans protested and wanted him to keep his word, Rooker turned a Pirates disaster into a positive event. When the season ended, he agreed to make the trek but asked fans to support what he called his "unintentional walk." It took thirteen days, but Rooker managed to make it by foot from Philadelphia to Pittsburgh and in the process raised eighty-one thousand dollars for Pittsburgh charities, including the Children's Hospital and Bob Prince Charities.

The Pirates continued to sputter and on August 19 reached the season's low point by falling twenty games below .500. They finished the season with a record of 74–88, in fifth place, nineteen games behind the division champion Chicago Cubs. After their dismal season, the Pirates had their fans wondering if, with all its injuries, their team was suffering from a "Syd Thrift curse." The fear was that the Pirates, without Thrift, were about to spin into another losing cycle as they entered a new decade of baseball in Pittsburgh.

CHAPTER THREE

LEYLAND AND BARRY BONDS LEAD THE WAY

The 1990 Season

No player arrived in the major leagues with more expectations of greatness than Barry Bonds. No player, however, generated more disappointment before he reached that greatness or more controversy after he became great. When he played his first game in Pittsburgh, he was the heir apparent to Roberto Clemente and Willie Stargell. When he played his last game in a Pirates uniform, he was on his way to becoming one of the most reviled figures in Pirates history.

Like a baseball Hamlet, Barry Bonds was born and bred a prince of the game, but he was haunted by his father's fate and legacy. He was the son of one of the greatest leadoff hitters in baseball history and the honorary godson of arguably the greatest player in the history of the game. His father, Bobby Bonds, made his major league debut in 1968 batting leadoff for the San Francisco Giants and hit a grand slam in his first game. During his career, Bobby Bonds broke major league records by hitting eleven leadoff home runs in one season and thirty-five in his career. An athlete gifted with great speed and power, he once said, "I knew I could do anything on a baseball field that any other man could do."[1]

The problem for Bobby Bonds was that one of those men on the baseball field was his teammate Willie Mays, who overshadowed him. While Mays was in the twilight of his career when Bonds made his major league debut, the "Say Hey Kid" was already one of the game's legends. In recognition of his excellence, the *Sporting News* named Mays the 1960s Player of the Decade. A brilliant center fielder, Mays made some of the greatest defensive plays in baseball history, including an over-the-shoulder grab that robbed the Cleveland Indians' Vic Wertz in Game 1 of the 1954 World Series and became known over the years simply as "the catch." Possessed of great speed and the base-running daring of a Jackie Robinson, Mays was also one of the greatest power hitters in baseball history. He twice hit more than fifty home runs in a season, and when he finally trotted off the field for the last time in 1973, he was second only to Babe Ruth in career home runs. He won the National League Most Valuable Player Award when he was only twenty-three years old and won the MVP award again at the age of thirty-four.

Mays befriended and tutored Bobby Bonds during the years they spent together with the Giants. He urged his younger teammate to have fun playing the game, while always striving to be the best. He also, however, warned him to be wary of the press, a lesson learned quickly by his protégé. Described by some as the next Willie Mays when he first put on a Giants uniform, Bobby Bonds soon discovered that no matter how well he played, he could never meet expectations.[2] Bobby Bonds struggled with alcoholism early in his life, and he reacted to criticism from the press by withdrawing into himself. He passed along this distrust and antagonism to Barry.

From the moment he put on a glove, threw a ball, and swung a bat, it was Barry Bonds's destiny to become a baseball great. Growing up in Riverside and San Carlos, California, he was always the best player on his team by far, and he knew it. He had what the *Post-Gazette*'s Gene Collier called "an unbelievable sense of entitlement."[3] He was the son of an MLB star and was so blessed with talent that he became the center of attention the moment he trotted onto the field. When he accepted a scholarship to play baseball at Arizona State University, one of the most successful baseball programs in the country, it seemed only a matter of time before Barry Bonds would play his way into becoming the top pick in the Major League Baseball draft.

Barry Bonds's problem at Arizona State was not his talent, which was extraordinary, but his attitude, which according to many was awful. Mario Moccia, who would go on to play his way into the New Mexico State University Sports Hall of Fame, remembered playing a practice game against Arizona State and its All-American center fielder. From his first base position, he watched Bonds "hit the ball over the right field fence at Parkland Stadium, and it was a monumental epic Ruthian blast." Moccia also remembered an arrogant Bonds, after he touched third base and slapped the hand of Arizona State head coach, Jim Brock, "walking straight into the dugout without the slightest inkling of making any move toward jogging the extra 90 feet and touching home."[4] As far as Bonds was concerned, his talent and his name commanded celebrity status and special treatment both on and off the field. Years later, Brock told *Sports Illustrated*, "I never saw a teammate care about [Barry]. Part of it would be his being rude, inconsiderate and self-centered. He bragged about the money he turned down, and he popped off about his dad. I don't think he ever figured out what to do to get people to like him."[5] His father's son, the more Barry Bonds received the adulation and coddling he demanded, the more he distrusted and antagonized those who gave it to him.

By the time Barry Bonds declared himself eligible for the MLB draft at the end his junior year, he was one of the top prospects in the country. He also, however, had aroused suspicions that his ego and flashes of surliness could become a problem for any team that drafted him. On June 3, 1985, after Bonds was passed over by the first five teams, the Pirates, who were desperate for an infusion of talent and excitement, took a gamble and named Bonds as their first round selection. While some sportswriters questioned the pick, Pirates scouts believed that Bonds was a "can't-miss" prospect and that, for once, the Pirates "weren't about to miss."[6]

Barry Bonds's major league debut failed to generate the electricity of his father's grand slam in his first game. He struck out three times and went hitless, but from the moment he walked into the Pirates clubhouse, Barry Bonds had one goal in mind. Walk, who would be Bonds's teammate throughout his years with the Pirates, said, "I've never met anyone before Barry who had Hall of Fame ambitions as a rookie."[7] That level of expectation, however, was complicated by the attention that came with being baseball's golden child. When Bonds struggled and hit only .223 in his 1986 rookie season, Mays told the press, "He's got all the pressure you guys are putting on him because of his father. I think his mind is not totally focused on what he can do. Instead, it's focused on what people say he can do."[8]

In 1987, in the middle of Barry Bonds's second season with the Pirates, Collier wrote an article in the *Pittsburgh Press* that captured the dilemma of Bonds. Collier pointed out that the level of expectation for Bonds, despite his early struggles, was incredible. Although he had done little on the field to merit national attention, he was treated like a celebrity by the media, "putting Bobby and Barry on 'Today,' putting Barry in the Vanna White Playboy issue, making Barry a *Pittsburgh Magazine* cover, sitting him down with TV sports talk host Roy Firestone."[9]

Putting even more pressure on Bonds was his father, who proclaimed to the press that his son was "gonna be a helluva player. I have numbers I think he can achieve, but I'm not going to tell you them." He added that "Barry wants to do those things. There's nothing wrong with wanting to do too much. . . . There are two things he's said the most in his life. 'I hate to lose. I want to be the best.'" As for the press, "I told him don't worry about what they write; don't pay any attention because it's not important."[10]

While Bobby Bonds was heralding the anticipated greatness of his son, Barry Bonds's manager was sounding a note of caution. Leyland warned fans and the press to be careful in their treatment of the twenty-two-year-old Bonds. "They think they have a hero, a superstar. Some guys just aren't ready to absorb all that. He hasn't really absorbed it. He has a pretty good feel for it and he's getting more mature all the time, but it is tough on him."[11]

In 1989, two years after Leyland's warning, Collier wrote another article on Bonds that could have served as a sequel to his earlier piece. Titled "Bonds Has Potential to Excite and Exasperate," it was written on the eve of Barry and Bobby Bonds's breaking the record for most career home runs hit by a father and son. This record was held jointly, at that time, by Yogi and Dale Berra and Gus and Buddy Bell. Collier was struck by the indifference and arrogance of Barry Bonds's comments on the historic significance of his next home run: "It's no biggie. It's for my father. It'll be just a homer to me. I plan to hit a lot more."[12] Collier saw Bonds's reaction as "part of a complex makeup" that was a combination of "his nearly undefinable potential" and his failure to that point to live up to that potential. Collier noted that there were nights when Bonds dazzled the crowds with his "wondrous bat speed" and his athleticism in the outfield and on the bases. Unfortunately, Collier observed, there were other nights when Bonds was careless on the bases, "brain-dead" in the outfield, and a showboat after hitting a home run, all out of proportion to his career .246 batting average and low run production. Collier also shared the belief of Jeff Pearlman, Bonds's biographer, that Bonds was fortunate to be playing in Pittsburgh, where there was "no media crush."[13] Pittsburgh sportswriters knew about Bonds's churlish behavior, but at least in his early years, Bonds escaped the scrutiny of the national press.

When questioned about Bonds's conduct, Leyland said, "He has his moments when he gets the manager upset." While Leyland pointed out that he also got upset with mistakes made by Van Slyke and Bonilla, he admitted that Bonds was a special case: "Barry Bonds has so much ability, extraordinary ability, that you forget he's only been playing a little more than two years and he still has a lot to learn."[14] Pirates GM Doughty echoed Leyland's frustration with Bonds: "I don't want to put any undue pressure on him. But when you see a player of his capabilities and you think he can hit well above .300 and he's flirting with .240, it's a little disappointing."[15] When Collier approached Bonds about the management's disappointment with his performance, Bonds expressed surprise and claimed that he had never received a word of criticism and could not understand why the Pirates would be "anything less than delighted" with him. As far as he was concerned, "I think I've done the job. I built a house here and I built it because I want to stay here. If they're not satisfied with me, there's nothing I can do about it. I don't want to leave, but if I have to I hope I go to California. That's the only thing I would say, send me home."[16]

For all the bravado, Barry Bonds struggled to adjust to his life as a Pirate. As Pittsburgh sportswriter John Perrotto wrote, "Bonds is an enigma. One day, he is friendly, outgoing and charming. The next, he is sullen, aloof and not a fun guy to be around."[17] While distancing himself from the press and alienating many of his teammates, Bonds did, however, have one close friend and defender in Bonilla. Despite their different backgrounds and personalities, they became friends while playing together at Class A Prince William in 1985 and remained close in the Pirates clubhouse. Unlike the privileged Bonds, Bonilla grew up in the South Bronx where drugs and violence were common. For Bonilla baseball was not a legacy. It was his escape: "That's why I'm always smiling. I appreciate being a major-league baseball player very much." While Barry Bonds put pressure on himself to do the same things that his father and Mays did on the playing field "and has a hard time accepting it when he fails," Perrotto wrote, Bonilla figured "having a bad day at the ballpark is a lot better than having a bad day in the Bronx. It helps you keep things in perspective." As for Bonds, Bonilla said, "He tends to put too much pressure on himself and I think he knows it. Once he learns how to relax. . . . He'll take this city by storm. . . . These fans will love him. He'll be the man."[18]

The Pirates' disappointment with his failure to be the man and Bonds's belief he was doing the job led to a major confrontation, the first of many, when Bonds balked at signing his contract for the 1989 season. Still a year away from being eligible for salary arbitration (a process wherein the team and the player both submit a proposed salary and an arbitration panel decides on the winning salary bid), Bonds had little leverage in contract negotiations. If he refused the Pirates' offer of $360,000 plus incentives, the club could automatically renew his contract at $300,000. When he finally did accept the offer just weeks before the start of the season, he became the last player in the major leagues to sign a contract.

Especially galling for Bonds was the three-year $5.5 million contract, with a $600,000 signing bonus, given in the offseason to the popular Van Slyke. Bonds put on a good public face, but he had a hard time understanding his own offer from the Pirates in light of Van Slyke's contract. "I was happy for Andy Van Slyke, and he deserved what he got. He is the best center fielder in baseball. But to say I'm not worth his signing bonus is wrong." While he had no choice but to accept the offer, which he considered well below market value, he warned, "I'll ring the bell next year" when he entered salary negotiations.[19]

Frustrated with Bonds and anticipating more contract problems once he was eligible for salary arbitration following the 1989 season, the Pirates, while claiming they were not shopping Bonds around, were clearly open to a trade. When Doughty was asked to name the untouchable players going into the 1989 season, he mentioned Van Slyke, Bonilla, Lind, Drabek, Smiley, and Gott. Conspicuously absent from the list was Bonds. When asked about the omission, Doughty said he was "borderline untouchable."[20]

One of the ironies of the Pirates' attempt to trade Bonds before the 1989 season was their complaint, after low-balling him in salary negotiations, that other teams were not willing to offer accomplished players in return. Doughty said, "We would have to be overwhelmed to trade Barry and we haven't had a proposal that is even close."[21] With the Pirates unable to find teams willing to overlook his attitude and pay the high price commanded by his talent, they faced the prospect, after the 1989 season, of dealing with a disgruntled Bonds in arbitration.

Going into the 1990 season the Pirates had nine players eligible for salary arbitration,. First up was Bonilla, a two-time All-Star who was seeking a $1.7 million contract for the 1990 season. Bonilla lost his arbitration hearing and was awarded a salary of $1.25 million. He had expected to win in arbitration, and though he said that he was not angry, he was "definitely hurt. . . . I like Pittsburgh, but arbitration has changed a lot of things. I'm very upset. It's a mystery to me why I lost."[22] The storm surrounding Bonilla's arbitration loss turned into a tempest when Bonds also lost his arbitration hearing. Bonds was seeking $1.6 million for the 1990 season, but he was awarded $850,000. His reaction was the same as that of his close friend Bonilla: "it used to be I'd never think of playing for another team but the Pittsburgh Pirates. I wanted to be a Pirate for my whole career. But this makes you realize this is a business. If I stay here, OK, but, if not, I'll work somewhere else. . . . We're going to win a championship here, and it will be about the same time everybody becomes eligible for free agency. And we're going to say, 'You didn't care about us when we were second- and third-year players. You didn't care about us when we went to arbitration.'"[23] Five other players, including Drabek and Smiley were arbitration winners, but even they were unhappy. Drabek said, "For the first, time it makes you realize how the team thinks. . . . Since the hearing, I've tried not to dwell on it."[24] But, after their losses in salary arbitration, none were as angry as Bonds and Bonilla.

When the Pirates defended their offer to Bonds, they pointed to his low run production, a criticism that infuriated Bonds because he felt he had little opportunity to drive in runs while batting in the leadoff spot. When they defended their offer to Bonilla, they pointed to the fact that he had led National League third basemen in errors for the preceding two years. At the beginning of the 1990 season, to make room for first-round draft pick Jeff King, the Pirates moved Bonilla back to right field where he had played for most of his career before the Pirates converted him into a third baseman. Bonilla's reaction was diplomatic: "It's fine with me. As long as I get 500 at bats. I always have fun at the plate and playing the outfield is no problem."[25] Leyland had moved Bonds into the fifth position behind Van Slyke and Bonilla to shake things up late in the disappointing 1989 season and decided to keep Bonds batting fifth for the 1990 season. The move thrilled Bonds and, with the shift of Bonilla to right field, gave the Pirates a potent middle of the batting order and arguably the best defensive outfield in baseball. Moreover, the changes gave Bonds and Bonilla an opportunity to maximize their talents and prove that the Pirates had made a grievous error in not paying them their worth.

A spring training lockout over the absence of a basic agreement briefly delayed the start of the 1990 season and forced some odd traveling quirks to squeeze in a full 162-game schedule. Mike LaValliere, who was the Pirates' player representative in the negotiations with the owners, said that the delay created some apprehension that players would not be ready for the start of the season. But it actually worked to the benefit of the Pirates who had several players, including LaValliere, coming back from major injuries.[26] Still rehabilitating from knee surgery, Bream remembered having trouble rounding a base and was grateful for the extra recovery time.

The Pirates were confident that they could bounce back in 1990, but they also knew that they would have to deal with a disdainful New York Mets team and what Bream called "their cocky attitude." With their strong starting pitching staff, led by ace Dwight Gooden, and a power-laden lineup, that included home-run threats Darryl Strawberry and Howard Johnson, the Mets were the overwhelming pick of most sportswriters to win the division in 1990, after they had finished second in 1989 to the NL East Division champion Chicago Cubs. Like the rest of his teammates, LaValliere believed that the Pirates "had been dogged by the Mets" and been their "whipping boys" over the last few seasons. Van Slyke said the Mets not only "beat the hell out of us," they talked about it "and made fun of us." That lack of respect was clearly on display when Gooden, asked what he thought of the Pirates, told reporters they were "a Little League team." Van Slyke said that Gooden's comment was posted on the clubhouse wall and would remain there for the rest of the season.

If ever a game was a warning shot, it was the Pirates' 1990 opener against the Mets in New York on April 9. Facing Gooden, the middle of the Pirates lineup exploded against the Mets' ace on the way to a lopsided 12–3 victory. The twelve runs were the most scored by a Pirates team on Opening Day since 1955. Van Slyke led the way with three hits, including two home runs, three runs scored, and four RBIs. Bonilla also had three hits, including a home run. He scored twice and drove in three runs. Bonds went 1-for-3 with two runs scored and was on base four times with two walks and a hit batsman. Collectively, Van Slyke, Bonilla, and Bonds had seven hits, including three home runs, were on base ten times, scored seven runs, and drove in seven.

But after all the fireworks on Opening Day, in the second game of a three-game series the Pirates fizzled against Mets left-hander Frank Viola, and were shut out, 3–0. With Bonds batting leadoff, they bounced back the next day, beating the Mets, 6–2. For the rest of the season Leyland would occasionally bat Bonds at the top of the order when the Pirates faced a left-handed pitcher. Back in his familiar spot, Bonds went 2-for-5 with three RBIs and a stolen base. His single with the bases loaded broke a 1–1 tie and sparked the Pirates to victory behind the strong pitching of left-hander Neal Heaton, who had re-signed with the Pirates after becoming a free agent in the offseason. After taking two of three in New York, the Pirates headed to Pittsburgh for their home opener against the defending division champion Cubs. In front of 44,799 disappointed fans, the Pirates were shut out, 2–0, by Greg Maddux, who allowed only three hits. The next day the Pirates managed to score just one run in a 4–1 loss to the Cubs in front of only 13,226 fans, before bouncing back in the final game of the series with a 4–3 win in extra innings on a base hit by Bream.

After splitting six games against the top two teams in the NL East Division, the Pirates hosted the St. Louis Cardinals for a three-game series. After splitting the first two games, the Pirates dropped their second straight home series when they were shut out by former Pirate John Tudor, who had been traded to the Cards in 1984 for George Hendrick. The third shutout loss of the season dropped the Pirates under .500 with a record of 4–5. While the Pirates' pitching, with the exception of Heaton, had been inconsistent, the major problem was an underachieving offense that had not produced many runs since their explosion in the opener against the Mets. While Bonds, Van Slyke, and Bream were struggling to hit above .200, King was batting .100, and LaValliere's average had dropped to .067.

Facing a long road trip that included stops in five different cities and two visits to St. Louis, the Pirates were slumping and appeared to be on the verge of an early-season collapse. To make up games postponed by the lockout, the Pirates had to play a game in St. Louis, go to Chicago for a three-game series, come back to St. Louis for another makeup game, before heading to the West Coast for eight games. The dreaded trip, however, unexpectedly turned into a triumphant tour for the Pirates. Longtime Pirates broadcaster Lanny Frattare believed that the successful trip was "the key" to the 1990 season.[27] It proved that the Pirates had what Van Slyke called "the nucleus of a good ballclub" and gave them the confidence to believe they could compete for a championship. The Pirates, behind a strong outing from Drabek and Bonds's first home run of the year, won on the road against the Cardinals, then swept the three-game series against the Cubs. After a loss in St. Louis, they flew out to the West Coast and won six straight games against the San Francisco Giants and the San Diego Padres. The Pirates won ten of their last eleven games in April and finished the month in first place with a record of 14–6.

The initial spark for the Pirates' turnaround in April was the strong pitching of starters Drabek, Smiley, and Heaton. Each won two games during the streak, while Walk, who was coming back from injuries, won his first game of the season. Only Walt Terrell, who was signed as a free agent to a three-year contract in the offseason, struggled as a starter. Heaton was particularly effective after developing a new pitch called a "screw-knuckle-curve." When asked to describe the oddly named pitch, all Leyland could do was smile and say, it was "very confusing" for batters.

With the pitching staff stabilizing, the hitters began to contribute to the team's success. While Bonilla remained the Pirates' best hitter and led the team in April with seven home runs, Van Slyke, Bream, and LaValliere finally started to round back into shape after the previous season's injuries. King still struggled, hitting only .103 for the month, but Wally Backman, his occasional replacement at third base, went 6-for-6 in a 9–4 victory over the Padres and was hitting well over .300 coming off the bench. Don Slaught was also hitting over .300, while platooning at catcher with LaValliere. Bonds, however, continued his slow start, and on Thursday, April 29, when he struck out as a pinch-hitter in a 2–1 victory in San Francisco, his average dipped to .205. Inserted back into the starting lineup the next day in San Diego, Bonds had by far his best game of the season. In the same game that Backman went 6-for-6 from the leadoff spot, Bonds, batting fifth, went 4-for-5 with two home runs, three runs scored, and two RBIs. Bonds went 3-for-4 the next day in a 4–3 victory and, on Sunday, hit his fourth homer of the season in a 10–1 romp. In the three-game sweep of the Padres, Bonds banged out nine hits, including three home runs, and raised his average from .205 to .317. His performance in just those three games was so spectacular that he was named the National League Player of the Week for April 23–29.

At the beginning of May, the Pirates lost the last two games of their road trip to the Dodgers, but when they returned home, they went on another impressive streak, winning five in a row against the Braves and the Padres, thanks to continued strong starting pitching and the clutch hitting of Van Slyke, Bonilla, and Bonds. By mid-May Drabek (6–1) and Heaton (5–0) had a combined record of 11–1. Bonilla was leading the Pirates in home runs and RBIs and was among the league leaders in both categories. Bonds and Van Slyke, after a 5–1 victory against the Houston Astros on May 15 gave the Pirates their eighth win in nine games, were both hitting .333 and challenging Bonilla for the team lead in home runs and RBIs.

The Pirates were solidly in first place by mid-May, and their fans had plenty to cheer about. But since the home opener, the turnout at Three Rivers Stadium had been disappointing. After only 17,108 fans showed up for a May 6 doubleheader against the Braves, attendance dropped the next night to 9,653 and only 10,694 the following night. During a home streak in which the Pirates won eight out of nine games and improved their record to 22–9, they had only one game at which more than 20,000 fans showed up. Pirates fans, as in the past, would not warm up to the Pirates until the summer months. But as disappointing as the early turnout was, the fans would eventually set an attendance record that season, surpassing the two million mark for the first time in franchise history.

The Pirates lost only one game during their nine-game homestand after their successful West Coast swing, but the defeat did sound a cautionary note for a team that had won eighteen of their last twenty-two games. In a 10–4 loss to the Reds, the bullpen imploded and gave up eight runs in the eighth inning. Until that game, the Pirates' relief pitching had been effective, but the team had no dominant closer since the loss of Gott. That vulnerability became evident when the Pirates lost seven of nine games on their next road trip, including four games in which Pirates relievers surrendered the winning run. To make matters worse, the Pirates lost starter Smiley on May 18 when he broke his pitching hand in an off-field accident and they had to replace him with Bob Patterson out of the bullpen. When they returned home and lost to the Giants, the Pirates fell out of first place for the first time in over a month.

Remembering the injury-plagued 1989 season, Leyland called a clubhouse meeting to remind his team that, even with Smiley out, "we still had a good team and that we could still win. I honestly believed that." The Pirates responded by winning five in a row at home against the Giants and the Dodgers and finished May back in first place with a record of 29–17. While Terrell continued to struggle, Patterson and Walk supplemented the outstanding starting pitching of Drabek and Heaton, who were on an early pace to win twenty games each. The bullpen, with Bill Landrum emerging as the closer, was also becoming more consistent. By the end of the month, Landrum had seven saves and an ERA of 1.07.

The real story in May, however, was the Pirates' hitting. At the end of the month the Pirates could field a team with six players batting over .300, led among the regulars by Van Slyke at .321. Bonilla and Bonds were on a home run and RBI tear that had them among the league leaders. Bonilla, with 12 home runs and 40 RBIs, was on pace to hit more than 50 home runs and drive in 150 runs for the season, while Bonds was not far behind with 9 home runs and 37 RBIs. The only question going into June was the confidence of a team that had the talent to win but also had a history of losing. For Van Slyke, whose antics would keep his teammates loose all season, it was just a matter of remembering that baseball was a game "played by adults acting like little kids." For the Pirates, there was no bigger kid in the clubhouse than Van Slyke, but no one was a more dedicated and demanding teammate on the field.

At spring training that year, a fan handed Leyland a ticket stub from the seventh game of the 1960 World Series preserved in a plastic case.

One of the trademarks of the 1960 Pirates team was its ability to come from behind in the late innings. It won twenty-three games in its last at-bat and topped that with a dramatic come-from-behind victory in the seventh game of the 1960 World Series. The fan told Leyland that the stub would bring the team good luck. In a game against the Dodgers on a miserably cold Memorial Day in 1990, the ticket seemed to work its magic. Walk, who was pitching on the tenth anniversary of his first major league appearance, struggled and, going into the bottom of the ninth, the Pirates were trailing, 5–1. The game had featured three ejections and two bench-clearing shoving matches after the opposing pitchers took turns throwing at batters. Dodgers manager Tom Lasorda was so confident that the Dodgers had the game won that he removed starting pitcher Tim Belcher from the game and turned the bottom of the ninth over to his bullpen. Backman led off the inning with a single, and Bell followed with a double that sent Backman to third base. After Backman scored on a wild pitch to make the score 5–2 Van Slyke walked to put runners at first and third. Representing the tying run, Bonilla bounced into a force out, while Bell scored to cut the Dodgers' lead to 5–3. When Bonds popped out for the second out of the inning, the rally seemed as if it were over, but Bream singled Bonilla to third, and Slaught followed with a walk. With the bases loaded, José Lind bounced a single into right field, and when Dodgers outfielder Hubie Brooks tried to throw out pinch-runner Gary Redus at the plate, Slaught scored all the way from first base with the winning run as the throw eluded the Dodgers' catcher. It was easily the most exciting win of the early season. Leyland called it "one of the greatest, memorable wins" of his career.

The ticket stub from the 1960 World Series was not the Pirates' only good luck charm. They also had the Teenage Mutant Ninja Turtles. In April, at the beginning of their long western road trip, Smiley and John Cangelosi were browsing through a St. Louis shopping mall when they came across a poster of one of the cartoon figures. In spring training Redus claimed that LaValliere looked like one of the anthropomorphic turtles when he was wearing his catcher's equipment. Smiley and Cangelosi decided to buy the poster—it cost all of four dollars—and hang it in LaValliere's locker.

Once the Pirates started winning, the Ninja Turtle became the Pirates' guardian against evil spirits. When the team played at home, the poster hung on the wall facing the clubhouse door. When the team went on the road, equipment manager John Hallahan would wrap the poster in a tube so it could be shipped with the rest of the equipment. If the Pirates fell into a losing streak, there were, fortunately, four Teenage Mutant Ninja Turtles. LaValliere told reporters, "We'll ride this guy as long as we can. Then we'll get another one."

In June, the Pirates needed their magic 1960 World Series ticket stub and their Ninja Turtles poster. They managed only a 14–13 record for the month, their worst for the season. If not for several late-inning rallies, June would have been a disaster. The month started well. After losing two out of three at home to Montreal, the team that gave them the most trouble during the season, the Pirates swept the Cubs and defeated the Mets to improve their record to 34–19. In a June 8 loss to the Mets, however, Walk pulled a muscle running the bases and joined Smiley on the disabled list. Walk would not pitch again for over a month.

With Terrell floundering with a 2–6 record in mid-June and Smiley and Walk out with injuries, the Pirates had to rely primarily on starting pitching from Heaton and Drabek for the rest of June. After a five-game losing streak that included games pitched by Heaton and Drabek, the short-handed Pirates fell into second place on June 23, a half-game behind the pesky Expos. The next day, however, Heaton pitched the Pirates back into first place and extended his season record to 10–2. The Pirates ended June with a five-game winning streak, a 43–30 record, and a two-and-a-half-game lead over the Expos.

At the beginning of July the Pirates won six of eight games leading up to the All-Star Game and, at the midseason break, had a 49–32 record and a half-game lead over the streaking Mets. The Pirates had some good news just before the break, when Smiley returned to the mound on July 8 and defeated the Dodgers in Los Angeles for his first win in two months. It was their victory the night before, however, that had national sportswriters taking notice of the Pirates as legitimate contenders and buzzing that the outfield of Bonds, Van Slyke, and Bonilla could well be the best in baseball. In the Pirates' 9–6 win over the Dodgers and their All-Star pitcher, Ramón Martínez, each member of this trio homered in the same game for the first time, and they were joined in the home run onslaught by Bream. Bonds made two spectacular defensive plays, one a sliding catch of a looping fly ball in short left field, the other a one-handed grab of a Kirk Gibson line drive that was headed for the outfield fence. Van Slyke added his own contribution to the circus catches when he fell while going back on a line drive but reached up and caught the ball as he lay on the outfield grass. Despite the media attention the game drew for the Pirates' outfield, Bonilla and Bonds were still upset about losing their contract arbitration hearings during the offseason. After the win, Bonilla told reporters, "Only time will tell how good we can be . . . or how long they'll keep us together. It's all up to the Pirates." To Bonilla's comments, Bonds added, "Yeah, and they'll mess it up."[28]

After outstanding performances in the first half of the season, both Bonds and Bonilla headed to Wrigley Field for the 1990 All-Star Game.[29] Whereas Bonds had hit only .248 with nineteen home runs and fifty-eight RBIs in all of 1989, halfway through the 1990 season, he was batting .340, with fifteen home runs and sixty-two RBIs. Bonilla, for his part, hit twenty-four home runs and drove in eighty-six runs in 1989, but already had hit nineteen home runs with sixty-one RBIs at the 1990 All-Star break. The All-Star Game itself was mostly a dud for Pirates fans. Neither Bonds nor Bonilla had a hit in their brief appearances in the game, while Heaton, who had also been selected, watched the game from the dugout. Bonds, however, generated his own excitement by expressing his unhappiness with Pirates management in a pregame interview. He told reporters that he was still angry after losing his salary arbitration case: "They better negotiate next time." When reminded that the Pirates were a small market team with limited resources, he scoffed: "They talk about Pittsburgh not having money. If Pittsburgh didn't have money, they wouldn't have a ballclub. None of these guys is going broke. Baseball teams are their toys. They have other things [businesses]."[30]

An unhappy Bonds and the Pirates started the second half of the season with a ten-game homestand against West Coast teams. Their first game was not as spectacular as their opening-day rout of the Mets, but it was one of the season's most dramatic wins. After Bonds hit a three-run homer in the first inning, San Diego fought back to tie the game at 3–3 and send it into extra innings. In the bottom of the fourteenth, King, who had struggled in the first half of the season, singled home the winning run.

The next night, Drabek easily defeated the Padres, 4–1, to improve his record to 10–4 on the season. The Pirates then split the remaining eight games against the Padres, Giants, and Dodgers before heading to Montreal for three games against the Expos. They struggled against the Expos, losing two out of three games, and when they lost the first three games of a four-game home series against the Phillies, they fell out of first place, one game behind the Mets. The next night, however, Drabek ended a four-game losing streak with a masterful two-hitter against the Phillies. When the Pirates beat the Cubs, 9–1, in Chicago on the last day of July, they finished the month with a record of 58–41 and moved into a first-place tie with the Mets.

By the end of July, it was clear that the Pirates' fortunes in the last third of the season depended upon Bonds and Drabek, two distinctly different individuals in character and level of talent. Bonds was a lightning rod for controversy, but he was by far the most talented player on the ballclub. In 1990, he finally was playing up to his immense talent and was on pace to become the first player in Pirates history to hit thirty home runs and steal thirty bases. Passed over for the All-Star Game, Drabek finished July with a 13–4 record and was poised to become the Pirates' first twenty-game winner since John Candelaria in 1977. Unlike Bonds, Drabek, in the words of his manager Leyland, was "not a great talent" but there was no questioning "the size of his heart." Despite his limitations, Drabek would go on to win the Cy Young Award that year and won 155 games in his thirteen years in the majors. Every time the Pirates struggled in 1990, it was Drabek who came up with a big game to stop the losing streak.

On August 1, the Pirates fell out of first place after a 5–0 loss to the Cubs, but they bounced back by winning six of their next seven games and moving back into first. The highlight of the surge was another brilliant pitching performance from Drabek. On August 3 he went into the bottom of the ninth of a game in Philadelphia with a no-hitter. With two outs and two strikes on the batter, Drabek lost his no-hitter when Phillies utilityman Sil Campusano lined a single into right field on a pitch outside the strike zone. Drabek was disappointed, but the 11–0 Pirates victory gave him an impressive 14–5 record for the season.

Drabek had become the ace of the Pirates' pitching staff, but the rest was a patchwork of spot starters called up from the minors or borrowed from the bullpen. With Smiley and Walk working their way back from injuries, Heaton struggling with arm problems since the All-Star break, and Terrell released at the end of July, Pirates GM Doughty decided he needed to bolster his pitching staff. On August 8, Doughty made his move by sending reliever Scott Ruskin and two top minor league prospects, Willie Greene and Moises Alou, to Montreal for left-hander Zane Smith. After a 1989 season in which he had gone 1–12 for the Braves before being traded to the Expos, Smith was having a good season in 1990. He was surprised by the trade, but he was happy to join the Pirates. He also recognized that one of the reasons the Pirates traded for him was his reputation as a "Mets killer." In particular, with a sinker that broke down and away from left-handed hitters, he had "owned Darryl Strawberry."[31] After joining the Pirates, Smith would go 6–2 with a dazzling 1.30 ERA. Leyland regarded Smith as necessary to the team's success: "We wouldn't have won without him."

Despite the addition of Smith, the Pirates lost their next five games and dropped back into second place, a half-game behind the Mets. But on August 14, the Smith trade began to pay dividends. After Drabek defeated the Braves 3–1 in the first game of a doubleheader for his fifteenth win of the season, Smith won the nightcap, 6–4, for his first victory in a Pirates uniform. After a Heaton loss to the Braves the following day, the Pirates went on a six-game winning streak that improved their record to 72–49 and gave them a three-game lead over the Mets. Seemingly on the verge of running away with the East Division title, the Pirates then lost six of their last seven games in August and finished the month at 75–55, with only a half-game lead on the Mets. They entered the month of September in a dramatic struggle with the team that had bullied, humiliated, and ridiculed them ever since Leyland had taken over in 1986.

Pirates fans had been slow to embrace the 1990 team, but by mid-season large crowds had become more and more common at Three Rivers. By the end of July, attendance had topped one million. Going into September fans not only had an exciting division race to draw them to the ballpark, they also had a popular fight song when Lawrence County native Ernie Pontiere, the mullet-haired lead singer for The Lettermen, recorded "You Gotta Believe." The song caught on with fans and was endorsed by the Pirates as the team's official fight song.[32] Meant as a tribute to long-suffering Pirates fans—"Remember the heartbreak, Remember the tears"—it urged fans, with a salute to Bob Prince's trademark "Kiss it good-bye," to cast the past aside and believe in the now high-flying Pirates. The Pirates tested their fans' faith when they lost their first game in September and fell into second place, a half-game behind the Mets. But they won their next three games against the Astros and the Phillies and moved back into first place, a half-game ahead of the Mets, who were then on their way to Pittsburgh for a critical three-game series. On September 5, 49,793 fans turned out for a twi-night doubleheader against a Mets team that, as LaValliere pointed out, had been "sticking it" to the Pirates for far too long.

In the first game of the doubleheader, Smith proved that he was indeed a Mets killer by pitching nine shutout innings and allowing only one hit. The Pirates were unable to score until the bottom of the ninth, when Redus brought the fans to their feet with a leadoff single. When Bell, who would sacrifice thirty-nine times during the season, laid down a perfect bunt, Mets reliever John Franco misplayed the ball, putting runners at first and second. After Van Slyke sacrificed the runners to second and third, the Mets decided to walk Bonilla and face Bonds. With Pirates fans in a frenzy, Bonds drove the ball deep to left field and over the head of Mets outfielder Kevin McReynolds. The game-winning RBI was his hundredth on the season. The Pirates kept their momentum going in the second game of the doubleheader, when King homered in his first two at-bats to give the Pirates a 3–0 lead. The ailing Heaton gave the Pirates five solid innings, and the bullpen held on for a 3–1 victory and a doubleheader sweep. The next night, with Van Slyke, Bonilla, and Bonds scoring or driving in six runs, Randy Tomlin, another midseason call-up, pitched the Pirates to an impressive 7–1 victory. The sweep moved the Pirates three and a half games ahead of New York in the standings.

After the exciting Mets series, the Pirates suffered a letdown against the Expos and lost two out of three games at home, before starting a ten-game road trip. They won two games in Philadelphia, then headed to New York for a two-game series. After the Pirates managed only four hits in a 2–1 loss to the Mets in the series opener, Drabek went after his twentieth win of the season but was defeated, 6–3, by Dwight Gooden in an Opening Day rematch. With their lead over the Mets cut to a game and a half, they headed to Montreal to play an Expos team they had struggled against all season.

The three-game series in Montreal was a disaster. The Pirates wasted two Bonds home runs in the first game and lost 4–2. Then in the second game, Smith suffered his first defeat in a Pirates uniform in a close 4–3 defeat. The next day, the Expos swept the series, beating Tomlin, 4–1. After the loss, their fifth in a row, the Pirates' lead over the Mets was down to a precarious half-game. After a day off, they traveled to Chicago where, in the opening game of a three-game series, Smiley gave up six runs to the Cubs in the first inning of an 8–5 loss. Although the Pirates still held a half-game lead over the Mets, they had dropped six games in a row.

On September 19, Drabek took the mound at Wrigley Field still in search of his twentieth win. All season, when the Pirates floundered, Drabek was the one who rescued them with a strong pitching performance. With Bonds leading the way with two home runs, the Pirates surged to a seemingly safe 8–1 lead. But Drabek faltered in the bottom of the eighth, and when Derrick May hit a three-run homer off reliever Ted Power, the Pirates' lead was cut to 8–7. Patterson, who had pitched well both as a starter and out of the bullpen, relieved Power and retired the Cubs, but when he got to the bench, he saw that Drabek was a nervous wreck. As Drabek drank "about eight cups of coffee," Patterson told him "to chill," that he would get the Cubs out in the bottom of the ninth.[33] After giving up a two-out double to Ryne Sandberg, Patterson retired Mark Grace on a ground ball to Bream to end the Pirates' losing streak and give Drabek his much-deserved twentieth win of the season. The next day, Bonds hit his thirty-second home run of the season, and Van Slyke homered twice as the Pirates, behind Walk, rolled over the Cubs, 11–2. When the Mets lost both games of a makeup doubleheader to the Expos, the Pirates' lead was back to two games.

The Pirates opened a three-game series in Pittsburgh against the Cardinals with a 1–0 win behind another brilliant pitching performance by Smith and a game-winning RBI by Bream. The Pirates split the next two games before heading on the road for six games with the Cubs and the Cardinals. When the Pirates returned home, they would face the Mets in a three-game season-ending series that looked like it would decide the division championship.

Behind the strong pitching of Smiley, Drabek, and Smith and the clutch hitting of Bonilla, the Pirates swept the Cubs and then headed to St. Louis with a two and a half game lead over the Mets and only six games left in the season. In the first game of the series, Pirates relievers Landrum, Patterson, and Stan Belinda pitched brilliantly after Smiley surrendered a 3–0 lead. With the score tied at 4–4, Bonds drove in the go-ahead run, and the Pirates went on to a 6–4 victory. When Walk shut out the Cards, 8–0, the next day and the Mets lost to the Cubs, the Pirates were four games up on the Mets with four games left to play. They needed just one more win or one Mets loss to clinch the division title.

On Sunday, September 29, the Mets lost again to the Cubs, but the Pirates did not need the help. With Drabek on the mound, the Pirates were locked in a scoreless tie until they broke through in the top of the eighth for two runs on RBIs by Van Slyke and Redus. When pinch-hitter Denny Walling bounced out to Lind to end the game, Bream and Drabek leaped into each other's arms. In the ensuing celebration the Pirates carried a tearful Leyland off the field on their shoulders. In the clubhouse a jubilant Van Slyke tossed Leyland over his shoulder and carried him into the shower. Observing all the madness, Steve Blass, who was now in the Pirates' broadcasting booth, said "the cork had come out of the bottle . . . the team went crazy . . . Leyland went crazy."[34] No one deserved to cut loose emotionally more than Leyland, who remembered fans and writers mockingly asking, "Jim Who?" when he was hired for the 1986 season. Facing several key injuries to his pitching staff, he had managed to capture a division title with nineteen different pitchers winning games, a major-league record. He gained the respect of his players with his knowledge of the game and what Walk called his "straight-shooting."[35] He also had taken an underachieving, surly player of immense talent and helped him break out into an MVP season. It was no wonder that when Leyland was carried off the field, one of the shoulders he rode on belonged to Bonds.

When the Pirates arrived in Pittsburgh after their flight from St. Louis, they were greeted at the airport by more than ten thousand exuberant fans waiting to cheer their heroes. The terminal was so jammed with people, Walk claimed, that if he fell down he would "never touch the ground." Walk described the scene as "a sea of people." Fans were "screaming, yelling," and seemed to be "hanging from the ceiling."[36] Relief pitcher Bob Kipper, who, like Van Slyke and LaValliere, had been unhappy when he was traded to Pittsburgh, said the airport scene "was the thrill of his career."[37] Leyland later described the reception as "unbelievably warm," an experience "near the top" of his impressive career.[38] Frattare simply called it "inspirational."[39]

Over the next few days more than 125,000 fans came out to Three Rivers to watch the Pirates play three inconsequential games against the Mets and help set an attendance record of 2,049,908. Once the season ended, the Pirates would board a plane to Cincinnati to play the Reds in the National League Championship Series. More than a decade after the

Pirates' last World Series appearance, a decade in which Pittsburgh had almost lost its baseball team, they were returning to Cincinnati to face an old playoff nemesis for the chance to return to the World Series and bring a baseball championship back to Pittsburgh.

CHAPTER FOUR

THE PIRATES TAKE ON THE NASTY BOYS

The 1990 National League Championship Series

Pittsburgh fans have good reason to see the Cincinnati Reds as a major rival. The Pirates and the Reds have been competing against each other in the National League since 1890. In the 1970s the rivalry reached its peak when the Pirates and the Reds met four times to determine the National League championship. Both teams won six division titles and two World Series in the decade, but not until 1979 did the Pirates finally defeat the Reds in the playoffs. Of the three playoff defeats, the 1972 NLCS loss to the Reds on a wild pitch in Roberto Clemente's final game was perhaps the most crushing.

The Pittsburgh fans finally received a measure of revenge when the Pirates swept the Reds in the 1979 NLCS, but the bad blood was still there in 1990. As the series began, T-shirts with the slogan "Reds are Communists" were circulating around Pittsburgh.[1] The Pirates and the Reds had split twelve games during the regular season, but the Pirates were healthier going into the playoffs. They also had won seven games in a row before clinching the division in St. Louis and finishing 20–10 in the last month of the regular season. In the midst of their celebration, however, there were a few ominous signs as the Pirates headed into the postseason. Andy Van Slyke had been in a 2-for-20 slump the past few weeks, and Barry Bonds had gone 0-for-9 to end the season.

Despite his slumping star players and the team's almost complete lack of postseason experience, Leyland was not going to allow any self-doubt in the clubhouse. Bullpen coach Rich Donnelly said that, during the season, it was the manager who convinced the players that they were championship caliber: "Leyland was the only person in America who believed we were going to win for all 162 games."[2] Besides Leyland's faith, the Pirates also had Bonds's talent and self-assurance. Bonds had been wanting to prove himself on the national stage since he entered the major leagues, and he believed he was destined to wear a World Series ring and win MVP awards on his way to the Hall of Fame.

Although they had a worse record, the more experienced Reds were heavy favorites going into the series. One of the major reasons was their bullpen and the hard-throwing "Nasty Boys." Relievers Rob Dibble, Randy Myers, and Norm Charlton were so dominant that if the opposing team did not have a lead after the sixth inning, it was not typically going to rally against the Reds' bullpen. Even with the Nasty Boys, however, the Reds had played only .500 baseball since early June. They also had a recent spate of injuries that included the strained back of Eric Davis, described as "the best center fielder in the National League" by his manager Lou Piniella.[3]

Leyland was aware of the Nasty Boys' dominance, but he hoped to take them out of the series by scoring early. He believed that if the Pirates could score in the early innings, the Reds' bullpen would not be a factor. Leyland also had a surprise for the Reds in Game 1. He decided to start Bob Walk, who had finished the season at 7–5, instead of Doug Drabek, who had won twenty-two games and lost only six. Sportswriters questioned the move, but Leyland did not want to start Drabek with only three days of rest. When confronted by the press, Leyland was adamant about the decision. "I'm not going to take any chance for one moment. I'm not going to risk anybody's career for a playoff, World Series or anything else."[4] Leyland also knew that, unlike Drabek, Walk had postseason experience. Walk started and won a game in the 1980 World Series when he was with the Phillies despite giving up six earned runs over seven innings. He also pitched one inning in the 1982 NLCS for the Braves, giving up one run. Nevertheless, since joining the Pirates,

Walk had been one of their most successful pitchers in pressure situations as a starter and in relief. With Walk, who had pitched eight shutout innings in his only start against the Reds during the season, Leyland hoped he could "steal" the first game in Cincinnati and have Drabek properly rested for Game 2. Meanwhile, Piniella did not have to be as calculating with his pitching choices. After clinching their division early the Reds' top starters, José Rijo and Tom Browning, were well rested for Games 1 and 2.

The 1990 NLCS opener was held on Thursday, October 4, at a sold-out Riverfront Stadium in Cincinnati. At the start it looked as if Leyland, who had a remarkable talent for putting his players in a position to succeed, had made a major blunder. In the first inning Walk appeared nervous and erratic. He walked leadoff batter Barry Larkin to start the bottom of the first and, after giving up back-to-back doubles to Davis and Paul O'Neill, surrendered three runs before retiring the side. Afterward, when asked if he was worried about Walk, Leyland said, "One thing about Walk. He's nervous as hell, but he ain't scared. I know that."[5]

Walk managed to settle down and gave up no runs and only one hit for the next six innings, while the Pirates, who had hoped to take the early lead, chipped away at the Reds' 3–0 lead. José Lind started the comeback in the third with an RBI triple to right field. A Bonds walk and a two-run home run from Sid Bream off Rijo tied the game at 3–3 in the fourth. The game remained tied until a miscue from Davis in the top of the seventh gave the Pirates the lead and the come-from-behind victory. With Gary Redus on second and Jeff King on first, Van Slyke launched a deep fly ball into left-center field. Davis, to the dismay of Reds fans, misjudged the ball after losing it in the late afternoon sun, recovered too late, and watched it land over his head and bounce into the seats for a ground-rule double. With their own less heralded bullpen shutting out the Reds in the last three innings, the Pirates held on for a 4–3 victory. They were up 1–0 in the series and had a rested Drabek ready for Game 2.

In Game 2, Drabek, like Walk, struggled in his first inning and gave up a run to the Reds on a bloop single by O'Neill just out of the reach of Lind, but then Drabek settled down and shut out the Reds for the next three innings. Trailing early once again, the Pirates failed to score on Browning until Lind hit a home run, only his second of the year, to tie the game at 1–1. With the game still tied in the bottom of the fifth,

O'Neill drove a ball to deep left field with a man on second. This time it was Bonds who struggled against the sun and lost track of the ball when he tried to use his sunglasses. "As soon as I dropped my glasses, I lost it," Bonds said. "So I tried to run back to where I thought it was going to go. I mean, I was in the vicinity."[6]

Bonds's misplay put the Reds on top, 2–1, but the Pirates had a chance to tie the game in the top of the sixth. Back-to-back hits by Bonilla and Van Slyke gave the Pirates two men on with no outs, but O'Neill, who had driven in both runs for the Reds, thwarted the rally by throwing out Van Slyke at third when he tried to tag up on a Bonds fly ball to right field. With the Reds still ahead, 2–1, in the seventh, Piniella brought in his Nasty Boys, Dibble and Myers, to close out the game. After they combined to retire the last nine hitters in a row to preserve the victory, all that Leyland could say was, "They got that name for a reason."[7]

Game 2 was a painful loss for the Pirates and the beginning of a hard-luck postseason career for Drabek that would culminate in Game 7 of the 1992 NLCS. It was also a game the Pirates could have won with more timely hitting. That would have given them a 2–0 advantage, with the next three games in Pittsburgh. To make matters worse, during the second inning of Game 2, King suffered a bruised lower back diving back to second on a pickoff play. As for Bonds, he offered no apology for his critical misplay nor took any responsibility for the loss. All he had to say was, "The teams are evenly matched. It'll probably go three and three, with the last one here."[8]

Game 3 brought the Pirates a welcome return to Pittsburgh, but despite the buzz surrounding the first postseason game in Pittsburgh since 1979, there were thirteen thousand empty seats at Three Rivers Stadium at the start of the game. Van Slyke was disappointed but not surprised. He had questioned the fans' support throughout the season, even though the team had drawn more than two million in attendance for the first time in its history. Bonds, who rarely missed an opportunity to express his feeling that he was underappreciated said, "I'm so upset right now I don't even want to comment on that. I might hurt somebody's feelings."[9]

Despite the empty seats, the Pirates were still playing at home and had more than forty-five thousand fans cheering them on as Zane Smith, who had pitched well after coming to the Pirates in a late-season trade, took the mound. The Reds countered with left-hander Danny Jackson, who had struggled with shoulder problems in 1990 and finished the season with only a 6–6 record. Smith had a solid 6–2 record with a spectacular 1.30 ERA after joining the Pirates on August 8, and he had won the two games he pitched against the Reds. With Smith facing Jackson, the Pirates seemed to hold a clear advantage going into Game 3. Smith, however, who felt that he had too much rest and that he needed a tired arm for his sinkerball to be effective, had his worst game as a Pirate. In the second inning, he gave up a two-run homer to Billy Hatcher, who had been traded by the Pirates to the Reds in April, and a three-run homer to light-hitting Mariano Duncan in the fifth. "I made two mistakes," Smith said, "They were awfully big mistakes."[10]

Smith's sinker was not sinking, and the Pirates hitters did not help matters. After tying the game, 2–2, in the fourth on a base hit by Bonilla and a double from Carmelo Martínez, they still had the bases loaded with only one out. Lind struck out, however, and Smith tapped the ball back to Jackson to end the inning. After falling behind, 5–2, on Duncan's home run, the Pirates loaded the bases in the fifth but again failed to score. While Leyland had hoped to build early leads, instead his team had fallen behind once again and faced the challenge of rallying against the Reds' Nasty Boys. The Pirates managed to score a run in the bottom of the eighth on an error, but the Reds added an insurance run in the top of the ninth on a Duncan base hit to increase their lead to 6–3. In the bottom of the ninth, Myers struck out the side, putting a disappointing end to Game 3.

The Pirates tried to put a good face on the defeat and on falling behind in the series. "We're not going to roll over and die," promised Van Slyke.[11] Bonds declared that it was only a matter of time before the Pirates' "Big Three" started to deliver, but no one seemed to have an answer for why the team was struggling or how to fix it. Bonilla pledged, "I'm going to keep swinging the bat," Van Slyke was looking for "more walks," and Bonds thought they all needed to show more "patience."[12]

Game 4 saw a rematch between Game 1 starters Walk and Rijo. While a win from Walk in Game 1 was a bonus, a win in Game 4 had now become a necessity. The Pirates were in danger of going down 3–1 and, with another loss, would be forced to win their final game at home and two games in Cincinnati to advance to the World Series. Attendance was slightly up for Game 4, and the crowd was noticeably louder, but there were still nearly ten thousand empty seats, hardly the hometown excitement and support the Pirates were looking for to help them mount a series comeback.

During the season, Pirates fans had dubbed Three Rivers Stadium the "Field of Dreams" after the 1989 Academy-Award-nominated movie of the same name, and they brought stalks of corn to Game 4. After Walk retired the Reds in the first, the Pirates finally took an early lead. Wally Backman doubled off Rijo to start the bottom of the first and eventually came around to score on groundouts from Jay Bell and Van Slyke. Walk looked strong at the beginning, but he gave up a solo home run to O'Neill to tie the game in the fourth. Before the inning was over, back-to-back base hits from Davis and Hal Morris, and a fly ball from Chris Sabo had the Pirates trailing again.

Behind 2–1, the Pirates tied the game in the bottom of the fourth when Bream hit a ground-rule double to bring home Van Slyke. Bream almost scored on a base hit from Lind, but slowed by a surgically repaired knee he was thrown out at home by Hatcher to end the inning. When Sabo hit a two-run homer off Walk to put the Reds up, 4–2, in the top of the seventh, the Pirates were behind yet again with the Reds' bullpen ready to close out the game. As Dibble put it, "If we have the lead by the sixth inning, the Pirates start thinking about us."[13]

After Bream led off the bottom of the eighth with a solo homer to cut the lead to 4–3, Piniella replaced Rijo with Myers, who had yet to give up a run in the series. The Reds hoped Myers would make quick work of the Pirates, but with one out Bonilla sent a line drive into deep center field. Both the ball and Hatcher banged into the outfield wall at the same time, and while the ball bounced back into the playing field, Hatcher came crashing down on the warning track. It was an easy double, but seeing an opportunity to get to third base with only one out, Bonilla took a chance.

Davis had been playing in pain the entire series. He was batting a dismal .158 and had driven in only one run. But as Bonilla's hit rolled on the outfield turf, he seemed to come out of nowhere to scoop up the ball and launch a perfect throw to third, where Sabo easily tagged out Bonilla. Instead of a man on third with one out and Bonds due up, the Pirates had no one on with two outs. Bonds gave the Pirates one last hope in the bottom of the eighth when he singled and stole second, but Bream, who was 3-for-7 against Myers with a home run during the season, struck out

The Pirates Take On the Nasty Boys

to end the inning. In the bottom of the ninth, Dibble struck out two Pirates in a one-two-three inning, and the game was over.

While the Reds were now up three games to one with only one game remaining in Pittsburgh, Leyland remained as committed as ever to his team. "I'm not going to look for faults in my team because I'm not going to desert my team. Ever."[14] The Reds, however, were hardly lacking in confidence, especially Dibble and Rijo, who gloatingly pronounced the series as good as over. Rijo was already discussing how the Reds would match up against the Oakland As in the World Series.

Larkin, on the other hand, was more cautious. "We just won three straight. Why can't the Pirates?"[15] A three-game sweep of the remaining contests in a postseason series, although rare, was not impossible. The Pirates had made baseball history in the 1925 World Series by coming back from a 3–1 deficit, and they had repeated the feat in the 1979 World Series. The Pirates had won four straight from the Reds in Cincinnati in mid-July, and now they had Drabek ready for Game 5. Asked if the critical importance of the game would alter his performance, Drabek simply said, "Why change now?"[16]

The Pirates had scored only eleven runs in the first four games. They would score only three in Game 5, but that would be enough for Drabek. After giving up a run in the first on a Larkin double and his own wild pickoff throw, Drabek was nearly perfect for the next six innings. In the bottom of the first, after Reds starter Browning hit Bell with a pitch, Van Slyke tripled Bell home with the tying run and scored later in the inning on a Bonds groundball to give the Pirates a 2–1 lead. In the bottom of the fourth, after Bonds walked and went to third on an R.J. Reynolds single, Don Slaught increased the Pirates' lead to 3–1 by scoring Bonds on a sacrifice fly.

In the top of the eighth, Drabek ran into his first trouble since the opening inning. He gave up a run-scoring two-out double to Larkin that cut the Pirates' lead to one, but he managed to get out of the inning without any further scoring. The Pirates' bullpen had been successful holding leads during the season, but it had no dominant closer for Leyland to turn to. In the top of the ninth, with the Pirates clinging to a 3–2 lead, Leyland decided to leave Drabek in the game. Afterward, he said, "If I had [Oakland As' All-Star reliever] Dennis Eckersley, I probably would have taken him out," but he claimed he had something better than a dominant closer. "I had Cy Young."[17]

Despite his manager's confidence, Drabek gave up back-to-back singles to O'Neill and Davis to start the ninth inning. When Morris sacrificed them to second and third, the Pirates were a base hit away from the end of their season. Leyland, at that point, decided to bring in left-handed Bob Patterson, who walked Sabo intentionally to face left-hand hitting catcher Jeff Reed. Just weeks earlier, Patterson had saved Drabek's twentieth victory of the season. He now faced the task of saving Drabek's first postseason win and the Pirates' season.

On Patterson's third pitch, Reed hit a groundball in between short and third that looked like it was headed into left field for a two-run game-winning single. Bonilla, who had moved in from right field to play third base when King's ailing back prevented him from starting the game, cut the ball off, fired it to Lind to force Sabo at second, then watched Lind pivot and flip the ball to Bream for a game-ending and series-saving double play.

After the dramatic victory, the Pirates, still down 3–2 in games, were confident they could win the series in Cincinnati. "It's not over yet," said an ecstatic Bonilla after the game.[18] Backman claimed he never doubted that Drabek would extend the series at least another game. He said that he had packed his bag for Cincinnati before the game even started.[19] "We might still be the underdogs," beamed Bell, "But in our hearts, we know we can win two games there and go on to the World Series."[20]

The only sour note after the Pirates' victory came from Bonds, who questioned King's absence from the lineup. King had played all of Game 4 despite his sore back but sat out Game 5. "It's kind of funny that he hurt his back a couple days ago but then was able to play the other day, then couldn't play tonight," Bonds said. He added, "There's a lot of minor league third basemen who would like to play everyday up here." King ignored the comments, but Leyland was upset with Bonds's criticism, especially after a game that should have, if anything, brought the team closer. Visibly agitated with Bonds, who was hitting only .176 in the series, Leyland told reporters, "It was my decision not to play Jeff King."[21]

At a press conference in Cincinnati before Game 6, Zane Smith said he would be starting against the Reds' Danny Jackson, but he knew that was not true. Leyland had decided that thirty-five-year-old Ted Power, signed as a free agent for 1990, would start Game 6 for the Pirates, but Leyland instructed Smith not to reveal his plan. Power had relieved in forty games that year but had not been used as a starter. Leyland's unorthodox and controversial strategy was to start a right-hander to force Piniella to insert his left-hand hitters into the lineup, then bring the left-handed Smith into the game after an inning or two.

Respected for his openness, Leyland was roundly criticized for his deception and manipulation of the press. His choice also seemed to backfire when Power gave up an unearned run in the bottom of the first on a Larkin single, a stolen base, and a bad throw from catcher Slaught. Power, however, kept the Reds from scoring in the second, and Smith, who took over in the third, gave up only one run in his four innings. While Leyland's strategy seemed to work against the Reds' offense, the problem for the Pirates, once again, was their own offense.

In Game 6, the Pirates' hitters would be at their worst. Jackson retired the first thirteen hitters he faced (just one short of a championship series record), and he did not allow a hit until an RBI double by Martínez (the only Pirates hit in the game) in the fifth that tied the score at 1–1. When Smith gave up an RBI single to pinch-hitter Luis Quinones in the bottom of the seventh, the Pirates trailed 2–1. Once again they had to face Myers, who struck out two batters, around a walk, to retire the Pirates in the eighth.

In the top of the ninth, down to their last at-bats, the Pirates came just inches short of staying in the series. With one out, Bonds drew a walk. Martínez followed by launching a ball into deep right field that appeared to be a home run. As the ball headed over the outfield fence, Glenn Braggs, who was put into the game by Piniella for his defense, leaped high into the air. When he came back down, the ball was in his glove. With two outs and Reds fans roaring in anticipation, Myers struck out Slaught on a high fastball to end the game. The 1990 Pittsburgh Pirates' season was over.

"It really is like a dream," Braggs said after the game.[22] For the Pirates, however, it was more like a nightmare. Every critical play in the series seemed to go against them. Braggs's catch was not the most spectacular play of the series (that belonged to Davis's throw in Game 4), but it was the most definitive. "That catch summed up the whole series," Bonilla said following the game. "If we pitched well, they pitched better. If we got a big hit, they got a bigger hit."[23]

When the Pirates arrived in Pittsburgh at 2:45 in the morning, there were about 120 fans waiting to greet them, a far cry from the mob scene they had encountered only a few weeks earlier after clinching the division. Van Slyke smiled and waved as the small crowd chanted "Let's Go Bucs." Leyland reached out to shake the hands of Pirates fans, while (perhaps not surprisingly) Bonds complained to reporters, this time about the generous strike zone for the Reds' pitchers.[24]

The Pirates did not make it to the World Series in 1990, but they brought winning baseball back to Pittsburgh. Going into the 1991 season, they would be favorites to win their division. By the season's end, they were the heavy favorite to win the National League pennant and play in the World Series.

CHAPTER FIVE

WINNING THE DIVISION, AFTER LOSING SID BREAM

The 1991 Season

The National League Championship Series loss to the Cincinnati Reds was a painful disappointment for Pirates fans after all the excitement of the 1990 season, but they had plenty of good news to comfort them as they waited until next year. Every major baseball award during the offseason went to a Pittsburgh Pirate, and in each case the voting was nearly unanimous. To no one's surprise, the National League Cy Young Award for pitcher of the year went to Doug Drabek, whose twenty-two wins were the most for a Pirate since Bob Friend in 1958. Drabek received first-place votes on twenty-three of the twenty-four ballots cast by the voting members of the Baseball Writers' Association of America (BBWAA). The only dissenting vote was for Dodger Ramón Martínez. Drabek became only the second Pirate to win the award. Vern Law received the award in 1960, which at that time was granted to the best pitcher in both leagues.

There was also little doubt about the NL Manager of the Year. Jim Leyland, an unknown when he was hired by Syd Thrift for the 1986 season, easily won the honor over Reds manager Lou Piniella, the Expos'

Buck Rodgers, and the Dodgers' Tom Lasorda. Leyland received seventeen votes to three each for Piniella and Rodgers and one for Lasorda. In the past, the *Sporting News* had selected Pirates managers, including Billy Meyer, Danny Murtaugh, and Leyland (who shared the honor with Lasorda in 1988) for their Manager of the Year Award; but no Pirates manager until Leyland had been selected as Manager of the Year by the BBWAA. Leyland's overwhelming popularity in Pittsburgh was evident when he received the Dapper Dan Sportsman of the Year Award.[1] When a tearful Leyland accepted the honor, he said that when the Pirates hired him he told them, "They've got a manager from the get-go. And I'll be here until they tell me they don't want me."[2]

In late August of 1990 Barry Bonds and Bobby Bonilla were having such outstanding seasons that they were asked to speculate on the possibility that they would share the NL Most Valuable Player Award. The award had been shared only once—in 1979, when Stargell was the co-MVP with the Cardinals' Keith Hernandez—but never with teammates. Bonilla pointed to Bonds and said, "It's him. I'm having a good year. He's having a m-o-n-s-t-e-r year." Bonds responded by saying, "I think I've had an MVP year," but, remembering his salary arbitration loss, he added that if he received the award, "I'll be compared to the best players in salary arbitration."[3]

When the award was announced, Bonds, with his .301 average, 33 home runs, and 114 RBIs, was a nearly unanimous choice, receiving 23 of the 24 first-place votes cast by the BBWAA. The only dissenting vote went to his teammate and close friend Bonilla. Bonds was gracious in accepting the MVP award and in recognizing the role that his teammates played in his successful season. It was also clear, from comments he made during the season, that the award would soon serve as leverage in his approaching salary negotiations with the Pirates.

Near the end of the 1990 season, as the Pirates were battling the Mets for the East Division title, the *Post-Gazette*'s Bob Smizik threw cold water on Pirates fans who were dreaming of a championship. No matter the outcome of the division race, he reminded fans, there were challenges facing the Pirates' front office during the offseason in salary demands and free agency: "Bobby Bonilla's agent is making staggering contractual demands. Barry Bonds regularly has wailed about his unhappiness with the terms of his contract. A gaggle of players, including Zane Smith, Sid Bream, Don Slaught, R.J. Reynolds and Ted Power, are eligible for free agency after the season." Acknowledging that the small-market Pirates did not have the resources to sign every player, Smizik wondered, "Who are the Pirates going to attempt to keep? How are they going to pay them?"[4]

The purpose behind Smizik's article was to convince the Pirates' upper management that, with all the challenges and uncertainties facing the team going into the 1991 season, the number one priority should be securing Leyland, who had only one year remaining on his contract. "The Pirates must realize what a prize they have in Leyland. They will get around to extending his contract but they shouldn't wait too long." After Leyland reminded the Pirates that the only thing he wanted "was to be working on two years," the team moved quickly to extend his contract for another year along with a promise to do everything possible to keep the team intact.[5]

One month after free agency began on November 5, the Pirates fell short when Sid Bream signed a three-year $5.6 million contract with the Atlanta Braves. Going into negotiations, Bream assumed that the Pirates, after making the playoffs, were "not losing anyone" and that he was the team's "first priority." That changed when Bream received an offer he described as "not even close to the marketplace." When he received a more substantial offer from the Braves, he spoke with Leyland, who expressed his fear that the Pirates were about to lose their first baseman. After talking with Leyland, Bream consulted his attorney, who advised him to take the Braves' offer. Knowing that they were about to lose many close friends, Bream and his wife "cried all night long." At the last minute Bream even offered to sign with the Pirates for less money than he wanted if they would improve their offer, but in the end he felt the Pirates left him with no choice but to sign with the Braves.[6]

The loss of Bream upset Leyland: "He was everything we stood for, a guy who was good for the community, a total team guy, and a damn good player."[7] A month later the Pirates lost another key player, when valuable utility infielder Wally Backman signed a $650,000 contract with the Phillies. They also lost R.J. Reynolds, who eventually left to play baseball in Japan after the Pirates expressed no interest in re-signing him.

The free agent news, however, was not all bad for the Pirates. They did sign two priority targets, pitcher Zane Smith and catcher Don Slaught, to multi-year contracts, though the signings also fueled the growing anger of Bonds and Bonilla, who were headed to salary arbitration if the Pirates did not offer them long-term contracts. The Pirates were working on a multi-year deal, reportedly at $17 million over four years, for Bonilla, but they refused to consider a multi-year contract for Bonds because he was not in his final year of arbitration.

Bob Hertzel of the *Pittsburgh Press* reported that Bonds wanted "a multi-year contract or a one-year deal that will pay him $3 million plus incentives and a salary bonus." If the Pirates refused and took him to salary arbitration, Bonds said, a "$100 million" offer "won't keep him with Pittsburgh once he becomes eligible for free agency after the 1992 season." Bonds, who had lost his 1990 arbitration hearing and ended up with an $850,000 salary, told Hertzel, "They are going to pay for what they did to me last year." When Hertzel pointed out that the Pirates had set a salary figure of $2.3 million for their arbitration hearing with Bonds, who set his own salary demand at $3.3 million, Bonds told Hertzel, "If I'm not a $3 million player, then there isn't a 3 million dollar player in baseball." He flatly stated, "I will not lose [in arbitration]. This time there's nothing against me." As for the Pirates claim that they were limited financially, Bonds said, "If they don't have the money let someone with money buy the club."[8]

The reaction to Bonds's outburst from Pirates fans and particularly the press was immediate and negative. The *Post-Gazette*'s Gene Collier mocked Bonds's surliness and ridiculed his performance during the playoffs. Pointing out that the annual Piratefest weekend was approaching, where fans would have the opportunity to meet the players and have them sign autographs, Collier wrote that it was a shame there would be no Bonds booth where he could supplement his salary by charging "Insults—$2; Sneers—$2.50; Random episode of unconscionable rudeness—$5; Brief self-absorbed tirade—$7; Extended infantile tirade—$10; Autographs—$13." Collier also advised Bonds not to criticize any of his teammates in light of his own performance in the playoffs: while batting only .168, "you had more strikeouts than hits in the playoffs . . . drove in only one run in the playoffs . . . lost Game 2 by misplaying a fly ball, then whined about the sun and the starting time because you're too stupid to realize that television dictates these things so they can pay you the $3.35 million you're asking for."[9]

The Pirates denied that they were actively trying to get rid of Bonds, but they were quietly making it known that he was available for the right offer. Sportswriter John Perrotto reported rumors "that the Yankees and the White Sox were preparing big packages in an effort to lure the multi-talented left fielder."[10] While the Yankees were reportedly offering their top prospect Bernie Williams as part of a trade, the most intriguing story had the White Sox willing to include Sammy Sosa in their package.[11]

The Pirates did not trade Bonds. Had they known what would happen over the next several weeks, they may have regretted that decision. On February 16, two days after Drabek won his arbitration hearing for a record-breaking $3.3 million salary (triple what he made the previous season) Bonilla lost his arbitration hearing and had to settle for $2.4 million rather than the $3.475 he was seeking. The next day, Bonds, who said he could not possibly lose his arbitration hearing, lost his bid for $3.3 million and had to settle for $2.3 million. When Bonds arrived in Bradenton for the start of spring training, he made his displeasure with the Pirates clear by refusing, at first, to talk with reporters. The *Post-Gazette*'s Paul Meyer reported that Bonds, after stowing his equipment in his locker, told an approaching reporter "Man, don't even talk to me." A few minutes later, when the Pirates' media relations director Jim Lachimia asked Bonds "if he were talking to the media, his answer was brief, 'Nobody.'" When another reporter approached Bonds and asked for an interview, he laughed and said, "No thank you."[12]

While Bonds practiced, at least momentarily, what Meyer called "the silence of the MVP," a seething Bonilla was embroiled in a last-ditch effort by the Pirates to sign him to a long-term contract. The Pirates were offering a four-year $16 million deal, but Bonilla was holding out for five years and $20 million. While Bonds would not talk directly about his own situation, he could not resist needling the Pirates. When asked what he would do if he were in Bonilla's situation, Bonds replied, "I don't have free agency. I can't be a free agent for two years. So I really don't know. But if they offered me that kind of money, I'd jump to sign it."[13]

The growing tension at spring training exploded a week later in a confrontation between Bonds and Leyland that would reverberate throughout the rest of their careers. It started during what should have been a routine outfield drill conducted by former Pirates player and manager Bill Virdon, who was now helping out as coach and instructor. Bonds had his own photographer taking pictures of him, but when Lachimia brought two television crews over to film the routine, Bonds, who was still boycotting the media, lashed out at Lachimia. When Virdon tried to intervene, Bonds got into a shouting match with Virdon.

When Leyland heard all the yelling, he ran over and engaged in what was described as "an obscenity-laced shouting match."[14] When challenged by Bonds, Leyland angrily shouted, "Don't fuck with me. . . . If you don't want to be here, get your fuckin' ass off the field . . . Let's get the fuckin' show over with or go home." When Bonds still appeared to question his authority, Leyland lashed out again: "I'm the manager of this team. That's who the fuck I am." Lanny Frattare, the longtime Pirates broadcaster, remembered Leyland's parting words to Bonds: "I've kissed your ass for three years. I'm not going to do it anymore."[15]

The incident was typical of Leyland when he lost his temper, but he usually exploded in the privacy of the clubhouse. Don Slaught remembered how Leyland would "rant and rave" at his players and then disappear into his office. The players would wait a few seconds, look at each other, and then Leyland would explode out of his office again. After he went back in, they would nod at each other because they "knew he was coming back."[16] Leyland did the same thing in his confrontation with Bonds. He shouted at him, began to walk away, then came back and shouted some more. The only difference this time was that there were cameras rolling.

Immediately after the incident was over, an upset Leyland told reporters, "I'm the goddamn manager and I'm going to run the goddam team." He added, "I don't give a damn what his problems are, he's not going to run this camp. He can just go home."[17] A subdued Bonds, now willing to talk to reporters, said he did not care if the incident damaged his reputation: "I'm just going to play baseball." To the astonishment of the gathered press, he denied being unhappy playing for the Pirates and could not understand why he had "such a negative image in Pittsburgh."[18] Once Leyland had a chance to cool down, he tried to get a proper perspective on his confrontation with Bonds, calling it "a family squabble that just boiled a bit. . . . I consider what happened minor." He admitted that "the tension was thick in camp," but he insisted that the Pirates were capable of taking care "of our business and go on, because we're a pretty damn good team." As for Bonds, Leyland said, "Barry's the best player in the league, the most talented player in the league and I haven't had any problems with him. But I'm the manager of the team and I've got to head off problems when I see them."[19]

Bonds's teammates, with the exception of Bonilla, were not as forgiving as his manager. In a television interview, pitcher John Smiley said, "Barry needs to grow up." He added, "Barry would be a great guy if he would just let some things go. I mean you don't have to say 'I this' and 'I that.' You know we're all here as a team and we have great members, but it's a part of a team effort."[20] Van Slyke, who reportedly had several run-ins of his own with Bonds and whose multi-year contract was an early catalyst for Bonds's and Bonilla's unhappiness, said that he could not understand Bonds's unhappiness with a $2.3 million salary, nearly triple what Bonds had made in 1990: "Baseball players are the luckiest people in the whole world. We're all making great money. . . . You should have nothing to complain about and it's unfortunate that we do have people in this camp who find themselves having to do that."[21]

Meanwhile, Leyland's managerial counterparts were effusive in their praise for his courage in standing up to a high-salaried star player. Sparky Anderson, manager of the Detroit Tigers, claimed that Leyland "saved a lot of people a lot of problems." He told a reporter that Leyland showed "a lot of courage. This may be one of the most important things he did for all our clubs in 1991. . . . I think what he did will improve all 26 clubs. My guys are certainly talking about it. What Leyland did he did for everyone."[22]

Leyland hoped that his confrontation with Bonds would bring an end to the growing tension in the ballclub and allow the club to focus on preparations for the upcoming season, but there was one more major distraction. When Leyland signed his two-year extension, general manager Larry Doughty promised his manager that "every effort would be made to sign the Pirates four star-caliber players." With the season approaching, Doughty was still trying: "We've got to get it done—for the immediate and the long term future."[23] When Bonds heard what Doughty had said, he responded, "I'll believe it when I see it."[24]

Bonds and Drabek would not become free agents for two more years, so Doughty's major target was Bonilla, who would become a free agent after the 1991 season, and Van Slyke, who was in the last year of his three-year contract. His effort to sign Bonilla reached a snag when Bonilla, once again, rejected a four-year contract for $16 million and told the Pirates he would not sign a deal unless it was for five years and $20 million. When questioned by the media about his refusal of such a large offer, Bonilla said, "It's not the money. It's the principle." Still smarting from his arbitration defeats, Bonilla added, "They said they wouldn't give Don Slaught a three-year deal. They gave Don Slaught a three-year deal. They said they wouldn't give Zane Smith a four-year deal and they gave him a four-year deal. Now I've been here when we lost 98 games. I've been here when no one wanted to play here. I'm asking for five years and I'm the one who is crazy. I want five years."[25]

With the chances of signing Bonilla slipping away, the Pirates turned their attention to Van Slyke. Two days before the season opener, any hope of keeping Bonilla in a Pirates uniform all but ended when the Pirates announced that Van Slyke had signed a contract extension covering the next four years. With a seething Bonilla headed for free agency and an angry Bonds alienated from teammates, reporters, and fans, the Pirates presented Van Slyke as the public face of the Pirates. In an effusive article that appeared in the *Pirates' Official 1991 Magazine and Scorecard*, John Mehno of the *Altoona Mirror* portrayed the newly signed Van Slyke as a fun-loving prankster "prone to outward flights of goofiness," like driving golf balls out of Three Rivers Stadium, but someone possessed "of an inner peace. Life has been good and Van Slyke is perceptive enough to know that." As for Van Slyke's recent contract negotiations, Mehno praised Van Slyke for taking a "mature, reasoned approach," which he characterized as something quite different "in an industry where egos demand one dollar more than the next guy." Mehno went on to describe Van Slyke's struggle with dyslexia in his youth and his lack of direction and maturity early in his career. Van Slyke, however, turned his life and career around, according to Mehno, when he committed himself to Christianity: "I had the ability to play baseball, but that was given to me. In a sense after I became a Christian I felt an obligation to do something with that ability and not waste it." That opportunity came when he was traded to Pittsburgh, where it all came together: "He has financial security, a manager who thinks he's the best center fielder in the game and an important job with a contending team. What's not to like?"[26]

While Mehno was writing that fans had plenty to like in Van Slyke as the Pirates approached their 1991 season, Bob Smizik of the *Post-Gazette* worried that they had plenty to dislike in Bonds. In "Give Him a Break, Don't Boo Bonds," an article that appeared just a day before the Pirates' opener against Montreal, Smizik pleaded with fans to go easy on Bonds even though he had proved himself a "big jerk" in the offseason: "How should tomorrow night's crowd deal with Bonds? Gently folks, gently. Give him a break. Does he deserve it? Probably not. But the Pirates do. He's their most important player. This is no time for vengeance; it's a time for compassion. Why start the season on a sour note." Smizik also pointed out that Bonds "has shut up for more than a month. . . . It's as if he realizes he has gone too far." Bonilla, putting aside his own frustrations, was quick to defend his best friend on the team: "People have to have a lot of patience with Barry. They forget that Barry had done all of his growing up in the big leagues and we tend to be a little spoiled up here." Even Van Slyke came to Bonds's defense: "Of course, booing bothers a player. How would you like to be standing out there in front of 50,000 people and have them booing you?" Jim Leyland added, "I hope there's total appreciation for Barry Bonds's effort because he has given us nothing but his best since he's been here. I would hope there's nothing but total applause for him."[27]

The 54,274 fans who attended the opener at Three Rivers did not need to boo Bonds. The Pirates' poor performance was enough in itself to begin the season on a sour note. With Cy Young Award–winner Drabek giving up four runs in only five innings, the Pirates lost, 7–0, to the Expos on a one-hitter by starter Dennis Martínez and two relievers. In their next game, in front of only 6,624 fans, they rallied late to defeat the Expos, 4–3, for their first win of the season. Behind the strong pitching of Smith and three hits and two RBIs by Bonilla, the Pirates took the series a day later with a 6–3 victory.

With another strong pitching performance, this time from Smiley, and the clutch hitting of Bonilla, the Pirates opened a three-game series in Chicago with a 3–1 win. But the next day, after another poor performance by Drabek, they lost 7–3 to the Cubs. The only Pirates runs in the game came on a three-run homer from Lloyd McClendon, who had gone into the game to replace Bonds after Bonds hurt his wrist and knee crashing into the outfield brick wall at Wrigley Field. With Bonds out of the lineup the next day, the Pirates wasted home runs from Bonilla and starting pitcher Walk in a 6–4 loss, then returned to Pittsburgh, where the Mets scored six runs in the ninth inning to defeat them 9–3 and drop the team a game under .500, with a 3–4 record.

The biggest problem for the Pirates at the start of the season, besides Drabek's erratic pitching, was their lack of hitting, the same problem that plagued them in the 1990 postseason. They went five games into the season before hitting a home run, and every regular, with the exception of Bonilla, struggled at bat. Bonilla soared to a .438 average in the early going, while a frustrated Bonds was hitting only .111 at the time of his injury. When he returned to the lineup, Bonds continued to slump, and twelve games into the season he was batting a dismal .069. The *Post-Gazette*'s Meyer, one of the few reporters who had a good working relationship with him, thought that Bonds was pressing and trying "to do too much."[28]

Despite the poor starts of their star performers, the Pirates began to turn things around with a combination of strong pitching, timely hitting, and outstanding fielding. They won nine of their next ten games, which included a six-game winning streak. On April 20, 1991, after a 9–3 win at home against the Cubs, they moved into a tie for first place, where they would remain for the rest of the season. In their next game, played on a rainy, chilly Sunday afternoon, the Pirates came up with their most dramatic win of the season and, in the process, made baseball history. The game started out as gloomily as the weather. Going into the bottom of the eighth, the Pirates trailed the Cubs 7–2. They rallied for four runs and, in the bottom of the ninth, to the joy of the few soggy fans still in the stands, tied the score at 7–7. In the top of the eleventh, however, the Cubs' Andre Dawson topped off a five-run rally with a grand slam and sent most of the remaining fans headed for the exits.

Laurie Graham, die-hard Pirates fan and author of the Pittsburgh memoir *Singing the City*, was at that game and remembers feeling "a crush of disappointment" when Dawson hit his grand slam. But the Pirates, with the help of a clutch base hit by Bonds, fought back in the bottom of the eleventh and trailed by only one run with the bases loaded. When Slaught drove a ball over the head of the Cubs' center fielder, Bonilla and Bonds scored to give the Pirates a miraculous 13–12 victory, it was the greatest extra-inning comeback in baseball history.

After the game, Leyland, who was barely able to face the television cameras, broke into tears as he said, "they showed why they're professionals. Nobody gave up. . . . They always give their best. I'm proud of that." Leyland went out of his way to praise the team, but for Graham, the victory belonged to the manager: "Leyland had become the face of the team, the one constant holding the team together. As a person, he was the embodiment of how we, as a city envisioned ourselves: unpretentious, straight-forward, self-deprecating, tough when we needed to be, a family man, a believer in work. He was proud of his players, proud of their effort."[29] The victory also fulfilled a pledge Leyland had made to Pittsburgh fans during spring training back in 1988: "We're developing a relationship with our fans and we're doing it by hard work. Pittsburgh is very much a workingman's city, and we're a perfect club for that city, because we've got a bunch of hungry players. . . . A lot of people say we were at a disadvantage as a ball club because Pittsburgh was so depressed. I think, sadly, that that was to our advantage because of the style of baseball we were going to play. We had a good chance to win the fans back if we busted our ass. That's all they would have asked."[30]

The Pirates won sixteen games in their last at-bat in 1991, but the 13–12 win over the Cubs, after scoring six runs in the bottom of the eleventh, was the most compelling and set the stage for another division title run. Despite Drabek's early struggles and Bonds's low .177 average, the Pirates ended April with a 13–7 record and a half-game lead over the Cardinals. With Drabek losing his first two games in May and Bonds still batting below .200, the Pirates managed a 6–4 record in their first ten games in the month. They fared worse in their next eight games, going 4–4. After losing the last two games of a three-game homestand against the Cards, however, the Pirates pounded the Phillies 9–1 and went on to close out May with seven straight wins and a commanding six-game lead over the Mets.

There was plenty to cheer about during the Pirates' winning streak. After starting the season with a record of 2–7, Drabek threw a one-hit shutout in St. Louis on May 27 in the first game of a three-game sweep of the Cardinals. In the third game of the series, Smith matched Drabek's one-hitter and raised his record to 7–2. While Drabek was struggling to get back in form, Smiley had become the Pirates' best starter. He finished May with a 7–1 record, while Walk, who had been out with a groin injury, picked up his first win in the last game of the month. Leyland's "bullpen-by-committee," led by Bill Landrum's fifteen scoreless innings on his way to fifteen consecutive saves, was also impressive.

While the Pirates were getting a solid early-season performance from Bonilla, who was hitting over .300 and leading the team in RBIs, Bonds had a horrendous start. He raised his average, though, to .236 by the end of May, and he was beginning to hit with power and steal bases again. The real offensive boost, however, came from Little League legend and future Pirates manager McClendon, who hit well coming off the bench, and from first baseman Orlando Merced, who finished May with a team-leading .326 average and hit a dramatic game-ending home run in the eleventh inning against the Phillies.[31] Merced grew up worshipping Pirates legend and fellow Puerto Rican Roberto Clemente.

Bream's new team, the Braves, paid their first visit of the 1991 season to Pittsburgh on May 10. Many Pirates fans remained loyal to Bream and had yet to forgive the Pirates for giving him up to free agency. For his part, Bream had left behind many friends and did not want to take the field against the Pirates. He did not start the game, but with the Pirates ahead 5–1, Braves manager Bobby Cox called on him to pinch-hit for Francisco Cabrera in the top of the ninth. When Bream homered against Stan Belinda and circled the bases, the Pirates fans gave him a standing ovation.[32] The Pirates won, 5–2, but lost the next two games in the series. They lost two more games to the Braves in late May. In Atlanta, Bream homered again, this time a grand slam against Bob Patterson, one of Bream's closest friends and a fellow participant in the Pirates' chapel circle. Bream later recalled the pain he felt and "the tears in his eyes" as he circled the bases.[33] At the time, no one was concerned about the early-season losses to the Braves, who had finished last in their division in 1990. It would be the upstart Braves, however, with their promising young pitchers, talented young hitters, and veteran free agent acquisitions, who would give the Pirates the most trouble during the regular season and stand in the way of a Pirates trip to the 1991 World Series.

For the time being, the Pirates extended their winning streak to nine games in early June, but they went on to play sluggish baseball for the rest of the month. They managed only a 4–5 record in a homestand against the Giants, Padres, and Dodgers, then traveled to the West Coast and went 4–6 against the same teams. When they returned home and lost the first game of a three-game series against the Cubs, their record fell to 40–27, and their lead in the division dropped to four games. Only a five-game winning streak at the end of June against the Cubs and the Expos prevented them from having a losing month. The winning streak also restored their division lead against the Mets to a healthy six games.

The story for the Pirates' pitching staff in June was the return to form of Drabek, who went 3–1 during the month, and the return from groin and hamstring injuries of Walk, who had a 4–0 record in June.

The bad news in June, and the reason the Pirates barely played .500 baseball for the month, was the struggle of Smiley and Smith. In the month of June, Smiley went 2–4, and Smith lost his first four games before finally winning his last start of the month. The good news for the Pirates' offense was the slow recovery of Bonds from his poor start. By the end of June, he had improved his average to .263—up nearly thirty points since the end of May—and was leading the team in home runs and RBIs. The Pirates badly needed Bonds to pick up its offense because Bonilla, after his sensational start, hit only one home run in June and was struggling to drive in runs. The Pirates were winning games, but mostly because of their flare for late-inning dramatics. Going into July, no Pirates regular was batting over .300 on a team that was supposed to have one of the best offenses in baseball. The Pirates began July with a 3–4 record before the All-Star break and saw their comfortable six-game lead cut to two and a half by the streaking Mets.

Despite his recent struggles, Bonilla was selected for the All-Star Game and started the game as the National League's designated hitter. Batting fourth, he singled twice and drove in a run in a 4–2 loss to the American League. Smiley, who made a brief appearance in the game, was also selected as an All-Star, but the surprise was the exclusion of reigning MVP Bonds from the game. An even bigger surprise for Pittsburgh sportswriters and fans was Bonds's silence after he was not selected for the All-Star team. Bonds did not complain to the media about the snub, but it may well have motivated him once the Pirates returned to action. He homered in three of the first four games, drove in eleven runs, and spurred the Pirates to a six-game winning streak and a four-and-a-half-game division lead. Bonilla, after a month-long home run drought, also exploded after the break, hitting four home runs in his first eight games and bringing his batting average back over .300. Van Slyke, who was coming back from knee surgery in the offseason, also broke out of his season-long hitting struggles and drove in key runs during the streak.

After the streak ended, the Pirates went on to win seven of their next ten games. After defeating the Astros on July 27 they were a season-high twenty-six games above .500, at 60–24, and had increased their division lead over the Mets to seven games. While Bonds, Bonilla, and Van Slyke were leading the way, the Pirates were also getting excellent starting pitching from Drabek, who won eight of his last ten starts, and Smiley, who won his first three starts after the All-Star break and improved his record to 12–6. Walk had gone down with another injury, but Smith and recent call-up Randy Tomlin were pitching well, as was Neal Heaton, who came out of the bullpen to take Walk's place in the rotation. The bullpen was also effective though Leyland, instead of relying on one closer, was now rotating Belinda and Landrum to finish out games.

After losing the last game of a three-game series in Houston, the Pirates closed out the month of July with four games in Atlanta. They had struggled against the Braves in their earlier meetings, and the series in Atlanta would prove no exception. Despite McClendon's two home runs, the Pirates lost the first game of a twilight doubleheader, 7–5, when Drabek struggled on the mound. In the second game, the Braves defeated Smiley, 5–3. The Pirates fared no better the next night losing, 10–3, after Landrum, one of their most consistent relievers, gave up eight runs in two innings. Then they blew a 6–2 lead in an 8–6 loss in the series finale and ended July with a five-game losing streak that saw their division lead reduced to four and a half games.

The Pirates opened August with a four-game series in St. Louis. The new month and the change in cities, however, did little to help the Pirates shake their losing streak. They lost the series opener to the Cardinals, 6–3, but in the second game, they took a 3–2 lead into the bottom of the ninth. This time Belinda gave up the tying and winning runs. The next day, the Pirates suffered another painful defeat when yet another of their best relievers, Bob Patterson, gave up the winning run in the tenth inning in a 6–5 loss. The defeat extended the losing streak, their worst of the season, to eight games. The reeling Pirates, however, saw their streak end in the series finale, when they defeated the Cardinals, 2–1, with the help of a key error by the usually sure-handed shortstop Ozzie Smith.

The Pirates' long road trip that had begun so promisingly with two wins in Houston and then quickly descended into the depths of the season's longest losing streak finally came to an end in New York. Losing two out of three to the Mets, the Pirates closed out the road trip with four wins and ten losses and came back home with a shaky four-game division lead. They limped back to Pittsburgh to open a ten-game home-stand that would either give them the boost they needed to take control of the division race or continue a slump that could eventually cost them their chance at a second straight division title.

The Pirates lost the first game of a four-game series against the Cardinals, but they bounced back to win the next three to improve their record to 65–45 and increase their lead to seven games over the Mets, who had begun to falter. If any moment in the 1991 season was iconic for Bonds, it came in the last game of the Cardinals series played at Three Rivers on the night of August 12. Bonds's two-run homer had given the Pirates a 2–1 lead, but the Cards rallied to tie the game and send it into extra innings. The Cardinals took a 3–2 lead in the eleventh, but with two outs and Bonilla on first, Bonds launched a slider from Cardinals ace reliever Lee Smith deep into the right field stands for a dramatic 4–3 victory. The second Bonds hit the ball, he dropped the bat and raised his arms in a gesture of elation.

On the morning of the game, an article written by Amy Niedzielka had appeared in the *Post-Gazette* under the title "Bonds Hasn't Changed, but His Image Undergoes Facelift." Niedzielka pointed to a shift in Bonds's recent conduct, if not in his attitude. She mentioned his appearance in a public service commercial for Pittsburgh's Children's Hospital, his participation in a free baseball clinic for inner-city kids, and his donation of one hundred dollars for every home run he hit to a foundation to help troubled children. Niedzielka even noted Bonds's willingness to sign autographs at charity events, something he had been loath to do in the past, including at an exhibition game played against the Pirates' farm club in Buffalo.[34] Greg Brown, who was the Buffalo Bison announcer in 1991 before joining the Pirates broadcasting team in 1992, was struck by Bonds's willingness to talk with reporters and his uncharacteristic act of taking a seat behind the dugout and signing "hundreds of autographs." A year later, Bonds would pass Brown in the hall without saying hello and another time cut him off when Brown tried to talk with him while driving Bonds to a television interview.[35]

When Niedzielka asked Bonds if he was trying to change, his response was, "Change what?" He told her, "I've always tried to lead myself in the right manner as far as the kids go. I'm not alcoholic. I don't do drugs. I love my wife and family to death. I'm not perfect, and I don't claim to be perfect, but I try to be a good person. . . . If you believe all that you read, you can think I'm bad person all you want to."[36]

The day after the dramatic win against the Cardinals, Pirates fans were reading another article about Bonds in the *Post-Gazette*, this time by Collier, one of his harshest critics, who once said that interviewing

Bonds "was like pulling teeth."[37] Collier admitted that what Bonds had done against the Cardinals "looked monumental" and that he "threatens to become the Pirates." But Collier preferred to spend most of the article—as its title, "Bonds Awesome, but Bonilla No. 1 Man," indicated—praising Bonilla as the Pirates' best player. Collier described Bonilla as "monstrously reliable in temperament and in dependability and in pride." While pointing out that the overlooked Bonilla saved the game against the Cardinals with two outstanding defensive plays and had singled ahead of Bonds's dramatic home runs, Collier's highest praise came for Bonilla's willingness to switch from right field back to third base when Jeff King's back problems put him on the disabled list and demanded surgery. Bonds was the Pirates hero for a night, but for Collier Bonilla was the "monumental" Pirate who did what was necessary to "steady the team" all season.[38]

Following the win against the Cardinals, the Pirates finished their critical ten-game homestand by taking two out of three against the Phillies. Then they swept a three-game series against the Mets. Bonds and Bonilla continued their hot hitting, but the Pirates were also getting a surprising boost from rookie third baseman John Wehner, a local product who grew up in Pittsburgh's Carrick neighborhood. He had dreamed of playing for the Pirates as far back as Little League and was thrilled when he first saw his Pirates uniform hanging up in the clubhouse. Wehner was also in awe of Leyland when he met him for the first time, but he quickly learned how sharp his new manager could be, especially in having fun with a new player. Just before Wehner was called up, Leyland had a health scare after he experienced some chest pain. When Wehner introduced himself, Leyland told him, "I heard you were coming and almost had a heart attack."[39] Brought up in late July, Wehner, in addition to giving Bonilla an opportunity to return to the outfield, went on a spree that included hitting 5-for-5 and 4-for-4 in separate games and batting well above .300.

As they approached the last month of the season, the Pirates were building team camaraderie and letting off steam in the clubhouse with a Nerf basketball set.[40] The "around the world" Nerf shooting contests and player tournaments that preceded home games brought the team together. There were great all-around athletes on the team, but the hoop was so low that even vertically challenged Mike LaValliere excelled at the game, finishing second to Curt Wilkerson in a clubhouse tournament. The only disruption was Lind, who kept running by and swatting away shots directed at the hoop. The pastime became so popular that as the Pirates approached the stretch run to the playoffs, Leyland led the team in layup drills before they took the field.

The Pirates stumbled briefly in late August, losing four of six, but they ended the month with a five-game winning streak that increased their division lead to a healthy eight games. They also solved their season-long problem at third base, which was complicated again when Wehner ruptured a disc in his back and was lost for the season. They acquired veteran third baseman Steve Buechele from the Texas Rangers for Kurt Miller, a top minor league pitching prospect. With Buechele in the lineup, the Pirates, after playing only .500 baseball in the first twelve games in September, won ten of their next twelve games and ran away from the rest of the division. The highlight of their division title run came on September 19, when utility infielder and clubhouse Nerf basketball champion Curt Wilkerson, who had not homered all season, came up in the bottom of the eleventh and hit a towering grand slam off Cardinals reliever Lee Smith, the same pitcher Bonds had victimized a month earlier, to give the Pirates a dramatic 5–1 victory. Wilkerson's teammates were so elated by his unexpected heroics that they laid towels on the clubhouse floor in lieu of a red carpet and had him walk under crossed bats to an easy chair hastily decorated as a throne.[41]

Three games later, on September 22, with Drabek on the mound and Bonds and Bonilla driving in the tying and winning runs, the Pirates clinched their second consecutive NL East Division title in front of 33,662 wildly cheering fans, with a 2–1 victory over the Phillies. When Drabek struck out the Phillies' Charlie Hayes to end the game, Drabek and Slaught leaped into each other's arms in a joyful embrace. As Van Slyke ran in from center field to join his exuberant teammates, Bonds and Bonilla embraced and congratulated each other in the outfield before jogging in to join the celebration. In the clubhouse Bonds told reporters, "This team is on a mission. These two years have been the best years of my life, but we've got more big games to play." Jay Bell said, "We want it all, we want the whole package. We want the playoffs, the World Series. Last year, I think we thought we can do it. Now we know we can do it." A tearful Leyland recalled that when he took over the team in 1986, it was coming off a season of 104 losses: "When I took this job nobody wanted it. Now there's a lot of guys who would like to have it." He added, "This was real sweet, doing it at home. It was great last year to come home and see all those people at the airport, but this was fun."[42]

The 1991 Pirates ended the season with a league-best record of 98–64, three games better than in 1990, and finished a comfortable fourteen games ahead of the St. Louis Cardinals. They also set another new attendance record, up from 2,049, 908 in 1990 to 2,065,302 in 1991. The offense led the National League with 768 runs scored and had the highest team batting average at .263. Their pitching staff, with the support of a defense led by five Gold Glove performers, finished second to the Dodgers with an earned run average of 3.44, while their relievers led the league with fifty saves.

Bonds once again led the Pirates offense, though his season home-run total of 25 was a significant drop from his 33 homers in 1990. His batting average also dropped, from .302 to .292, but his team-leading RBIs increased from 114 to 116. Bonilla also had a significant drop in home runs, down to 18 from 32 in 1990, but he drove in 100 runs and was the only Pirates regular to hit over .300. The rest of the lineup had solid years—including Van Slyke who hit 17 home runs and drove in 83 runs, Bell who had a career-high 16 home runs, and Merced who filled in capably for Bream, with 10 home runs, 50 RBIs, and a .275 average.

Drabek failed to match his Cy Young performance of 1990, but after starting the 1991 season 2–7, he went 13–7 for the rest of the year and finished at 15–14. The Pirates did have a twenty-game winner, but it was Smiley, described by LaValliere as "locked in" all season, who finished with a 20–8 record.[43] Zane Smith was undefeated in September and finished the season with sixteen wins, while Walk battled injuries all season and had a 9–2 record. Landrum, with seventeen saves, and Belinda, with sixteen saves, shared the closer's role, but five other pitchers also earned saves.

Based on their batting, pitching, and fielding performances in the 1991 season, the Pirates were rated the all-around best team in the National League and the odds-on favorite to win the division playoff and go to the World Series. With Bonilla almost a certainty to sign with another team once he became a free agent, the Pirates knew that this was their best, and perhaps last, chance to win a World Series. All they had to do was defeat a dark horse Atlanta Braves team that had bedeviled the Pirates during the season by winning nine of the twelve games played between the two teams.

CHAPTER SIX

TOO MUCH STEVE AVERY

The 1991 National League Championship Series

After the Pirates fired Chuck Tanner as manager at the end of the 1985 season, Atlanta Braves general manager Bobby Cox hired him to manage the Braves during a major rebuilding program. For Tanner, after his recent ordeal in Pittsburgh, the move was the baseball equivalent of leaping from the frying pan into the fire. With the Braves shedding veteran players and their high salaries, the team struggled to a 72–89 record in 1986 and sank to a 69–92 finish in 1987. When the Braves opened the 1988 season with a 12–27 record, Cox fired Tanner and replaced him with former Cincinnati Reds manager Russ Nixon.

After finishing the 1988 season with a 54–106 record, the Braves did not fare much better under Nixon in 1989, winning just 63 games, while losing 97. They had the unique distinction that season of finishing last in their division, while also finishing last in the major leagues in attendance and in player payroll. The attendance in Atlanta was so low that the Pirates AAA farm club in Buffalo drew more fans.[1] Going into the 1990 season, *Financial World* estimated that only one National League franchise, the Montreal Expos, was worth less than the Atlanta Braves.

When the Braves continued to play poorly in 1990, Cox fired Nixon at midseason and took over himself as manager. Under Nixon, the Braves had gone 25–40 that year. Under Cox, they played just as poorly, going 40–57 and ended the season at 65–97. At the end of the season, the team decided to replace Cox as the general manager so that in 1991 he could focus on managing the team he had been rebuilding for the past five years. Cox was no stranger to managing in the major leagues or for the Atlanta Braves. His first managing job was with the Braves in 1978, but after four unremarkable seasons, he was fired by owner Ted Turner. Cox spent the next four years managing the Toronto Blue Jays, where he had a much more successful run. After Cox led the Blue Jays to a division title in 1985 and was named the American League Manager of the Year, Turner, admitting that he had made a mistake in firing Cox, lured his former manager back to Atlanta by offering him the general manager's job. Going into the 1991 season, Cox's good fortune as manager was that he was about to benefit from the hard work he had put in as general manager. The 1991 Braves were the team that Cox built. Young and talented outfielders Ron Gant and 1990 National League Rookie of the Year David Justice, both products of the Braves' farm system, were the strength of the lineup, but the team had also added veteran free agents with playoff experience, like former Cardinals third baseman Terry Pendleton and former Pirates first baseman Sid Bream.

This Braves team became the first team in National League history to go from last to first place in a single season. They did this with an impressive balance of talent and experience in their starting lineup, but this impressive accomplishment would not have been possible without the coming-of-age of starting pitchers Tom Glavine, John Smoltz, and Steve Avery. The solid and consistent Smoltz won fourteen games, while Glavine had a breakthrough Cy Young–worthy season with twenty wins. The biggest story for the Braves, however, was the performance of twenty-one-year-old Avery who, in his first full season, won eighteen games and lost only eight.

The Braves needed every one of their wins in 1991. Trailing the Dodgers by nine and a half games well into the season, they started to win at a remarkable pace that Smoltz described as "magical." Cox said that the turnaround not only gave his team confidence, it "energized the city" for the first time in over a decade.[2] The streaking Braves managed to move into first place by late August, then they spent the last month of the season in a dramatic see-saw struggle with the Dodgers.

On October 3, 1991, in their penultimate game of the season, the Braves, behind the pitching of Smoltz and a home run by Gant, completed their remarkable season by defeating the Houston Astros and clinching the NL West Division title. Their opponents in the NLCS would be a well-rested and playoff-experienced Pittsburgh Pirates team that, while struggling with the Braves during the season, had easily won the NL East Division and were favorites going in to the series. Looking back on the 1991 NLCS, Pirates catcher Don Slaught thought that the Pirates may have been too well rested, that clinching the division so early worked against them by costing them momentum and intensity going into the playoffs.[3] If there was any rust on the Pirates, however, it was hardly evident to the 57,347 fans who came out to Three Rivers Stadium for the opening game of the playoff series and cheered the Pirates to an easy victory over the Braves.

Jim Leyland chose Doug Drabek to open the series. After he retired the Braves in order in the top of the first inning, Andy Van Slyke brought the crowd to its feet with a towering home run into the right-field stands off left-hander Glavine. Leyland had loaded the Pirates lineup with right-handed hitters, but it was the left-handed Van Slyke who first got to Glavine. Rattled by the home run, Glavine walked two of the next three Pirates around an error by shortstop Jeff Blauser, but he managed to get out of the inning trailing only 1–0 when Slaught grounded out to third with the bases loaded.

Giving up only a single to Bream, Drabek had little trouble with the Braves in the top of the second and third innings. In the bottom of the third, Van Slyke struck again. After Jay Bell led off with a single, Van Slyke hit a line drive into the right-center gap to score Bell from first base with the Pirates' second run. When Bobby Bonilla bounced a single into left field to score Van Slyke from second, the Pirates took a 3–0 lead.

Drabek allowed a single and a walk in the top of the fourth with only one out, but he got out of the inning without giving up a run. He gave up only harmless singles in the fourth and fifth and took his 3–0 lead with him into the bottom of the sixth. After Steve Buechele doubled to lead off the bottom of the sixth, Drabek did something that the Braves were incapable of doing—he knocked himself out of the game. With two outs and Buechele still on second, he hit a line drive over the head of center fielder Lonnie Smith. Buechele scored, but Drabek was easily thrown out at third base after pulling a hamstring running the bases.

Drabek had been pitching masterfully, but Leyland was unwilling to risk sending him back out to the mound in the seventh inning and turned to his bullpen to finish out the game. He decided to bring in Bob Walk, the pitcher he trusted most in pressure situations. Walk regarded himself as "a jack of all trades" on the mound and, in an interview, said he never "bitched or moaned" about the way he was being used. He was Leyland's favorite, his "teacher's pet," and the perfect pupil for pitching coach Ray Miller. Walk saw Miller as "a father figure," and he compared him to a "psychologist" who could instill confidence in his pitchers with his simple mantra: "Work fast, throw strikes, change speeds."[4]

While Walk had suffered from groin and leg injuries in his career, he had never had arm problems and was capable of pitching effectively as a starter or reliever. He had no trouble in relief on this night and retired the Braves in order in the top of the seventh and eighth innings. When José Lind drove in Bobby Bonilla with a sacrifice fly in the bottom of the eighth, the Pirates took a 5–0 lead into the ninth. Walk gave up a leadoff home run to Justice, but he easily retired the next three batters and gave the Pirates a 5–1 victory and a 1–0 lead in the series.

If any Pirates pitcher was going to suffer from too much rest going into the NLCS, it would be Leyland's choice for Game 2, left-hander Zane Smith. The Pirates sixteen-game winner relied on a sinking fastball that sank more effectively when he was pitching with a tired arm.[5] The 57,533 fans were a little soggy from pregame showers, but they cheered on the Pirates and Smith, who gave up only a check-swing single to Gant in the top of the first inning. However, broadcaster Tim McCarver noticed that Smith's pitches were high, usually a sign of trouble for a sinkerball pitcher.[6] In the bottom of the first, the Pirates looked like they would need Smith at his best if they were going to take a 2–0 lead to Atlanta. Avery, who had won his last five games for the Braves, including a near no-hitter, walked Gary Redus to lead off the Pirates' half of the first inning, but then struck out Bell, Van Slyke, and Bonilla, all on called third strikes.

When Zane Smith came out for the second inning, he still had trouble keeping his pitches down and gave up consecutive singles to Brian Hunter, Greg Olson, and Mark Lemke to load the bases. After a visit to the mound by Miller, Smith settled down and retired the former Pirates shortstop Rafael Belliard on a force out at home, then struck out Avery. Lonnie Smith worked the count full but grounded sharply to shortstop Bell to end the inning. With the crowd roaring "Let's Go Bucs," Barry Bonds led off the second inning with an infield single that bounced off Avery's heel. After Slaught struck out, Bonds stole second base. With two outs, Bonds stole third, but Lind bounced out to Avery to end the inning. In the top of the third, Gant reached first after being hit with a pitch. It was a questionable call, but Gant took advantage of it and duplicated Bonds's feat by stealing second, then, after being nearly picked off on another questionable call, stole third before Hunter flied out to Van Slyke.

For the next three innings, Avery dominated the Pirates hitters, retiring eleven in a row before allowing a harmless single to Lind in the bottom of the fifth. Zane Smith was not as masterful, but he settled down and matched Avery's shutout innings going into the top of the sixth, where one bizarre play decided the game and became the turning point in the 1991 playoffs. Justice led off the sixth with a line single to left-center field, but Smith struck out Hunter for the first out of the inning. On a hit-and-run, Olson grounded out sharply to Buechele, who threw Olson out at first as Justice advanced to second. With a two-strike count, Dennis Menke bounced a ball down the third-base line. Buechele, who led the American League in fielding percentage before his late-season trade to the Pirates, moved in to backhand the ball, but it took a freakishly high bounce and just eluded his glove. Buechele may have been distracted by Justice running toward third. Perhaps he intended to tag out the Braves' runner instead of throwing to first base, but he took his eye off the ball and missed it completely. The ball rolled down the left-field line, scoring Justice with what the official scorer generously ruled as a double.

Trailing 1–0, the Pirates went down in order against Avery in the bottom of the sixth, but after the Braves failed to score in the top of the seventh, Bonilla raised the Pirates' hopes with an infield single to lead off the bottom of the inning. With the crowd roaring, Bonds stepped to the plate, but he ended the rally by bouncing into a double play. After Roger Mason retired the Braves in order in the top of the eighth the Pirates threatened again, when, with two outs, Redus lined a single into center field and stole second. Bell then grounded the ball sharply past

Avery, but second baseman Lemke made a sliding backhanded stop to keep the ball in the infield and prevent Redus from scoring the tying run. With the crowd in an uproar, Van Slyke hit a groundball to short that Belliard easily handled and stepped on second to end the inning.

After Stan Belinda retired the Braves in order in the top of the ninth, Bonilla brought fans to their feet one last time by leading off the bottom of the ninth with a drive down the left-field line that bounced on one hop off the fence for a double. Braves manager Cox visited the mound but decided to leave the left-handed Avery in the game to face Bonds. On a 3-and-1 count, instead of attempting to pull the ball and move Bonilla to third base, Bonds tried to drive a fastball to the opposite field but undercut the ball and lifted a high pop fly that Belliard caught in shallow left field. As fans groaned in disappointment, Bonds slammed his bat and helmet into the artificial turf in frustration.

Bonds's failure to move Bonilla to third was critical to the outcome of the game. Braves closer Alejandro Peña came in to relieve Avery, and his first pitch sailed wide of the catcher and straight to the backstop, allowing Bonilla to advance to third base. Had Bonds advanced the runner, the wild pitch would have scored the tying run. Instead, with Bonilla now at third base, any hope of tying the game ended when Buechele bounced weakly back to the mound and pinch-hitter Curt Wilkerson struck out on three pitches. The 1–0 loss tied the best-of-seven playoffs at one game apiece and sent the series to Atlanta, where rabid Braves fans, including owner Ted Turner, his wife, the actress Jane Fonda, and their guests Jimmy and Rosalynn Carter, were waiting to cheer on their Braves. Particularly distracting for opposing teams was the war chant and tomahawk chop used by Braves' fans to urge on their team.

It would not be the first time in their long postseason history that the Pirates were distracted by opposing fans. In the 1903 World Series against the Boston Americans, for example, a group of fans calling themselves the Royal Rooters began to sing special lyrics to "Tessie," a popular song of the day. Instead of "Tessie, you make me feel so badly / Why don't you turn around?" they sang, "Honus, why do you hit so badly? / Take a back seat and sit down." One Pirates player from that team, Tommy Leach, looked back on what baseball historians now regard as the first modern World Series and believed that Boston fans singing that song had an effect: "Sort of got on your nerves after a while. And before we knew what happened, we'd lost the World Series."[7]

The Pirates did not need yet another distraction, but Bonds, once again, managed to draw attention to himself by responding to Bob Smizik's claim in the *Pittsburgh Press* that Bonds had called Van Slyke the "Great White Hope," and that Van Slyke had criticized fans for not selling out Three Rivers for playoff games. Bonds defended both himself and Van Slyke in a first-person column in the *Press*, but he could not resist reminding readers that, though he had failed to advance Bonilla in Game 2, it was Buechele who could have brought Bonilla home after the wild pitch: "We had Buechele up at the plate. He is an outstanding third baseman and an outstanding hitter. What happens? He grounds out to Peña."[8]

The Pirates had one day off to recover from their frustrating and painful loss in Game 2, and they had twenty-game winner John Smiley ready to face the Braves in Game 3. After losing all six games they played at Atlanta-Fulton County Stadium that year, the Pirates would need a strong effort by Smiley, who had won his last seven games of the season. His opponent for Game 3 was Smoltz, who was 2–11 at the All-Star break, then went 12–2 in the second half. Smoltz had won his last eight games of the season, including a division-clinching victory against the Astros. Facing the Braves in Atlanta for the next three games, the Pirates needed to win at least one game to bring the playoffs back to Pittsburgh.

With the right-handed Smoltz starting for the Braves, Leyland countered by inserting left-hand hitters Orlando Merced and Mike La-Valliere into the lineup, and the move paid an immediate dividend. On the first pitch of the game, Merced silenced the tomahawk-waving and chanting crowd by lining a fastball over the center-field fence to give the Pirates a 1–0 lead. Bell followed with a looping single to right field, but Smoltz settled down and retired Van Slyke, Bonilla, and Bonds to end the inning.

In the bottom of the first, Smiley easily retired the first two Braves, but Gant lined a pitch over Bonilla's head in right field for a double. Justice grounded a changeup down the left-field line for a game-tying double, and then Hunter lined another changeup down the left-field line to give the Braves a 2–1 lead. With the crowd in a frenzy, Olson lofted yet another Smiley changeup over the left-field fence to give the Braves a 4–1 lead.

After Smoltz retired the Pirates in order in the top of the second, the Braves struck again with two outs in the bottom of the inning after

Smiley hit Lonnie Smith with a pitch. With two strikes on Pendleton, Smiley threw to first and caught Smith, the Braves' most dangerous base-runner, in a run-down between first and second. But when first base-man Merced's throw to second base sailed into left field, Smith made it all the way to third. A frustrated Smiley then gave up a double to Pendleton to increase the Braves' lead to 5–1. After the Pirates failed to score in the top of third, Leyland replaced Smiley with Bill Landrum, who gave up a run in the bottom of the inning on a walk, a stolen base, and an RBI single from weak-hitting Belliard.

Down 6–1 after only three innings, the Pirates chipped away in the fourth with a Bonds single and stolen base, and a Lind single, but after Bell homered in the top of the seventh, Gant answered with a solo home run off Bob Kipper in the bottom of the inning to give the Braves a 7–3 lead. In the top of the eighth, after Cox replaced Smoltz with left-hander Mike Stanton, the Pirates mounted their most serious threat, by loading the bases on singles by Buechele and Slaught, and a walk to Lloyd McClendon. With only one out in the inning, Cox brought in the closer Peña. With the tying run at the plate, Peña retired Merced, who had homered in the first inning, on a pop fly and struck out Bell, who had three hits in the game, including a home run.

In the bottom of the eighth, Leyland brought in little-used left-hander Rosario Rodríguez, who had pitched in only eighteen games during the regular season. A rusty Rodríguez walked the first two bat-ters he faced; then, after Belliard moved the runners up on a sacri-fice, he gave up a three-run homer to Bream, who had come into the game for his defense. It was the last inning the twenty-two-year-old Rodríguez would ever pitch in a major-league uniform. Peña retired Van Slyke, Bonilla, and Bonds in the top of the ninth, and the Braves walked off the field with a lopsided 10–3 victory and a 2–1 lead in the series.

After the humiliating loss, Van Slyke, when asked about the Pirates' repeated failure to perform well in the playoffs, responded, "You've got to start wondering if we're a bunch of gaggers or not. We're the same 14 or 15 guys who got us through this year. I don't think we're all going to gag now." Before the start of Game 4, Leyland added, "I'm not doubting them. I hope they're not doubting themselves."[9]

The biggest concern for Leyland was the inability of the Pirates to hit in clutch situations, especially Van Slyke, Bonilla, and Bonds, who were a combined 1-for-7 with runners in scoring position. Added to Leyland's worries, however, was the pitching matchup for Game 4. Left-hander Randy Tomlin had a solid 1991 season, going 8–7 with a team-leading 2.98 ERA, but he had just completed his first full year in the majors. His opponent was veteran left-hander Charlie Leibrandt, who had pitched for more than a dozen big-league seasons and had fifteen wins for the Braves in 1991. Nicknamed "Whispers" by his teammates, Bonilla said of him, "Sometimes, you don't even know if he's around." Leyland admitted that Tomlin was "a shy kid," but he also pointed out he was "competitive." Tomlin did not throw very hard, and he did not strike out many batters, but he was a "pitch-to-contact" hurler for a team that had one of the best defenses in baseball.[10]

Unfortunately for Tomlin and the Pirates, Game 4 started out much like Game 3. After Leibrandt retired the Pirates in order in the top of the first, Lonnie Smith lined a ground-rule double, went to third on Pendleton's fly out to right, and scored on Gant's groundout to Bell. Trailing 1–0, Tomlin gave up three singles in a row, and the Braves, with the help of a Bonds throwing error, took a 2–0 lead going into the second inning. The Pirates, however, bounced back in the top of the second when Bonilla led off with a walk. After Bonds popped out, Bonilla came around to score on singles by Buechele and Lind to cut Atlanta's lead to 2–1. For the next few innings, Tomlin and Leibrandt both pitched in and out of trouble, but neither team was able to score again until the top of the fifth. With two outs, Redus lined a single to left field. He was able to come around to score on a Bell single to right when Gant threw wildly to third base. Leibrandt blamed himself for not backing up third base properly, but the Gant throwing error allowed the Pirates to tie the game at 2–2.

After Tomlin retired the Braves in order in the bottom of the fifth, both the Pirates and the Braves threatened in the sixth but failed to break the tie. In the seventh, the Pirates threatened again, but Bonilla bounced out to first against reliever Jim Clancy to leave the tie-breaking run at second base. Leyland pinch-hit for Tomlin in the top of the seventh, so in the bottom of the inning, he brought in Walk who retired the Braves in order. Bonds led off the Pirates' eighth with an infield single and made it to third base with two outs, but Lind struck out against Stanton to end the threat. When Walk retired the Braves in order, the game went into the ninth inning still tied at 2–2.

Too Much Steve Avery

After the Pirates failed to score in the top of the ninth, Leyland brought in Belinda, who retired the Braves without a threat and sent the game into extra innings. In the top of the tenth, Van Slyke led off with a walk against left-hander Kent Mercker. Bonilla and Bonds failed to advance the runner, but Van Slyke put himself in scoring position by stealing second base. After a Buechele walk, Cox brought in right-hander Mark Wohlers to face Slaught, but Leyland countered with left-hand hitting LaValliere. With two strikes, LaValliere fouled off several pitches before lining a base hit into the right-center-field gap, scoring Van Slyke with the go-ahead run. Buechele was thrown out at home on the play, but Belinda did not need the extra run. He retired the Braves in order in the bottom of the tenth to save the Pirates' 3–2 victory.

In winning Game 4, the Pirates had tied the series at 2–2 and, with only one game left in Atlanta, assured themselves of a return trip to Pittsburgh. Game 5 should have been a repeat pitching matchup of Game 1, but Leyland said that Drabek was "not quite ready" after his hamstring pull, and he decided to move up Zane Smith to face the Braves' Glavine.[11] Any hope that the Pirates would jump on Glavine in the first inning, as they had in Game 1, was dashed when the Braves' starter struck out leadoff hitter Redus then retired the Pirates in order. Zane Smith gave up a leadoff single to Lonnie Smith, but with the help of a Pendleton double-play groundball he was able to hold the Braves scoreless in the bottom of the first. Bonilla led off the Pirates' second with a double, but after advancing to third on a Bonds fly ball, he watched from third base as Buechele struck out and Slaught flied out. After the heart-breaking 1–0 loss on a bad hop in Game 2, it looked as though Zane Smith was in for another frustrating outing, especially when the Braves loaded the bases with no one out in the bottom of the second. This time, however, it was the Braves who made the key mistake. After Smith struck out Belliard and had two strikes on Glavine, Cox decided to put on the suicide squeeze. The strategy backfired. With Hunter coming down the line, Glavine failed to make contact with the pitch and struck out. Trapped between third and home, Hunter was an easy out in a rundown to end the inning.

In the bottom of the fourth, with the game still scoreless, the Braves had another opportunity to take the lead but blundered again. With two outs and Justice on second base, Lemke singled Justice home, but Justice, in his haste to score, stumbled rounding third. The Pirates appealed, and the umpires ruled that Justice had failed to touch third base and called him out. For the second time in three innings, the Braves were on the verge of taking the lead, but a botched play and a running blunder kept the game scoreless.

In the top of the fifth, after Bonds popped out, the Pirates put together a Buechele walk, a Slaught single, and a Lind RBI base hit to take a 1–0 lead. Zane Smith proceeded to shut down the Braves' offense for the next three innings, while Glavine kept the Pirates from extending their lead. With Bonds struggling in the playoffs, the Braves walked Bonilla intentionally with runners in scoring position in the sixth and the eighth innings so that they could pitch to Bonds. Bonds failed to drive in a run, but in the bottom of the eighth, he made a sensational catch just before Pendleton tripled off Smith with two outs.

Mason came on in relief of Zane Smith and retired Gant on a pop fly to third to strand Pendleton, but the Pirates, who were still hanging on to 1–0 lead, failed to score in the top of the ninth. In the bottom of the ninth, Mason struck out Justice to lead off the inning, but singles by Tommy Gregg and Olson put the tying and winning runs on base with Lemke coming to the plate. Leyland stayed with Mason, who retired Lemke on a force out at second. When Blauser hit a soft liner to Bonilla in short right field to end the game, the Pirates, who had seemed on the verge of disaster two days earlier, had taken a 3–2 lead in the series and were headed back to Pittsburgh, where they hoped there would be no tomahawk chops to torment them.

Heading into Game 6, the good news for the Pirates and their fans came with Leyland's announcement that Drabek had recovered from his hamstring injury and was ready to take the mound. Drabek's pitching opponent, however, would be Avery, who had dominated the Pirates in Game 2. After Drabek pitched out of trouble in the first inning, Avery struck out Redus, Bell, and Van Slyke in the bottom of the inning, all on swinging strikes. After Drabek retired the Braves in order in the top of the second, Avery struck out two of the three Pirates he faced in the bottom of the inning. The Pirates managed to get their first hit off Avery in the bottom of the third, but Slaught was thrown out trying to stretch his hit into a double. They would not get another hit until the sixth inning when Lind singled, but he was erased on a double play. Through six innings Avery faced only nineteen batters, one over the minimum, and struck out eight Pirates.

While Drabek was not as overpowering, he matched Avery inning for inning. The Braves managed to put a runner in scoring position in the top of the sixth, seventh, and eighth, but each time Drabek, described by Leyland in an interview as having "the heart of a lion," managed to pitch out of trouble.[12] In the seventh the Braves made their most serious threat when Gant made it to third base with only one out, after an infield single, stolen base, and ground out, but he was thrown out at home by Bell on a bouncer to short. After eight innings, Avery and Drabek had still not allowed a run and, combined, had tossed over thirty innings of shutout baseball in the 1991 NLCS.

In the top of the ninth, with Gant at first on a walk and two outs, the Braves finally broke the scoreless tie and ended Drabek's string of scoreless innings. Gant stole second and scored when Olson doubled just inside the third-base line to give the Braves a 1–0 lead. The Pirates threatened in the bottom of the ninth when Gary Varsho led off with a pinch-hit single, went to second on a sacrifice bunt, and with two outs advanced to third on a wild pitch, but Van Slyke, after fouling off several fastballs, was fooled by a Peña changeup and took the pitch for strike three.

After the game, the Pirates had high praise for Avery. Bell said that Avery was "lights out," while Van Slyke quipped, "Poison Avery. You can't get near him."[13] His rival on the mound, Drabek, said, "Composure . . . he stays within himself. Doesn't try to do too much. And he's working two games against a heck of a lineup in the other team's park. At twenty-one, he's something." Remembering Drabek's own stellar performance, pitching coach Miller put Game 6 into a proper perspective: "I don't know where you'll see better ball games. . . . My guy, Drabek, is the best in the game for my money, but Avery is going to be one of the best. He's there now. To do what he's done in two pressure games like these, puts him in the same company as Bob Gibson, Sandy Koufax, pick a name."[14]

The Pirates would not have to bat against Avery in the deciding Game 7, but they would have to face Smoltz, who gave up home runs to Merced and Bell but easily won Game 3. Smoltz's pitching opponent, Smiley, was a twenty-game winner during the 1991 season, but he lasted only two innings and gave up five runs in Game 3. Smiley was a concern going into Game 7, but the Pirates' biggest problem was the playoff collapse of Van Slyke, Bonilla, and Bonds for the second straight year.

Since Game 1 of the 1991 NLCS, Van Slyke and Bonilla had failed to drive in a run. Bonds's failure to drive in a run now extended through two NLCS and twelve playoff games. He also had no extra base hits in those twelve games.

For Game 6, there were 54,508 fans who watched the Pirates' heartbreaking loss, and far fewer were willing to pay their way back to Three Rivers for Game 7. If the Pirates were hoping for a great turnout to cheer them on to victory, they must have been demoralized to hear the morning before the game that over ten thousand tickets were still unsold. The official attendance for Game 7 was listed at 46,932, but that figure included a large contingent of Atlanta fans who came to Pittsburgh and had no trouble buying tickets for the game.

Those Pirate fans who did come to the game watched in frustration as Smiley started the game by walking Lonnie Smith. Pendleton then grounded a ball up the middle that glanced off the glove of a diving Lind and rolled into center field. With runners at first and third, Gant launched a deep fly ball to the warning track in center field to give the Braves a 1–0 lead. After a visit to the mound by Miller, Smiley settled down and struck out Justice, but Hunter drove Smiley's first pitch deep down the left-field line. The ball stayed fair and landed in the left-field stands to give the Braves a 3–0 lead. When Olson followed with a single, Leyland, with the sound of the Braves fans' cheers cascading from the stands at Three Rivers, brought in Walk to close out the inning.

In the bottom of the first, the Braves fans were quickly drowned out by Pirates fans when Merced and Bell lined singles into center field to bring up Van Slyke. With Pirates fans chanting "Let's Go Bucs," Van Slyke drove a Smoltz pitch deep into right field. The ball appeared to be headed for the stands, but it seemed to die at the last moment and ended up in the glove of Justice. Instead of being tied 3–3, the Pirates were still down 3–0 with one out. When Bonilla popped out and Bonds grounded out, the rally was over, and so was the Pirates' best chance to win Game 7.

The Pirates' bullpen held the Braves to a single run over the next eight innings, but Smoltz was even better. Over the next six innings after his shaky start, the Pirates threatened to score only once, when Bonds doubled to lead off the fourth (his first extra-base hit in a playoff game) and made it to third base with two outs on a Lemke error. But Lind bounced into a force out to end the inning. Looking back, Smoltz admitted that he started the game with a "case of nerves" and thought Van Slyke's drive was a home run—but when Justice caught the ball at the base of the fence, "I knew we'd win."[15]

Trailing 4–0, the Pirates had one more chance to rattle Smoltz. In the bottom of the eighth, with one out, Bell bounced a single off Belliard's glove, and after Van Slyke struck out, Bonilla blooped a broken-bat single into right field that sent Bell around to third and Bonds coming to bat. With the crowd roaring "Barry, Barry," Bonds, however, swung at the first pitch and lofted a fly ball to left field to end the inning. Bonds's failure tied the championship series record of 0-for-22 with runners on base held by Oakland As' Gene Tenace. In the bottom of the ninth, Smoltz easily retired the Pirates in order to give the Braves a 4–0 win and the National League pennant.

For the Pirates, the loss was incomprehensible. The team had played so well during the season. LaValliere still believed that the Pirates "were the better team." Redus did not think there was any "way the Pirates could lose at home." Van Slyke did not think the Pirates "choked" in the series, but Walk said that the "Big Three didn't scare anyone." Smoltz seemed to confirm Walk's view when he told reporters after the game that Braves pitchers, who shut out the Pirates three times, were "aggressive" in going after Pirate hitters.[16] While his second NLCS loss was "tougher to take," Leyland offered no excuses or blame in his postgame interview. He wanted to "tip his hat" to the Braves and thought their remarkable performance was a "good story for baseball." As for his own team, he simply said, "we didn't do the job."[17] The Pirates and their fans would have to wait until next year and hope for one more chance at winning their way into the World Series, but with the almost certain loss of Bonilla and several other key players, next year seemed clouded over with uncertainty.

Syd Thrift is deep in conversation with Jim Leyland.

Jim Leyland waves to Pirates fans. Photo by Peter Diana.

Barry Bonds watches a home run sail out of Wrigley Field. Photo © David Arrigo.

Bobby Bonilla tracks down a fly ball.

Sid Bream, followed by R.J. Reynolds, accepts congratulations. Photo © David Arrigo.

Barry Bonds congratulates Andy Van Slyke. Photo © David Arrigo.

Andy Van Slyke blows a bubble. Photo by Peter Diana.

Sid Bream and Gene Lamont restrain Barry Bonds.

Barry Bonds crashes into the left-field wall at Three Rivers Stadium.
Photo © David Arrigo.

Andy Van Slyke is seen with his kids at Pirates father-son game.

Doug Drabek delivers a pitch. © Pittsburgh Pirates / David Arrigo.

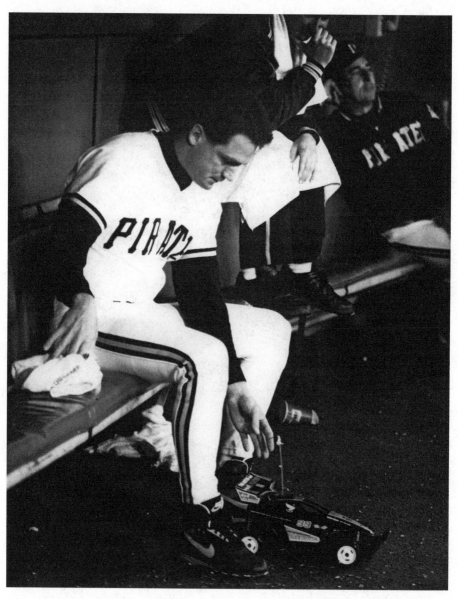

Andy Van Slyke plays with remote car (with Ray Miller in the background).
© Pittsburgh Pirates / David Arrigo.

Bobby Bonilla congratulates Barry Bonds.

Don Slaught and Mike LaValliere celebrate the 1990 division title.
Photo © David Arrigo.

Jay Bell and Jeff King chat with Cardinal Ozzie Smith.

Jim Leyland and Barry Bonds manage to find a relaxed moment.
Photo © *Pittsburgh Post-Gazette*.

Barry Bonds watches batting practice.

Jim Leyland argues with umpire. © Pittsburgh Pirates / David Arrigo.

Barry Bonds and Lloyd McClendon carry Jim Leyland off the field after Pirates clinch the 1992 NL East Division title at Three Rivers Stadium.

Sid Bream makes his infamous slide.

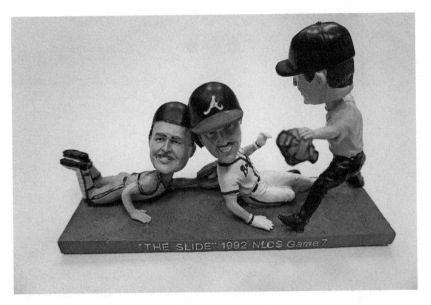

A Sid Bream bobblehead that depicts the slide.

BARRY BONDS'S LAST HURRAH

The 1992 Season

After the disappointing playoff loss to the Cincinnati Reds in 1990, Pittsburgh fans could take some comfort from the major postseason awards won by Pirates players and their manager. The 1991 postseason awards, however, would simply add to the frustration of Pirates fans after another painful loss in the NLCS. John Smiley had an outstanding 1991 season, finishing with a 20–8 record and a 3.08 ERA. He looked like a strong contender for the Cy Young Award, which his teammate Doug Drabek won in 1990. The best he could do, however, was a third-place finish in the Baseball Writers' Association of America (BBWAA) balloting, behind the Atlanta Braves' twenty-two-game winner Tom Glavine and the St. Louis Cardinals' ace reliever Lee Smith, who set a National League record with forty-seven saves. Pittsburgh fans could console themselves with the knowledge that Glavine had lost two games in the NLCS to the Pirates, and that two of Smith's three regular season losses came from dramatic extra-inning home runs off the bats of Barry Bonds and Curt Wilkerson.

With all the divisiveness and turmoil during the 1991 season, Jim Leyland probably overcame more challenges than he had in 1990 when he was named Manager of the Year. But he, too, lost out to an Atlanta Brave when the BBWAA selected Bobby Cox for its managerial honor. Leyland received several first-place votes but finished a distant second to Cox in the balloting.

The Braves made a sweep of the major awards for 1991 when the BBWAA elected Terry Pendleton as the National League Most Valuable Player. Pendleton received twelve first-place votes to ten for Bonds and one for Bobby Bonilla. Pendleton batted .319 to Bonds's .292, but Bonds had 25 home runs to Pendleton's 22 and drove in 116 runs to only 86 for Pendleton. However, while the baseball writers, perhaps remembering his animosity toward the press, snubbed Bonds, the *Sporting News* focused more on Bonds's on-the-field performance and named him its National League Player of the Year and its Major League Player of the Year.

The Pirates hoped to bounce back from their second consecutive NLCS loss and contend for a third straight division title, but these hopes took a major, though not unexpected, blow when, on December 3, free agent Bonilla signed a five-year, $29 million contract with the New York Mets, making him the highest paid player in team sports. The contract called for a base salary of $27.5 million and a $1.5 million promotional arrangement. Its annual salary of $5.8 million topped the $5.38 million of pitcher Roger Clemens. Growing up in the South Bronx, Bonilla saw his signing as a dream come true. He told the New York media, "I've got a soft spot in my heart for New York."[1] Bonilla also had to be happy with the Mets' signing of free agent Eddie Murray just a week earlier. Murray averaged over twenty-six home runs in his fifteen-year career to that point with the Orioles and Dodgers and would serve as protection for Bonilla in the batting order now that he would not have Bonds batting behind him. With the signings of Bonilla and Murray, the Mets appeared to have bought themselves into contention for the 1992 NL East Division title and weakened the Pirates in the process.

As for Bonilla's years with the Pirates, their longtime broadcaster Lanny Frattare believed that "Bonilla never intended to stay in Pittsburgh."[2] The *Post-Gazette*'s Gene Collier, while finding Bonilla cooperative, thought he "was not genuine" and had the same "sense of entitlement" as Bonds.[3] Pirates broadcaster Greg Brown shared the view that behind the smiling, friendly facade was a character as self-absorbed as that of Bonds.[4] The only difference between Bonds and Bonilla, in the commonly held view by those in the media who had to deal with them, was that if you called Bonds in the middle of a cold, wintry night and told him you were stranded with a flat tire, he would tell you to go to hell. If you called Bonilla, he would tell you he would be right there and never show up.

Losing Bonilla was not the only change the Pirates were dealing with during the offseason. Team president Carl Barger, after accepting a similar position for 1992 with the expansion Florida Marlins, stayed on with the Pirates during the 1991 season until Major League Baseball executives ruled late in the season that he had to step down. After the departure of Barger, the Pirates announced on October 30 that Mark Sauer, a former executive vice president and chief operating executive with the St. Louis Cardinals, had accepted the position of president and chief executive officer. One of Sauer's first decisions was to fire general manager Larry Doughty, who had been criticized for making costly late-season trades and free agent signings and had become a scapegoat for the Pirates' playoff losses. While Sauer conducted a search for a new general manager, he named Doughty's assistant, Cam Bonifay, as acting general manager. Bonifay's immediate and unenviable task was to deal with arbitration for several key players, including Drabek, Smiley, Jay Bell, José Lind, Bill Landrum, Bob Patterson, and the biggest challenge of all, a disgruntled Bonds, who had lost arbitration hearings during the last two offseasons.

Going into his third and what would be his last arbitration hearing with the Pirates, Bonds, who played for $2.3 million in 1991, filed for a salary of $5 million for 1992. The Pirates countered by filing an offer of $4 million. Just days before the hearing, the Pirates announced that they had signed Bonds to a one-year, $4.7 million contract. The contract also had bonus incentives for Bonds, including an additional $250,000 if he won the National League MVP Award and lesser amounts for being the MVP of the All-Star Game, the National League Championship Series, and the World Series. This contract finally placed Bonds in the upper echelon of baseball salaries. It surpassed the $4.5 million contract signed just a few weeks earlier by Detroit Tiger Cecil Fielder as the largest one-year contract. Several players, including Bonilla, would make more money in 1992, but they were under long-term contracts.

When asked if the signing opened the door to negotiations for a long-term contract, Bonifay said, "I wouldn't read anything into this." He did add that "I do believe we are now in good standing with Barry Bonds and this puts everyone into a good frame of mind going into spring training."[5]

Bob Hertzel writing in the *Pittsburgh Press*, speculated that Bonifay's coup in signing Bonds and avoiding the circus atmosphere of the previous year's spring training camp would give him the inside track in the search for a new general manager: "Bonifay may have benefited almost as much as Bonds from this deal." When approached about Bonifay's candidacy, Sauer responded that his acting general manager was certainly impressing him: "He is growing on the job."[6] Bonifay was one of five finalists for the permanent general manager's position. The others on Sauer's list included Walt Jocketty, director of baseball administration for the Oakland Athletics; former Detroit Tigers GM Bill Lajoie; former New York Yankees GM Murray Cook; and former St. Louis Cardinals All-Star and current director of player development, Ted Simmons. On February 5, just days after the Bonds signing, Sauer announced that the Pirates had hired Simmons as senior vice president and general manager. As for the disappointed Bonifay, he agreed to stay on in his old position as the Pirates' assistant general manager.

The hiring of Simmons out of the Cardinals organization raised questions of cronyism. Of the five candidates, including Bonifay, Simmons was the only one with no experience as a general manager, but he worked under Sauer when they were both in St. Louis. The hiring also raised larger concerns about the direction of the Pirates, now that they had lost Bonilla and likely would lose Bonds after the 1992 season. Simmons's background in evaluating and developing young talent as the Cardinals' farm director had many wondering if the Pirates were getting ready to start reducing salary by dumping high-priced veterans and replacing them with younger and cheaper talent out of their minor league system. Many, including some Pirates players, believed it was no coincidence that Doughty was fired after signing veteran Bob Walk to a new contract. In an interview, Walk called his two-year contract "the straw that broke the camel's back."[7]

Once spring training started, Bonds dashed any hope that he would be willing to sign a long-term contract when he told the media, "I'm going to test the market and see what's out there." He said, "If you're a ballplayer, where you lay your hat is your home." The prevailing opinion was that either he would join Bonilla and be wearing a Mets cap in 1993 or he would return home and put on the Giants cap that his father, Bobby Bonds, and his godfather, Willie Mays, had worn in their careers.[8]

The Pirates were hoping for a smooth spring training after the previous year's acrimonious camp, but player personnel decisions made by the new GM seemed to confirm the worst fears about the new leadership and its cost-cutting plans. One controversial decision was the release of relief pitcher Landrum, a stalwart in the Pirates bullpen since he signed as a free agent in 1989. By releasing Landrum, the Pirates were obligated to pay only $425,000 of his projected salary of $1.7 million for 1992.

When Landrum found out about his release, he was devastated. He felt that the Pirates' ownership had "punched a hole in his heart." He loved playing in Pittsburgh and felt that Leyland had placed him in a position time and time again to be successful. In an interview, Landrum remembered that when Leyland called him into his office to tell him that he had been released, the manager "had tears in his eyes."[9] Landrum filed a grievance against the Pirates, claiming that they had violated Rule 7b-2 of the collective bargaining agreement, protecting a player against a club releasing him for financial reasons. Landrum eventually signed a free agent contract with the Montreal Expos, but he was never the same after his release, which he claims crushed him both emotionally and mentally.

Leyland was upset over the release of Landrum, but he was furious when he learned that Simmons, with the blessing of Sauer, had traded twenty-game winner Smiley to the Minnesota Twins for two prospects, outfielder Midre Cummings and pitcher Denny Neagle. While the loss of one of his best starting pitchers was disturbing, what angered Leyland was the failure to consult him on the trade. He went on record as saying that "the general manager doesn't owe me any explanation," but he added, "it hurt me that I wasn't involved." While Leyland put a good face on the matter and called it a miscommunication "that's all been ironed out," some Pirates players were not as kind. Andy Van Slyke wondered if "Sauer and Simmons were still on the Anheuser-Busch payroll."[10]

Leyland's concern going into the 1992 season was that the Pirates had lost players who were a key part of what he called the team's "comfort zone," including veteran Neal Heaton who, in another cost-conscious deal, was traded to the Kansas City Royals for Kirk Gibson, whose game-winning home run in Game 1 of the 1988 World Series is one of baseball's most iconic moments. As the projected replacement for Bonilla, Gibson would be making $1.9 million, $4 million less than Bonilla's 1992 salary with the Mets. The Pirates also shed Heaton's $1 million contract in the trade.

Leyland noted the Pirates were losing more than talent: "John Smiley was a popular player. Neal Heaton was a popular player. Bill Landrum was a popular player." While he lamented their departure, he also felt it was time "to get on with our business." As Opening Day approached, he worried about his bullpen after the release of Landrum, the trade of Heaton, and the free agent loss of valuable left-hander Bob Kipper to the Minnesota Twins, after the Pirates made no effort to re-sign him. Leyland, however, still felt the Pirates had "a heckuva ballclub. . . . When you have Andy Van Slyke, Barry Bonds, Jay Bell, Chico Lind, Kirk Gibson, Steve Buechele, Doug Drabek, . . . we're not talking about a bunch of donkeys. We talking about a pretty good team."[11]

Leyland's pretty good team opened the 1992 season in front of 48,800 fans at Three Rivers Stadium against the Montreal Expos. For the second year in a row, the longest ovation at the pregame ceremonies honoring the division champions went to Leyland. Frattare, who was the master of ceremonies, remembered Leyland signaling him to cut off the ovations in 1991 and in 1992 and, in exasperation, yelling "get on with it." Frattare had become close friends with Leyland and knew the Pirates manager believed "it was all about the players if the Pirates won" and "about him when they lost."[12]

With Bonilla gone, the Pirates moved Bonds into fourth spot in the batting order and inserted Orlando Merced behind him. Replacing Merced at the top of the order was Gibson, who batted leadoff on Opening Day and started in Bonilla's spot in right field. At first Bonds had balked at batting in the cleanup position rather than his customary fifth spot, but going into spring training, he told the *Post-Gazette*'s Paul Meyer he was willing to make the move: "I don't mind hitting fourth. If Leyland thinks that's our best chance to win, I don't mind."[13]

Batting fourth in the order on Opening Day, Bonds led off the bottom of the second with a base hit and came around to score the Pirates' first run of the season. That was all the Pirates would need as they went on to shut out the Expos 2–0 on a strong outing by Drabek and a ninth inning save from Roger Mason, who had taken Landrum's place as one of Leyland's closers. Drabek had his own incentive going into the 1992 season. A year away from becoming a free agent, he had asked for $4.9 million heading into salary arbitration before signing a one-year contract for $4.6 million. When negotiations for a long-term deal stalled during spring training, it looked like Drabek was headed for free agency unless the Pirates were able to reach an agreement with their pitching ace after the season was over. With their recent cost-cutting moves this seemed highly unlikely even though Drabek, unlike Bonds, made it clear he wanted to stay in Pittsburgh.

In the second game of the season-opening series against the Expos, Zane Smith gave the Pirates another strong pitching performance, and this time Belinda came out of the bullpen to record his first save of the season. Once again, Bonds provided the offensive highlight when he launched his first home run of the season, a two-run shot that gave the Pirates a 3–2 lead on their way to a 4–2 victory. In 1991 Bonds did not hit his first home run until the fourteenth game of the season. The Pirates lost the final game of the opening series, 8–3, when the bullpen, Leyland's greatest concern, collapsed. Then they headed to Philadelphia and began a remarkable winning tear that propelled them into first place and confounded the baseball experts who picked them as also-rans for the 1992 season behind the Bonilla-led Mets. The Pirates split the first two games against the Phillies before taking the final contest of the three-game series. That victory was the beginning of an eight-game winning streak that moved them four and a half games ahead of the Mets. After the streak ended in a loss to the Expos in Montreal, the Pirates won three of the next five games and finished April with a record of 15–5 and a three and half game lead over the Mets.

The Pirates' unexpected surge in April owed much to its starting pitching and Leyland's ability to manage a bullpen that lacked a dominant closer. Zane Smith and Randy Tomlin, with four wins each, finished the month with a combined record of 8–1. Drabek went 3–2 in April, while Walk won his first two starts, before being forced to leave the game early in his third start with a pulled muscle. In that game, left-hander Patterson came out of the bullpen to pitch several innings to complete the game and preserve the shutout victory. Leyland's decision to rotate Belinda and Mason as the closer paid early dividends when the two of them combined for eight saves in April.

Barry Bonds's Last Hurrah

The Pirates needed all the help they could get from their pitchers because their hitting attack was soft for most of April. At various points in the month, most of the regular lineup was hitting under .200, including Van Slyke at .120, Gibson at .118, Lind at .115, and Jeff King at .048. With the exception of Bonds, no Pirate hit a home run until bench players Gary Varsho and Lloyd McClendon homered in the eleventh game of the season. The next day Gibson hit a grand slam, his first homer in a Pirates uniform and, two days later, homered to lead off the game in a 2–0 victory over the Expos that capped the Pirates' eight-game winning streak.

With the regulars struggling, McClendon came off the bench to give the offense a lift, but it was Bonds who carried the Pirates' offense in the first month of the season. In sharp contrast to his poor start in 1991, Bonds was phenomenal at the beginning of the 1992 season. He homered in four of the first six games of the season, drove in seven runs, and immediately drew the attention of the national media. Hal Bodley of *USA Today* in "No Bonilla Proves to Be No Problem for Bonds," wrote that people had mistakenly thought that with Bonilla "not batting ahead of him in the order, Bonds would struggle, but they failed to take into account Bonds's motivation if, or more likely when, he became a free agent at the end of the season."[14]

When queried about his early success, Bonds simply said, "I'm just trying to swing the bat and play defense." Leyland, however, claimed that Bonds "came out of spring training much more ready than he was last year" after missing part of camp in 1991 when he went home for the birth of his son and stayed for an extended period of time when complications developed.[15] Whatever the reason, Bonds continued at a torrid pace for the rest of April and finished the month with seven home runs, seventeen RBIs, and a .317 batting average. The title for the cover story in *Sports Illustrated* said it all. For the Pirates in early 1992, it was "Bonds Away."[16]

After their remarkable start in April, the Pirates, with Bonds hitting at an MVP pace and Van Slyke and other regulars bouncing back from early slumps, had no reason to believe that they would not keep up their winning pace in May. Their only adjustment came on May 5, when they released Gibson, who had been projected as a replacement for Bonilla. Gibson had a dramatic home run for the Pirates in April, but he was hitting only .196 at the time of his release.

The team did manage to go 8–5 in the first half of May and maintained its hold on first place, but after a loss to the Padres on May 15, they went on a six-game losing streak. After one win against the Dodgers, they lost five more games in a row and fell out of first place for the first time that season. They managed to break that streak and win two out of three against the Giants, but they finished with an 11–17 record during May and trailed the now-division-leading Mets by a half game. Leyland's reputation for putting his players in the right position to win games had been sorely tested that month. His most reliable starting pitchers struggled, and his bullpen faltered in the late innings. Drabek finished the month under .500 at 3–4, while Smith and Tomlin, after winning a combined eight games in April, won only two games between them in May and lost six. Walk, who was still struggling with injuries, failed to win a game in May, and his replacements, including rookie pitcher Neagle, pitched erratically. The bullpen blew several late-inning leads, including two in the bottom of the ninth by Belinda.

With Gibson gone, Leyland rotated several players between first base and right field but could find no permanent solution to the hole in the lineup created by the loss of Bonilla. He discovered that players like McClendon, Cecil Espy, and Varsho were effective coming off the bench but struggled when they were placed in the starting lineup over an extended period of time. Among the regulars, Van Slyke, after his poor start, was hitting .360 and was among the league leaders in average. Van Slyke, however, had only one home run going into June, as did Bell, after hitting a personal best sixteen homers in 1991. Bonds, whose average fell below .300 early in the month, bounced back at the end of May, hitting again with power and driving in runs, but it was not enough to carry the faltering Pirates.

June started on a sour note for the Pirates when their former reliever Jim Gott was the winning pitcher in an 8–6 loss to the Dodgers at Three Rivers. Former Pirate John Candelaria made the loss even more bitter when he picked up the save. The Pirates managed to win the next two games against the Dodgers, but the real challenge in turning their season around awaited them as the Mets came to town for a four-game series. This would also mark Bonilla's first visit to Pittsburgh since he signed a lucrative contract with the Mets.

On June 4, with the Pirates just one game ahead of the Mets and the Cardinals in the division standings, 24,907 fans came out to watch

Drabek pitch against Dwight Gooden in the series opener, but many in the crowd also came out to taunt and boo Bonilla for leaving the Pirates. Signs in the crowd read, "Bobby Boooonilla," "Bobby Bo-Traitor," and "Do You like NY Monilla."[17] When Bonilla stepped to the plate for the first time, the organist played "Take the Money and Run" as a torrent of boos rained down. The game, delayed by rain for two hours, turned out to be a perfect delight for bitter Pirates fans who wanted to see Bonilla lose. With Bonds leading the way with two hits, including his fourteenth home run of the season, three runs scored, and two RBIs, the Pirates, behind a strong pitching performance from Drabek, easily defeated the Mets, 7–2. Bonilla went 0–4 in his first game back. His hitless night dropped his average to .253, while Bonds's two hits raised his average to .313.

After the game Bonilla claimed he was not bothered by the booing, but his close friend and former teammate was furious. Bonds accused the fans of being racists: "Hell, they didn't do that to Sid Bream last year . . . they gave him a standing ovation." Noting that Bonilla, while standing in the outfield in the eighth inning, was hit in the leg with a golf ball in an incident reminiscent of the battery thrown at Dave Parker in July 1979, Bonds claimed, "They wouldn't do that to Andy Van Slyke . . . Mr. Pittsburgh. Bobby contributed as much to this team as anybody and he gets booed like that?"[18] In *Love Me, Hate Me: Barry Bonds and the Making of an Antihero*, Jeff Pearlman, while personally regarding Bonds as a "mean, selfish, and indulgent" human being, wrote that in this case his "outburst was justified. . . . Bonds was merely echoing the sentiments of dozens of black players before him—from Dock Ellis to Dave Parker to Bonilla." Pearlman quoted longtime Pittsburgh sportswriter Bob Smizik as saying, "Racism certainly played a part in Barry's unpopularity. This town does not like uppity black guys. They liked (Mean) Joe Greene and Willie Stargell because those guys were very humble. But black guys who strut take a beating."[19]

It is not surprising that Bonds would single out Van Slyke in his outburst. Bonds and Van Slyke had a complicated relationship that reflected differences not only in race but also in personality and in their relationships with the team and the city. Both players were confident in their abilities, and neither would back down from a confrontation. They had been adversaries since Leyland moved Bonds to left field so that Van Slyke, who had a stronger arm, could play center field. When

Van Slyke signed a long-term contract while Bonds was losing his salary arbitration hearings, the antagonism between the two grew worse. They were also different in their attitude and approach to the game. Darnell Coles, who played with Bonds and Van Slyke in the 1987 and 1988 seasons, remembered Van Slyke playing "with a chip on his shoulder" and as someone who was "not afraid to get in a player's face," including Bonds's.[20] In his book, Pearlman recalled an incident in which Van Slyke physically confronted Bonds after he thought Bonds had loafed on a play and embarrassed the team: "Barry, if you ever fuckin' do that again—embarrass me or this team while I'm in uniform and we're playing together—I'll punch you right on the spot. Play the game the way it's supposed to be played."[21]

Perhaps remembering his earlier confrontation with Van Slyke, Bonds told reporters that Van Slyke would not dare defend the booing of Bonilla "because he knows Bobby would come in here and kick the [shit] out of him."[22] Bonilla had his own way of responding to the boos, however. After the Pirates, sparked by a Van Slyke home run, defeated the Mets in the second game of the four-game series, Bonilla led the Mets to a 15–1 romp over rookie pitcher Neagle by banging out four hits, including a home run, and driving in four runs.

After Tomlin shut out the Mets in the final game of the series, the Pirates took two out of three games in Philadelphia before moving on to New York for another three games against the Mets. They continued their earlier success by sweeping the series and taking a five-game lead in the East Division, but it turned out to be a costly series. On June 14, in the top of the ninth of the final game in New York, Bonds strained a muscle in his side while swinging at a pitch and would be out until early July. With Bonds on the disabled list, Leyland had yet another outfield position to fill with players who were better suited for coming off the bench for spot starts rather than playing full time. With Bonds out of the lineup, the Pirates lost four of their next six games, but they managed to win five of their following nine, thanks to clutch hitting from Van Slyke and Merced and strong pitching from Tomlin, who won three straight starts to lead the staff with ten victories and only three defeats. Even after losing seven of their last eleven games, the Pirates ended the month with a 17–11 record in June, and going into July, had a 43–33 record overall and a healthy six-game lead over the Chicago Cubs and a seven and a half game lead over the fading Mets.

With Bonds just days away from returning to the lineup, the Pirates looked poised to run away with their third straight division title and another shot at playing in the World Series. On July 4, to stabilize the ballclub's revolving door situation in right field, they traded a minor league prospect to the Cleveland Indians for Alex Cole. Inserting Cole at the top of the order, the Pirates hoped he would provide an immediate spark to the lineup. He was no power threat, but he had a knack for getting on base and disrupting teams with his speed. A week later, the Pirates made another trade, this time to strengthen their starting pitching, which lacked depth after Drabek, Smith, and Tomlin. They sent third baseman Steve Buechele to the Cubs for veteran left-hander Danny Jackson. Jeff King, who had been playing first base, was completely recovered from his back problems and was ready to return to third base to fill the void left by Buechele's departure.

The Pirates also expected that Bonds's return would be a big boost to the lineup, but Bonds was rusty from his stay on the disabled list, and he struggled to hit with power. He may have been feeling the aftereffects of his injury and went nearly three weeks before hitting a home run. The Pirates lost six of their first nine games in July. Only a three-game sweep of the Astros just before the All-Star break kept them in first place.

Although they reportedly were antagonists in the clubhouse and barely talked to each other, Bonds and Van Slyke played side by side, not only in the Pirates' outfield but in the 1992 All-Star Game as well. Van Slyke was batting .340 and among the league leaders in RBIs, and Bonds was batting .313 and among the league leaders in home runs and RBIs. Both were easily voted in as starters. The All-Star Game did not, however, produce a reunion of the Pirates' old outfield. Bonilla was struggling in his first year with the Mets and was not voted into the game or selected as a reserve by All-Star manager Bobby Cox.

The Pirates resumed play with a 2–1 victory over the Cubs, sparked by a strong pitching performance from Drabek and a home run from Van Slyke. Any hope of taking control of the division race faded, however, when they lost nine of their next twelve games. After being swept by the Cubs at Three Rivers, the Pirates fell into a tie for first place with their old nemesis, the Montreal Expos. The only thing that prevented them from falling out of first place in late July was a strong pitching performance on July 26 by rookie Paul Wagner, who was called up from the AA Carolina team for a spot start after Smith had to miss a turn with a sore shoulder. In an interview, Wagner remembered that he was excited by the call-up until he noticed that his ticket to Pittsburgh was for a round trip.[23]

On July 31, the Pirates moved a game ahead of the Expos when Jackson pitched a 4–0 shutout for his first win as a Pirate. As encouraging as Jackson's victory was for the Pirates, it was the pitching performance the next night from another unproven rookie that would send them surging into August and on their way to another date with the Atlanta Braves in the playoffs. As Wagner headed back to the minors and waited for a September call-up, the Pirates decided to promote another rookie, knuckleball pitcher Tim Wakefield from their AAA Buffalo farm club.

Wakefield was the unlikeliest of heroes for the Pirates in the 1992 season. Selected in the eighth round of the 1988 draft as a first baseman, Wakefield batted only .189 in his first professional season. When he was told he would never make it to the major leagues as a hitter, he turned in desperation to pitching. He could not throw particularly hard, so he developed a knuckleball that danced toward home plate at about fifty-five miles per hour. He pitched well enough for Carolina in 1991 to earn a promotion to Buffalo, where he started the 1992 season. He was 10–3, with six complete games, in Buffalo when the Pirates called him up to the majors because Walk and Smith were struggling with nagging injuries. Leyland recalled that he had "no idea what to expect . . . I didn't know who Wakefield was. A lot of people didn't." Leyland, however, soon discovered that Wakefield was "the fuckin' Elvis Presley" of the 1992 season: "At that time that was probably the biggest impact of anybody that's ever come into the big leagues. That kind of stuff just doesn't happen. That's a fairy tale."[24] As for Wakefield's knuckleball, Leyland later described it as "a keg of dynamite."[25] He just hoped it would explode against opponents' batters and not in the face of his manager.

Wakefield made his big-league debut on July 31 against the St. Louis Cardinals. With the help of a Bonds two-run homer, Wakefield defeated the Cardinals, 3–2, for his first major league win. He struck out ten batters and pitched a complete game. The win preserved the Pirates' one-game lead over the Montreal Expos going into August. With Wakefield in the rotation, the Pirates were never out of first place for the rest of the season. He would win three more games in August and finished the season with a remarkable 8–1 record.

While Wakefield gave the Pirates a much-needed lift in the last third of the season, he did create a few problems along the way. A master at deciding when to turn to his bullpen in a game, Leyland could not figure out when the soft-throwing Wakefield was tired, so the chain-smoking Leyland would light up cigarette after cigarette and usually let Wakefield finish the game. Wakefield also caused what LaValliere called "emotional stress" for his catchers, who had little experience with a knuckleball, especially one that darted so sharply.[26] When Redus, who had done some catching in his career, told LaValliere and Slaught that he could not understand why they were having so much trouble with a pitch moving so slowly, they challenged Redus, who normally played first base or the outfield, to catch ten Wakefield knuckleballs. When Redus was unable to catch half of Wakefield's pitches, he had little to say about catching a knuckler for the rest of the season.

While Wakefield helped stabilize the Pirates' pitching staff, Leyland made a key move that solidified his lineup and helped the Pirates to a 19–8 record in August and a three-and-a-half-game lead over the Expos going into the critical last month of the season. Instead of shuffling players in and out of right field, he began using a platoon system with the left-hand hitting Cole batting against right-handers and the right-hand hitting McClendon batting against left-handers. He also decided to make a similar move at first base, where he platooned the switch-hitting Merced with the right-hand hitting Redus.

With Bonds regaining his timing, Van Slyke driving in key runs, and a healthy King hitting for power and playing regularly at third base, the Pirates won their last two games of July and extended their winning streak to a season-best eleven games by winning their first nine games in August. The only snag came in mid-August, when they lost three out of four at home against the Braves, including a 15–0 trouncing in which Smith, bothered by shoulder problems since late July, lasted only one-third of an inning. They did, however, bounce back with a three-game sweep of the Padres at home before heading to the West Coast, where they finished the month winning five out of nine against the Giants, Dodgers, and Padres.

The Pirates began September in the middle of another long winning streak, this time of seven games, though they still could not shake the Montreal Expos, who remained only four games back. The Pirates managed only five wins in their next nine games. Going into a two-game home series against Montreal in mid-September they still had only a four-game lead over the Expos. When they lost the first game in the series, their lead fell to a precarious three games.

On September 16, the Pirates and Expos, tied at 3–3, battled into the thirteenth inning in a crucial division game. An Expos victory would close the gap between the teams to only two games with sixteen left to play in the season. Time and time again, all season long, bench players had been the key to Pirates wins, and this game would be no exception. While Bonds had kept the Pirates in the game with four hits, two stolen bases, and an RBI, it was a leadoff triple in the bottom of the thirteenth by Espy that put the Pirates in position to win the game. When a Bell single brought Espy home with the winning run, the Pirates had their four-game lead back. The win launched a five-game winning streak for the Pirates, while the Expos lost three of their next four games and fell seven games behind the division leaders.

On September 29, the Pirates held a seven-game lead with only eleven left to play and headed to Montreal for a two-game series. The series was the last chance for the struggling Expos to make a run at the division leaders. In the opening game, the Pirates received a reminder of what they gave up to acquire Smith, when their former minor league prospect, Moises Alou, hit a grand slam in the bottom of the fourteenth to defeat the Pirates, 5–1. The next night, however, sparked by Bonds's thirty-first home run and three RBIs plus a strong pitching performance from Drabek, who won his staff-leading fifteenth game, the Pirates easily beat the Expos, 9–3, and once again held a seven-game division lead with only nine games left to play.

When the Pirates returned home for a three-game series against the Mets, they knew that any combination of three Pirates wins or Expos losses would give them their third division title in a row and another—and likely final—chance at getting to the World Series. With Tomlin winning his fourteenth game of the season, the Pirates defeated the Mets, who played without Bonilla in the lineup, in the first game of the series. The next day, Bonds, Van Slyke, and McClendon hit home runs, and the Pirates scored twelve runs in the first two innings on their way to a 19–2 romp that clinched at least a tie for the division championship.

On Sunday, September 27, there were 31,217 fans who flocked to

Three Rivers in hopes of watching the Pirates beat the Mets and win the East Division title. After Jackson retired the Mets in the top of the first inning, the Pirates took a 1–0 lead in the bottom of first when Bonds hit a sacrifice fly to score Bell. The Pirates increased their lead to 3–0 in the bottom of the third, when Bell and King hit RBI singles, and they added another run in the bottom of the fifth on Bell's second RBI single of the game. Jackson shut down the Mets for seven innings, allowing only one run. After late-season pick-up Danny Cox retired the Mets in the top the eighth, Leyland brought in Belinda to close out the game.

Belinda had made his major-league debut with the Pirates in September 1989. Growing up in State College, Pennsylvania, Belinda saw his first Pirates game in 1974 when his father drove the 140 miles to Pittsburgh to take his son to a twi-night doubleheader against the Padres at Three Rivers. For Belinda, it was love at first sight. By the time he became a star pitcher on the State College Area High School team, all that he could dream about was "what it would be like to play for the Pirates."[27] When the Pirates drafted Belinda in the tenth round of the 1986 draft, his dream was on the verge of coming true. By the 1992 season, he was the relief pitcher most used by Leyland in closing situations. Belinda enjoyed the role of closer, but he had an incentive beyond his teammates when he took the mound against the Mets. He remembered the unused ticket for the seventh game of the 1960 World Series that his father kept in a drawer because he had to study for a pharmacy exam while attending the University of Pittsburgh and could not make it to Forbes Field that monumental day in Pirates history. In an interview early in the 1992 season, Belinda said, "It would be a big thrill for me to pitch in the World Series in front of him. He's always been a Pirate fan. So have my mother and my five brothers. To get a chance to pitch for the Pittsburgh Pirates in front of all of them would be the ultimate."[28]

Belinda surrendered a run to the Mets to make the score 4–2, but then struck out pinch-hitter Jeff McKnight on a sweeping breaking ball to end the game. It was his seventeenth save on the season, but none was bigger than the one that now sent the Pirates into the playoffs for a rematch against the Atlanta Braves. With six games left in the season, the Pirates were now able to rest some of their starters and play September call-ups like outfielder Kevin Young, Carlos García, and Al Martin, the heir apparent to Bonds. While Leyland sorted out his pitching strategy for the playoffs, he was also able to showcase his young pitchers, like

Wagner, who filled in so admirably for Smith in an earlier call-up, and Steve Cooke, who was regarded as the best prospect in the Pirates' farm system.

The Pirates finished the 1992 season with a 96–66 record, only two wins off their 98–64 pace in 1991. Their season attendance was down by 237,907, but general manager Simmons blamed a newspaper strike that began in May for the drop: "It killed us. . . . We're working very hard to take a small market team and put people in the park, but when a newspaper strike hits, I believe people get out of the custom of following the team."[29] The resulting loss in revenue all but doomed the prospect of negotiating long-term contracts for players on the cusp of free agency, especially Bonds and Drabek.

Even with the loss of Bonilla and Smiley, the Pirates' offense led the National League in runs scored, and their pitching staff finished third best in the league with a 3.36 ERA. Bonds hit a career-high 34 home runs, second best in the National League. He drove in a team-high 103 runs and batted .311 on his way to his second National League MVP Award in three years. Playing injury-free, Van Slyke scored 103 runs, drove in 89, and hit a career-high .324, good for second among league batting leaders. After his slow start, Drabek finished with a team-high fifteen wins, just one ahead of Tomlin who, in his first full season, was the Pirates' most consistent starter. The bullpen, led by Belinda's eighteen saves, finished the season with an impressive forty-three saves, including nine by Patterson and eight by Mason.

Behind all the success of the 1992 season was the manager. The most valuable Pirate was clearly Leyland, who held the team together after the loss of key players. With a huge hole in right field, he rotated several bench players in and out of the lineup to compensate for the departure of Bonilla. With the loss of a twenty-game winner and key relievers, he was able to patch together a consistent pitching staff that was plagued by injuries during the season. Eighteen different pitchers won games in 1992, one off the major-league record, while nine recorded at least one save.

After the Pirates clinched the East Division title back in 1990, one of the shoulders that carried Leyland off the field belonged to emerging star Barry Bonds. This time, it was part-time starter McClendon who helped lift a tearful Leyland into the air. It was bench players like Mc-Clendon who, thanks to Leyland, were given the opportunity during the season to be a key part of the Pirates' success. It was the same McClendon who would have spectacular success in the upcoming playoff series against the Braves and just nine years later, with Leyland's blessing, became the manager of the Pirates.

For the present moment, as he was carried off the field, Leyland could wave his cap at cheering Pirates fans and ride the emotional wave of clinching the 1992 division title after overcoming so many challenges and obstacles. Once the cheering and celebration were over, however, he would have to figure out a way to defeat an Atlanta Braves team that had upset the Pirates in 1991 but now, after coasting to the West Division title, were the favorites to repeat . It was the third time that Leyland would have the chance to lead the Pirates to the World Series and likely his last.

CHAPTER EIGHT

SID BREAM'S SLIDE INTO HISTORY

The 1992 National League Championship Series

After the Atlanta Braves defeated the Pirates in the 1991 National League Championship Series, they played the Minnesota Twins in a World Series selected by ESPN as the "greatest of all time."[1] Five of the seven games were decided by one run—four of the five in a team's final at-bat, and three in extra innings. When the Braves lost the first two games in Minnesota, it looked like their Cinderella year would fall short of a world championship, but they bounced back to win the next three games in Atlanta to take a 3–2 lead in the series. With Steve Avery poised to pitch Game 6 and John Smoltz, if needed, available to start Game 7, the Braves appeared to be ready to win their first World Series since 1957, when the underdog Milwaukee Braves defeated the New York Yankees in seven games.

Unfortunately for the Braves, Avery was not as dominant against the Twins as he had been against the Pirates. He gave up two runs in the first inning and one more before he was relieved after six innings. The Braves rallied to tie the game, but eventually lost to the Twins, 4–3, in eleven innings. With the World Series tied at three games apiece, Smoltz gave the Braves another outstanding postseason performance, pitching shutout baseball into the eighth inning, but the Twins' Jack Morris was just as impressive. With the game scoreless in the bottom of the tenth, Braves closer Alejandro Peña gave up a pinch single to Gene Larkin that gave the Twins a 1–0 victory and the World Series championship.

The 1991 World Series loss was a disappointing end to the Braves' season, but they had good reason for feeling optimistic while they waited until next year. With Smoltz, Avery, and Cy Young Award–winner Tom Glavine, they had an outstanding core of young starting pitchers. With Ron Gant, David Justice, and National League MVP Terry Pendleton, they also had a potent offense, capable of hitting for average and power. In addition, they had a strong bullpen and one of the best defensive teams in baseball. Confident that they had the players to return to the World Series, the Braves made no major trade and only a few free agent signings during the offseason. One of their signings, however, would have a major impact on the season ahead and on the outcome of the 1992 NLCS. Near the end of the 1991 season, center fielder Otis Nixon received a sixty-game suspension after testing positive for cocaine. As a result, he missed the 1991 NLCS and the World Series and still had eighteen days remaining on his suspension going into the 1992 season. Few teams had an interest in Nixon, who had become a free agent during the offseason, but the Braves decided to take a chance and re-signed him.

For all the excitement and expectations going into the 1992 season, the Braves got off to a disappointing start, and by the end of May were under .500 at 23–27. They bounced back in June with a record of 19–6 and, by the end of July, had moved into first place in the West Division. In early August, they began to pull away and finished the season a comfortable eight games ahead of the Cincinnati Reds with a record of 98–64. While Avery had a disappointing 11–11 record, Glavine tied for the National League lead with 20 wins, while Smoltz led the league in strikeouts. Pendleton had another MVP-worthy season with 21 home runs, 105 RBIs, and a .311 average. Justice matched Pendleton with 21 home runs, and Gant added 17 to the Braves' offense. Underdogs in 1991, the Braves were now the favorites. Sid Bream, who said he finally felt comfortable in a Braves uniform, believed that, for the Braves, the NLCS "was theirs to lose."[2]

For the first game of the 1992 NLCS, Braves manager Bobby Cox passed over twenty-game winner Glavine in favor of Smoltz. While

Smoltz had confessed to an attack of nerves before facing the Pirates in Game 7 of the 1991 NLCS, he claimed that the pressure of starting the opening game was "a piece of cake" compared to pitching in the seventh and deciding games of the NLCS and the World Series.[3] He felt confident, focused, and eager to take the mound against the Pirates.

On the Pirates' side, Leyland's pitching options were limited by the absence of Zane Smith, who had injured his shoulder near the end of the season. Smith had taken injections to help with the pain and felt that he was ready to pitch against the Braves, but Leyland, who had said in the past that he would not use a player to win a game if it meant jeopardizing the player's career, decided not to use Smith in the series.[4] For Game 1, he still had an interesting choice between sensational rookie Tim Wakefield and his veteran ace Doug Drabek, but he decided not to pitch Wakefield in Atlanta and went with Drabek. Steve Blass, who won the World Series as a pitcher with the Pirates and was now part of their broadcast team, admired the decision because Drabek "gets it . . . he knows what he's doing . . . he knows how to pitch."[5]

The starting lineups for Game 1 were similar to those of a year before, but there were a few significant changes. The Pirates had traded away Steve Buechele in July for veteran pitcher Danny Jackson. Alex Cole, acquired in another midseason trade, would be starting in Bonilla's place in right field, while Jeff King was at third base. The most serious loss for the Braves occurred on September 18, when catcher Greg Olson, one of the heroes of the 1991 NLCS, suffered a broken leg and dislocated ankle in a collision at home plate with Astro Ken Caminiti. Damon Berryhill, acquired from the Cubs at the end of the 1991 season, would be the Braves' catcher for the 1992 NLCS. The Braves would also have a different starting center fielder in Nixon and shortstop in Jeff Blauser. Veterans Lonnie Smith and Rafael Belliard were still with the team, but the Braves turned to Nixon because of his superior defensive skills and Blauser because he was a much better hitter than the former Pirate, Belliard.

When Smoltz and Drabek each retired the side in order in the first inning, it looked like the Braves and the Pirates were headed for another classic postseason pitching duel, but all that changed in the bottom of the second when Bream singled and, with two outs, went to second on a walk to Berryhill. In a harbinger of things to come, it was Bream's baserunning, on surgically repaired knees, that gave the Braves a 1–0 lead in Game 1. When Mark Lemke bounced a single up the middle, Bream, thinking the ball was going into center field, rounded third base and headed for home. What he did not know was that second baseman José Lind had made a diving stop of the ball and prevented it from rolling into the outfield. Bream ran right through third-base coach Jimy Williams's stop sign and, catching the Pirates by surprise, scored on the play. Bream later explained, "I was running because I couldn't stop . . . I knew if I did stop my knees would end up in the stands. I saw Williams' hands go up, but I couldn't do it. Even if I had stopped I would have ended up three-quarters of the way down the line any way."[6]

In the bottom of the fourth, with Atlanta holding on to a 1–0 lead, Bream's hitting and baserunning helped the Braves take a 3–0 lead. After Justice walked, Bream brought him home with a double into the left-center-field gap. When Gant laid down a bunt, Merced bobbled the ball then threw wildly past Lind, who was covering first base, as Bream hobbled around third and scored on the error. After Smoltz retired the Pirates in the top of the fifth, Blauser launched a home run down the left-field line to give the Braves a 4–0 lead. Later in the inning, after a Justice double, Leyland brought Bob Patterson into the game to relieve Drabek.

After an RBI single by Pendleton in the bottom of the seventh increased the Braves' lead to 5–0, the Pirates finally broke through against Smoltz in the top of the eighth when Lind homered to lead off the inning, but they failed to mount a threat against Smoltz after the homer had cut the lead to 5–1. In the top of the ninth, reliever Mike Stanton gave up a two-out double to King, but Merced struck out to end the game. When questioned about the Pirates' poor showing in Game 1, Bonds, who had gone hitless once again in a playoff game, told reporters, "You know we won the first game last year, so it's just one game. I'm not worried about it. If you worry about it, it's not worth it."[7]

If Bonds and the Pirates were not worried after Game 1, they had plenty to worry about after Game 2. Before the NLCS started, Braves manager Cox announced that he would go with a three-man rotation, with Smoltz, Avery, and Glavine pitching in that order. That meant that in Game 2 the Pirates, already down a game, would have to face Avery, who had shut them out twice in the 1991 NLCS.

With Smith out with a sore shoulder, Leyland had the option of pitching Randy Tomlin, who had finished second on the Pirates' staff with fourteen wins, or Danny Jackson, who had gone 4–4 after coming to the Pirates in a midseason trade. Recognizing that Tomlin had completed just his first full season in the big leagues, Leyland decided to go with the veteran Jackson, who had pitched in two World Series and had pitched well for the Reds against the Pirates in the 1990 NLCS. For Jackson, after two years of struggling with injuries and hard-luck seasons, Leyland's decision was a chance for a comeback: "I've learned a lot. I've been through hard times. It got to be a mental thing with me." Reminded that he had a reputation while with the Reds of being nastier than the Nasty Boys, he said, "I've still got that same attitude."[8]

After a scoreless first inning, any hope that Jackson was ready to bounce back after his recent struggles collapsed in the bottom of the second when he walked Brian Hunter and Gant to lead off the inning, then gave up an RBI single to Berryhill. After the runners advanced to second and third on Bonds's throw to home plate, Lemke singled a run home, and Avery made the score 3–0 with a sacrifice fly. When Blauser tripled home Avery with two outs, Leyland brought in Roger Mason to finish the inning.

With a 4–0 lead, Avery continued his scoreless streak by shutting down the Pirates, allowing only one hit through the first five innings. While the Pirates' hitting woes continued against Avery, Bob Walk, in relief of Mason, kept the Braves scoreless until the bottom of the fifth when he loaded the bases with two outs and gave up a grand slam to Gant. Down an embarrassing 8–0, the Pirates went out in order in the top of the sixth, giving Avery twenty-two and a third scoreless innings in a row against the Pirates and extending his NLCS record.

After the Braves failed to score in the bottom of the sixth, the Pirates finally broke through against Avery. Bonds led off the top of the seventh with a base hit, and after King flied out, Lloyd McClendon brought Bonds home with a double into the right-center-field gap. Perhaps shaken by McClendon's hit, a tiring Avery walked Don Slaught, then gave up a two-run triple to Lind. When a Cecil Espy single drove home Lind with the fourth run of the inning, Cox walked slowly out to the mound and brought in reliever Marvin Freeman. After the game, Avery would tell reporters that the streak of shutout innings "was fun while it lasted. That might have been a case of being too fired up and losing a bit. I'll have to work on that."[9]

The Pirates may have thrown a brief scare into the Braves by cutting the lead to 8–4 in the top of the seventh and knocking out Avery, but the Braves put the game out of reach by scoring five runs in the bottom of the inning against rookie Denny Neagle. Trailing 13–4, the Pirates picked up a run in the top of the eighth, but Jeff Reardon closed out the game to give the Braves a lopsided 13–5 victory and a 2–0 lead in the NLCS. Heading to Pittsburgh, the Braves had outscored the Pirates 18–6 and, with Glavine and Smoltz scheduled to pitch, looked ready to sweep the Pirates in four games.

After the game, a grim Leyland said, "it's tough to be fighting up hill all the time. That's what we've been doing." With Van Slyke and Bonds going 1-for-11 in the first two games, he told reporters, "we've got to score some runs and we've got to win a game. It's that simple. There's no secret to that. That pretty much sums it up."[10] An upbeat Cox had no such problem, "I didn't expect all those runs. We hit some heavy artillery." A confident Bream added, "we know what we have to do," but a more cautious Blauser warned, "To say they're going to give up and feel they're likely out of it would be naive."[11]

The Game 3 matchup between the Braves' twenty-game winner Glavine and the Pirates' rookie Wakefield, who had pitched in only thirteen games in his major-league career, looked like a baseball David trying to bring down Goliath with nothing more than a knuckleball. The Braves, however, recognizing Wakefield's sensational 8–1 season record, which included a 4–2 complete game victory over Smoltz, brought in Bruce Dal Canton, the former Pirates knuckleballer and now the pitching coach for Atlanta's AAA farm club in Richmond, to pitch batting practice. When asked about Wakefield, Dal Canton said, "The thing that's impressed me with him is he throws [the knuckleball] for strikes. If he gets ahead in the count, he can get it over when he wants."[12]

One of the biggest concerns for Leyland and his players was how Wakefield would handle the pressure of pitching such a critical game, especially since they were already down two games in the series. Van Slyke said, "I'm sure everyone is asking him if he feels pressure. I don't know what his answers have been. But he should be feeling the pressure." When asked by reporters, Wakefield responded, "I'm sure I'll be nervous. But once I get the security of pitching, once I get the baseball in my hands, I'll be fine." As for his unpredictable knuckleball, "I don't want to get beat with nothing else."[13]

The Pirates were appearing in their ninth NLCS and playing in their seventeenth NLCS game at Three Rivers, but they had never had a sellout there—until 56,610 fans filled Three Rivers for Game 3. Armed with rubber foam hooks to counter the Braves fans' tomahawk chop, Pirates fans filled Three Rivers to watch the pitcher Leyland called the "fucking Elvis Presley" of baseball and see if he could bring the Pirates' postseason hopes back to life.

Pirates fans roared and waved their hooks as Wakefield started Game 3 by striking out Nixon and retiring the Braves in order in the top of the first inning. In the bottom of the inning, Gary Redus brought the fans to their feet with a leadoff triple off Glavine, but Bell, Van Slyke, and Bonds could not get the ball out of the infield and stranded Redus at third base. The Braves managed to put runners in scoring position in the next two innings, but Wakefield ended each threat with a double play ball. Redus hit a double with two outs in the bottom of the third, but Bell bounced back to the mound to end the inning.

With two outs in the top of the fourth, Bream swung and appeared to miss a knuckleball for the final out of the inning. When the ball popped out of Slaught's mitt, he tagged Bream, but the umpire ruled that Bream had tipped the ball. With new life at the plate, Bream silenced the crowd by driving Wakefield's next pitch over the right-center-field fence. Instead of ending the inning with a strikeout, Bream had homered to give the Braves a 1–0 lead.

Glavine retired the Pirates in the fourth after hitting Bonds with a pitch, but in the bottom of the fifth, Slaught, who had failed to hold Bream's foul tip, reenergized Pirates fans with a leadoff home run over the left-center-field fence to tie the score at 1–1. After Wakefield retired the Braves in the top of the sixth, the Pirates took a 2–1 lead in the bottom of the inning when Van Slyke doubled and, one out later, scored on a King double.

Wakefield retired the first two batters in the top of the seventh, but Gant launched a knuckleball deep down the left-field line that easily cleared the fence and tied the score at 2–2. In the bottom of the seventh the Pirates regained the lead, when Redus walked with one out and went around to third on a Bell double down the left-field line. At that point Cox decided to relieve Glavine and bring in another left-hander, Stanton. With one out, first base open, and the slumping Bonds on deck, Cox decided to let Stanton pitch to Van Slyke, who lofted a fly ball to right to score Redus.

Ahead 3–2 and only six outs away from a victory, Wakefield retired the first two Braves in the top of the eighth, but Nixon doubled to put the tying run in scoring position for Blauser. Wakefield, who had given up two home runs on the night, gave Pirates fans one more heart-stopping moment. He threw a knuckleball that Blauser lifted deep down the left-field line. The ball sailed toward the foul pole, but at the last moment, it curled foul. As the fans' groans turned into cheers, Blauser grounded out to King to end the inning.

After the Pirates failed to score in the bottom of the eighth, Leyland decided to let Wakefield go back out to the mound for the ninth inning. Wakefield rewarded his manager's confidence by retiring Pendleton on a ground ball to Lind and getting Justice with a fly ball to Van Slyke. With the hook-waving crowd on its feet and roaring with each pitch, Bream, who had homered earlier in the game, popped up a knuckleball to Bell to end the game.

In his postgame interview, Wakefield told reporters, "I'm not an emotional person," but admitted, "tonight was really special. It's amazing how good that crowd can make you feel. It was a dream come true to get into a championship game and come out of it like that."[14] Leyland earlier had said that Wakefield was living a baseball fairy tale, but his postgame comments focused on his team's effort after two embarrassing losses in Atlanta: "That's the real Pittsburgh Pirates you saw tonight. Not just because we won, but because we played like we're capable of playing."[15] As for Leyland's players, Redus best summed up their feelings: "I tell you, it was very uplifting to look up in the stands and see hooks and not chops up there. It made a big difference. I've still got goose bumps from the way the crowd reacted."[16]

After Game 3, Van Slyke declared, "We're out of the emergency room," but thought they still had to see about the "long-term prognosis."[17] Van Slyke had good reason to be hesitant about the Pirates' performance in the remaining playoff games. While he had bounced back from his hitting woes with a key double and the game-winning RBI, the Pirates had scored only three runs in the game and were still struggling offensively. Several players, including Bell, King, Merced, and Mike La-Valliere were batting under .200, but the biggest problem was Bonds, who had only one hit in three games and again was failing to hit with runners in scoring position. A frustrated Bonds, said, "I don't know what happens to me in October. I can't explain it." Jim Leyland thought Bonds's problem was that he was "trying to hit a five-run home run. . . . He's pressing a little bit."[18]

The starting pitchers for Game 4 were Drabek, who felt he had pressed too hard in his Game 1 loss, and a relaxed and confident Smoltz. Drabek knew that he and his teammates would "have to make sure that we don't go out there and start overdoing stuff. . . . We have to go out there and make it happen in the game at hand and not worry about what's happened in the past."[19]

Before a hook-waving crowd of 57,164, even larger than the night before, Drabek struggled in the top of the first inning when Nixon singled to lead off the game, stole second, and went to third on a sacrifice bunt. But Drabek retired Pendleton on a short fly ball to Bonds and Justice on a pop out to first. The Pirates mounted their own threat in the bottom of the first when Van Slyke tripled after Smoltz had struck out Cole and Bell, but after walking Bonds, Smoltz struck out King.

In the top of the second, the Braves threatened again, but this time Drabek was not able to pitch out of trouble. With two outs and Gant on second, Leyland ordered Drabek to walk Lemke intentionally so as to bring up Smoltz, but the strategy backfired when Smoltz singled Gant home and Nixon followed with a base hit to give the Braves a 2–0 lead. In the bottom of the inning, the Pirates rallied to tie the game with the help of base hits by LaValliere and Lind and a key error by Blauser. With the bases loaded and one out, Blauser made a diving stop on a ball hit by Cole. But he had trouble getting the ball out of his glove and threw wildly to home plate as LaValliere and then Lind raced home.

After Drabek settled down and retired the Braves in order in the top of the third, the Pirates took the lead in the bottom of the inning when Smoltz walked Bonds to lead off the inning. When King lofted an easy fly ball to right field, Justice muffed the ball but recovered in time to force out Bonds at second. Merced then lined a double into the left-center-field gap to score King and give the Pirates a 3–2 lead. Drabek and Smoltz had no trouble retiring the side in the fourth inning, but in the top of the fifth, the Braves broke through to take the lead and knock Drabek out of the game.

Once again it was Nixon who was the key to the Braves' rally when he led off the inning with a base hit and raced to third on a Blauser single. Drabek struck out Pendleton for the first out of the inning, but Justice tied the score with a broken-bat single. With runners on first and third and Bream coming to the plate, Leyland decided to replace Drabek with left-hander Tomlin, but Cox countered by having right-hand hitter Hunter bat for Bream. The strategy seemed to work for Leyland when Hunter bounced a ground ball to third, but King threw wide to home, and on the error Blauser was able to avoid the tag and score.

With a 4–3 lead, Smoltz shut down the Pirates in the bottom of the fifth. In the top of the sixth, with Danny Cox pitching, the Braves struck again, thanks to key hits, once again by Smoltz and Nixon. With two outs, Smoltz singled, and when the Pirates failed to hold him at first, Smoltz took off and stole second base. When Nixon followed with an RBI double and Blauser singled Nixon home, the Braves surged to a 6–3 lead.

The Pirates failed to score in the bottom of the sixth, but they gave their fans one last hope in the bottom of the seventh. With the crowd still on its feet after the seventh inning stretch and pleading for a Pirates rally, Cole led off the inning with a walk. One out later, Van Slyke sent the crowd into a frenzy when he lined a double off the right-center-field wall that easily scored Cole. With Bonds representing the tying run, Bobby Cox brought in hard-throwing left-hander Stanton in relief of Smoltz. With the crowd desperately chanting his name, Bonds stepped to the plate and, to the groans of Pirates fans, struck out on four pitches. As Bonds walked back to the dugout, fans let loose with a torrent of boos.[20]

After King bounced out to end the inning, the rest of the game was anticlimactic. As fans began to leave Three Rivers, Stanton struck out two Pirates on the way to retiring the side in order in the bottom of the eighth. When Reardon struck out Espy and Cole to start the bottom of the ninth, then retired Bell on a ground ball to third to end the game, there were thousands of empty seats at Three Rivers.

After the game, Leyland said, "We just didn't pitch well. We made some bad pitches when we got the lead and it cost us."[21] Others saw the game as a tale of two hitters. The Braves' Nixon, who was in a Georgia drug rehabilitation center during the 1991 NLCS, had gone 4-for-5 with two runs scored and two RBIs. Bonds, after leading the Pirates to three division titles, had failed once again in a pressure situation and had now gone 0-for-22 with runners in scoring position.

Going into Game 5, Leyland admitted that the Pirates had their "backs to the wall." To get to the World Series, the Pirates would have to become the first team in NLCS history to come back from a 3–1 deficit. To do that, they would have to find a way to defeat Avery, Glavine, and Smoltz in three straight games, including the last two in Atlanta. Leyland's strategy in Game 5 was to pass over Jackson and start Walk, as he had done often in the past in critical situations. When asked for his reaction, Walk, seemingly unruffled, said, "I'm a utility pitcher. But the manager felt I was the man who should be on the mound, and then I start to think I'm good enough to be out there."[22]

While Leyland was confident in Walk, he also made sure Bonds knew that, despite his continuing poor performance in the postseason, he still had faith in him. After Bonds went hitless in Game 4, Leyland sat down with his struggling star for nearly an hour and a half for a talk. Bonds also received a boost after his wife, Sun, urged Bonilla to fly to Pittsburgh for a visit. When Bonilla and Bonds walked into the Clark Bar and Grill near Three Rivers Stadium, Pirates fans applauded.[23]

Before the start of Game 5, retiring groundskeeper Steve "Dirt" DiNardo took the mound and threw out the first pitch in front of a crowd of 52,929. This was four thousand less than the sellout crowd of Game 4 but still impressive, considering the Pirates were now on the verge of elimination. The fans who did come to the game may have had low expectations. Instead they would see the Pirates explode against Avery, and Bonds have by far the best game of his postseason career with the Pirates.

Admitting to an attack of nerves in the first inning, Walk gave up two bases on balls, but he got out of trouble when Bream lined out to third. In the bottom of the first, Redus got the crowd into the game with a leadoff double and came home on a Bell single. The crowd erupted when Bonds lined a double off the fence to score Bell and finally ended his long hitting drought with men on base. As he stood out on second base, he mouthed, "Yeah, it's finally over!"[24] When King and McClendon followed Bonds with ringing RBI doubles, the Pirates had a 4–0 lead, and Avery was out of the game. Afterward, Avery said, "I had nothing. There isn't an explanation. . . . You never think that is going to happen."[25] His exit in the first inning was the earliest by an NLCS starter since the Pirates' Bob Moose lasted less than an inning twenty years earlier in the 1972 NLCS.

Whether it was Leyland's talk, the support of the fans, or Bonilla's visit, Bonds had finally come to life. In his next at-bat, he singled, stole second, and came home on a McClendon base hit to give the Pirates a 5–0 lead. He also made a dazzling catch after chasing down a Gant line drive that Leyland called one of the best of his career. With Walk settling down and pitching three-hit baseball through eight innings, the Pirates went on to an easy 7–1 victory and sent the series back to Atlanta. As for Bonds, he told the media, "Three years in a row . . . it wasn't making any sense." In a clear signal that he was playing his last games for the Pirates, he also said, "I didn't want it to end the way it was ending."[26]

A sellout crowd of 51,975 fans in Atlanta felt that there was no way the Pirates could do to Glavine in Game 6 what they had done to Avery in Game 5, but Braves fans would see an even worse performance. Unlike Avery, Glavine had no trouble with the Pirates in the first inning, but after Wakefield retired the Braves in the bottom of the first, the Pirates exploded against Glavine in the second. Bonds showed that his performance in Game 5 was no fluke by leading off the top of the second with a long home run to right-center field to give the Pirates a 1–0 lead. It was Bonds's first home run after eighteen postseason games. Glavine then gave up three straight hits, including a two-run double by Slaught. After an error gave the Pirates a 5–0 lead, Bell hammered a three-run homer to give the Pirates an 8–0 lead and knocked Glavine out of the game. Before the inning was over, Bonds batted again and singled, but he was thrown out at home trying to score for the inning-ending out.

With an 8–0 lead and in command of his knuckleball, Wakefield held the Braves scoreless until he gave up a run in the fourth, but the Pirates responded with four runs in the top of the fifth to take a lopsided 12–1 lead. Justice homered in the seventh and ninth innings, but Wakefield coasted to a complete-game 13–4 victory. After the game, Leyland, when asked if he thought of taking Wakefield out after the top of the second inning with such a big lead to save him for Game 7, simply said, "No. We've been in an oxygen tent for the last few days. No way I would take him out."[27] In the midst of a relaxed, confident clubhouse, it was Bell who put things into perspective, "Our task is not done yet, and neither is theirs."[28]

The atmosphere in the rival clubhouses before Game 7 was a study in contrasting emotions. After losing the most recent two games by embarrassing margins, the Braves were in a somber mood. Two of their pitching aces, Avery and Glavine, had been hit hard by the resurgent Pirates, and their offense, except for a few meaningless home runs, had been ineffectual. They had Smoltz ready for Game 7, but even Smoltz admitted to "pouting" in the clubhouse.[29] What looked like a playoff romp for the Braves had turned into a grim battle in a final and deciding game.

While the Braves pouted the Pirates, despite Bell's warning, were in a relaxed and confident mood. After two years of losses in the NLCS and on the verge of elimination for a third year, they had fought back and were one game away from going to the World Series. In the clubhouse, the Pirates were loose and playful. They shot Nerf basketball before the game and seemed more unified than they had been since the start of the series. There was some concern among reporters about Drabek, who had struggled against the Braves and lost to Smoltz in Game 1 and Game 4, but Drabek's manager and teammates had confidence in him. Leyland said, "momentum is your next day's starting pitcher," and the Pirates felt that they had the momentum.[30]

There was some speculation that Leyland would forsake his platoon system and stay with right-hand hitters Redus, McClendon, and Slaught instead of starting the left-hand hitting Cole, LaValliere, and the switch-hitting Merced. Cole, LaValliere, and Merced were batting only .190 in the series, while Redus, McClendon, and Slaught were collectively hitting .487, and McClendon was hitting a spectacular .727. The only move that Leyland made, however, was to move Merced into the fifth spot in the batting order behind Bonds and dropping King to sixth.

While the Braves were sulking in the clubhouse, another sellout crowd was waiting to cheer their home team to victory and a second straight trip to the World Series. When the game started, however, they had to be disappointed when a pressing Smoltz walked leadoff batter Cole. Bell, the Pirates' best bunter, failed to sacrifice Cole to second, but Van Slyke drove a double into right field, sending Cole to third base. In the previous year's NLCS the Braves intentionally walked Bonilla twice to get to a slumping Bonds, but this time the Braves walked the hot-hitting Bonds to get to Merced. Leyland's strategy of moving Merced behind Bonds paid off when Merced lofted a sacrifice fly to right field to score Cole with the first run of the game.

Any fear among Braves fans that the Pirates would mount a big inning and drive Smoltz out of the game ended when Smoltz retired King on a pop fly behind home plate for the final out of the inning. Any hope that Braves fans had that the Braves would score quickly against Drabek, as they had in two earlier games, ended when Drabek retired the

Braves in order in the first and second innings. Berryhill brought fans to life with a leadoff double in the third, but Drabek stranded Berryhill at second base and did not give up another hit until the sixth inning.

While Drabek was sharp and focused, Smoltz also found his pitching rhythm after a shaky first inning and matched Drabek's shutout innings. Drabek and Smoltz, after five innings, were locked in a pitchers' duel reminiscent of the 1–0 cliffhangers of the 1991 NLCS. In the top of the sixth, however, the Pirates struck again when Bell led off with a double and scored on a Van Slyke ground single into center field. Trailing 2–0, Smoltz, as he had in the first inning, bore down and retired Bonds, Merced, and King to end the threat of a bigger inning.

In the bottom of the sixth the Braves finally mounted a rally against Drabek when Lemke led off the inning with a single. Bobby Cox decided to lift Smoltz for pinch-hitter Jeff Treadway, and the move paid off when Treadway looped a single in front of Bonds. With runners at first and second, Nixon tried to lay down a bunt to advance the runners. When the ball took a high bounce and Merced misplayed it, the Braves had the bases loaded with nobody out. With the crowd roaring and waving their tomahawks, Blauser hit a soft line drive right at King, who stepped on third for an easy double play. When Pendleton hit a line drive on a 3–2 count that was caught by Bonds in left field, the Pirates, after two years of missteps and bad breaks, left the field looking very much like destiny's darlings.

With Smoltz out of the game, the Pirates threatened in the seventh and eighth innings, but they failed to break through against the Braves' relief pitching. The Pirates loaded the bases with two outs in the top of the seventh, but Van Slyke, after his two earlier hits helped the Pirates to their 2–0 lead, flied out to centerfield to end the inning. In the top of the eighth, Bonds led off with a single. After Merced forced Bonds at second base, King lined a base hit down the right-field line. Merced tried to score, but Justice's perfect throw to home plate easily beat Merced by several feet. The missed opportunities to score in the eighth and ninth would come back to haunt the Pirates.

Drabek gave up a one-out double to Bream in the bottom of the seventh but pitched out of trouble. In the bottom of the eighth, Drabek dominated the Braves' hitters, striking out Deion Sanders and Blauser and getting Nixon to pop out. In the top of the ninth, McClendon walked and advanced to second base on a wild pitch, but the Pirates failed, once again, to increase their lead. When Drabek walked to the mound for the bottom of the ninth, the Pirates were clinging to their two-run lead, but Drabek had been outstanding and needed only three more outs.

In the Pirates' clubhouse, workers were wheeling in the champagne and putting up plastic covers for protection against the wild celebration that was soon to take place. The MVP trophy had also been brought in, and Wakefield's name was already in place. In the Braves' dugout, however, Bream and his teammates thought that if they could get Drabek out of the game, they could still win because the Pirates had no dominant closer.[31]

Walk was so nervous at the start of the bottom of the ninth that he left the Pirates' dugout to pace in the runway leading to the clubhouse. When he heard Braves fans chanting and then wildly cheering, he made it back to the dugout to hear Leyland tell pitching coach Ray Miller that maybe they should get Walk warmed up in the bullpen.[32] What Walk had missed was the beginning of a baseball nightmare for the Pirates. Pendleton had led off the bottom of the ninth with a drive to right field on a pitch that LaValliere claimed was inside and out of the strike zone. The ball barely stayed fair and landed in the corner just beyond the glove of Espy. It was at that point that, as LaValliere stated it, "everything went wrong."[33]

With Pendleton on second base, Drabek induced Justice to hit a ground ball to Lind. When Lind, one of the best second basemen in baseball, failed to get in front of the ball, it skipped off his glove for an error and sent Pendleton to third base. As Pendleton made it to third, he thought "here we go," and that Lind's error had "opened the door."[34] Leyland had Stan Belinda and Patterson warming up in the bullpen, but he decided to leave Drabek in the game to face Bream. When Drabek walked Bream on four pitches, Leyland slowly walked to the mound and summoned Belinda from the bullpen.

Looking back on Game 7, Post-Gazette writer Paul Meyer thought that people forget what a nearly impossible situation Belinda faced in the bottom of the ninth.[35] With the bases loaded and no outs, he had to pitch to Gant, the Braves' biggest home run threat. When Gant swung and lifted a fly ball deep to left field, it look like Belinda had given up a dramatic game- and series-ending home run; but the ball seemed to die at the last moment and landed in the glove of Bonds.

Gant had cut the lead to 2–1 with a sacrifice fly, but the Pirates had the first out of the inning. With slow-footed catcher Berryhill at the plate, the Pirates were looking for a double play ball to end the game, but Belinda walked Berryhill on pitches that appeared they could have been in the strike zone. When asked later about the umpire's calls, LaValliere said, "Could Randy Marsh have called a better game? Yes. Could I have called a better game? Yes."[36]

The bases were loaded with one out, and Cox sent Hunter to the plate. But Hunter, who had done so much to hurt the Pirates in the playoffs, popped up for the second out of the inning. With two gone, the Pirates were one last out from winning the series, and Cox was down to one last bench player, catcher–first baseman Francisco Cabrera, to bring in as a pinch-hitter.

In 1992 Cabrera had appeared in only twelve games, batting eleven times, but he was the last player added to the Braves' playoff roster when he hit a late season home run. While Cabrera had some power, Van Slyke anticipated a play at home plate and motioned to Bonds to move in a few feet, but Bonds, according to Van Slyke, looked over and gave him the finger. Van Slyke thought, "Fine, you play where you want."[37] After umpire Marsh called Belinda's first two pitches balls, Cabrera lifted a deep fly ball that curved foul into the left-field stands. On the next pitch, he grounded a ball between King and Bell that sent Justice home with the tying run and Bream laboring around third on bad knees and a cumbersome knee brace. While Bonds was still playing deep, he was also one of the best outfielders in baseball at charging a base hit and throwing home. He made a clean pick up of Cabrera's hit and a quick throw home, but his throw was slightly off line. LaValliere had to move out to catch the ball as Bream slid across home plate ahead of LaValliere's lunging but late tag. After their comeback in the series, the slide was a crushing moment for the Pirates. It also would become one of the most iconic plays in baseball history and one of the most haunting in the Pirates' history.

As Bream's teammates poured out of the dugout and piled on top of him in a joyful celebration, Walk looked in from the bullpen and refused to think the game was over: "That can't be it."[38] If he had looked over to center field, he would have seen a distraught Van Slyke sitting on the grass in disbelief. In the clubhouse Blass, who was set to broadcast the Pirates' celebration back to Pittsburgh, saw workers rushing to take down the plastic and remove the champagne. He also watched as Wakefield's name was taped over on the MVP trophy and Smoltz's name hastily written on the tape before the trophy was carried to the Braves' clubhouse.[39]

Meyer recalled how "eerily quiet" it was in the Pirates clubhouse.[40] John Wehner, who would become a Pirates broadcaster, remembered the "heavy breathing. That's how quiet it was."[41] Before meeting with the media, Leyland asked for a few minutes for his players. Walk remembered Leyland's eyes "tearing up" as he went around, patting players on the back, including a "red-eyed" Barry Bonds.[42] "Everybody was speechless," Redus recalled. "How did this happen. So close to the World Series and just gone." LaValliere was so numb that he "couldn't do anything. I couldn't yell. I couldn't scream. It was devastating." No one blamed anyone, including, as McClendon later said, Belinda: "Stan came in with the bases loaded and almost got us to the World Series. He was one pitch away." Wakefield, who pitched so brilliantly in the series, could not recall "a word spoken in the clubhouse."[43] As Leyland faced the media, Van Slyke sat naked in the shower, still in complete shock. He was the last player to leave the clubhouse. When Leyland returned to the clubhouse, he sat in his office by himself until Pirates broadcaster Lanny Frattare, at the urging of Leyland's wife, went down to be with his close friend.[44]

The flight back to Pittsburgh was just as solemn as the clubhouse. "No one was talking," Belinda said. "That's when it really hit me. It was tough."[45] It was the end of one of the greatest runs in Pirates history, and it was the last time one of the greatest teams in Pirates history would have a chance to bring a world championship to Pittsburgh. The game and "the slide" would haunt Pirates players and teams for decades to come, including Leyland who would sometimes tear up when asked to talk about his Pirates of the early 1990s. In the end, though, he came to see that final devastating loss "as a part of life" and "no reason to sulk." It was like a "Little League game," where the winning team celebrates and the losing team "hangs its heads"—then life and baseball move on.[46]

CHAPTER NINE

THE PIRATES SLIDE INTO HISTORY

The 1993–2010 Seasons

The 1992 National League Championship Series was not the first time that the Pirates had ended a three-year division championship run with a heart-breaking loss in the playoffs. Twenty years earlier, after winning their third straight division title, they were one inning away from their second straight pennant and a return trip to the World Series. In that case the Pirates had the opportunity to win back-to-back world championships for the first time in franchise history.

With the Pirates leading the Cincinnati Reds 3–2 in the bottom of the ninth inning of the fifth and deciding game of the 1972 NLCS, Pirates manager Bill Virdon called on Dave Giusti, who had saved twenty-two games during the regular season, to close out the victory. Johnny Bench, who would be named the 1972 National League MVP and go on to the Hall of Fame, led off the bottom of the ninth with a towering home run to right field that stunned the Pirates and tied the score. After a shaken Giusti gave up consecutive singles and threw two pitches out of the strike zone to the next batter, Virdon brought in Bob Moose from the bullpen to hold down the Reds and send the game into extra innings. Moose managed to get two outs, but with the winning run on third base he threw a wild pitch that handed the playoff victory to the Reds. It was the most devastating loss for the Pirates since the Cubs' Gabby Hartnett knocked the Pirates out of a chance to win the 1938 pennant with his infamous "homer in the gloamin.'"[1]

It was a bitter moment for the Pirates and their fans in 1972, but at the end of the year, disappointment was overshadowed by tragedy. At 9:22 p.m. on December 31, a DC-7 cargo plane filled with supplies for the victims of a devastating earthquake in Managua, Nicaragua, crashed into the Atlantic minutes after taking off from an airfield in Puerto Rico, killing everyone on board, including Pirates great Roberto Clemente. There were many tributes to Clemente in the following days, but in Pittsburgh the collective grief and affection of the city was literally writ large on a neon sign perched on a Mt. Washington hillside looming high over the city that read, "Adios Amigo Roberto."[2]

At the beginning of the 1992 season, nearly twenty years after Clemente's tragic death, the Pirates, led by Barry Bonds, were off to a great start and in the middle of a nine-game winning streak. Bob Smizik wrote a column in the *Pittsburgh Post-Gazette* titled "Bonds Gets Head Start on Clemente's Greatness." He began the column by writing, "Roberto Clemente is the greatest Pirate of the past fifty years, no question about it. To compare him with Barry Bonds would be ridiculous. . . . But not the way you think."[3] Smizik went on to argue that if Pirates fans compared the offensive statistics of Clemente and Bonds after their first six seasons they would see that, despite a lower batting average, Bonds was the leader by a wide margin in home runs, runs scored, runs batted in, and stolen bases. Smizik also pointed out that, while Clemente was "arguably the greatest right fielder in history," Bonds, with the exception of a weaker throwing arm, was comparable as an outfielder, playing left field as well as Clemente played right field. Smizik noted that "Jim Leyland has called Bonds the best left fielder he has seen."[4]

Anticipating the counter argument that Clemente was a team leader while Bonds was "a poison in the clubhouse," Smizik claimed that neither view was "entirely accurate." He pointed out that Clemente, in his first six seasons, "struggling with the language and trying to learn a new culture . . . filled no leadership role. . . . His leadership emerged late in his career." While agreeing that the divisive Bonds "exerted little positive leadership in his first six seasons," Smizik wrote that he seemed to be maturing: "He might never be a great leader, but he does not figure to be a detriment to a team." Noting that Bonds "seemed destined" to accomplish even more than Clemente, Smizik urged Pirates fans to come out to watch Bonds while he was still in a Pirates uniform: "Clemente played 18 seasons in Pittsburgh. Bonds has played six and will play no more. Get a look while you can. He's headed for Cooperstown."[5]

Smizik's concluding remark, that Bonds would accomplish more in his career than Clemente, proved entirely accurate, though a steroid scandal would derail or at least delay his trip to Cooperstown.[6] Smizik was also accurate about Bonds leaving the Pirates. After the 1992 season, to no one's surprise, Bonds signed a six-year $43.75 contract, the largest in baseball history at that time, with the San Francisco Giants. At his introductory press conference, he told reporters that playing with the Giants—the team of his father, Bobby Bonds, and his godfather, Willie Mays—was a dream come true. After six years of alienation in Pittsburgh, Bonds believed he was finally coming home: "All I've ever wanted to do was share something with my father. Every time I step on that field, I know my godfather's in center field and my dad's in right field."[7]

In 1993 a happy and relaxed Bonds led the National League in home runs and RBIs and batted .336 for the Giants, all career highs, on his way to winning his third MVP Award. For the rest of the decade, Bonds was among the league leaders in home runs and RBIs. In 1997 and 2000 he returned to the postseason but did not hit well as the Giants lost those playoff series. In 2002 he finally had a chance to play in a World Series, and even though the Giants lost to the Angels in seven games, he batted .473 with four home runs. The year before, in one of the most controversial seasons in baseball history, he had shattered Mark McGwire's single-season record by hitting seventy-three home runs on the way to the first of four consecutive National League MVP awards.

In 2001, nine years after he wrote his column predicting Bonds would likely surpass Clemente's career accomplishments, Smizik wrote another column in the *Pittsburgh Post-Gazette* comparing Bonds and Clemente and validating his earlier claim. In "Unpopular Fact: Bonds Best Pirate," published on May 2, 2001, Smizik wrote that Bonds was "better than Wagner, better than Stargell, better than Paul and Lloyd Waner, better than Ralph Kiner, better than Bill Mazeroski, better than Pie Traynor and, yes, better than Clemente." He added, "No one in Pittsburgh wants to hear that. No one wants to acknowledge that Bonds, who for all his excellence is detested by Pirates fans, is that good. But he is. In fact, it's not even close."[8]

The night before, when Bonds played his first game at the newly opened PNC Park, a few fans of the 22,926 in attendance greeted him with boos and signs, one reading, "Where were you when Sid slid," but it was nothing like the thunderous boos and taunts that cascaded from the stands during his appearances at Three Rivers Stadium in his first season with the Giants in 1993. In "Bonds Gets Some Jeers, but Many Cheer Former Pirate," Paul Meyer wrote in the *Post-Gazette* that fans at PNC Park, unlike those at Three Rivers, cheered loudly when Bonds "dumped six baseballs into the Allegheny River behind the right-field seats" during batting practice. When Bonds batted for the first time in the game, fans "cheered again, some rising to their feet."[9]

While the fans were generally well behaved, the Pirates, aware that the left-field wall at PNC Park was only six feet high, took no chances and increased the number of security people in the stands in anticipation of some fan using abusive language or throwing an object at Bonds. That night Pirates pitchers, apparently after watching Bonds in batting practice, were equally cautious and walked Bonds in his first four times at bat in an 11–6 loss to the Giants. As for Bonds, he was in a good mood. He spent some time with Lloyd McClendon, his old teammate in the early 1990s and now the manager of the Pirates. Afterward, he told reporters, after looking around at PNC Park, "This is a nice ballpark. It's beautiful. . . . I might want to retire back in Pittsburgh."[10]

The Pirates and their fans were also in a more positive state of mind than they had been in years. The team had suffered through eight consecutive losing seasons after Bonds left Pittsburgh at the end of the 1992 season, but they had a beautiful new ballpark and the hope that there would soon be winning seasons ahead and another World Series. The Pirates' record was 9–15 when Bonds paid his first visit to PNC Park, but surely, fans thought, there had to be better days on the horizon. What they did not know, as they watched Bonds that night, was that the Pirates were not even halfway to losing for twenty consecutive seasons, the most for any professional franchise in the history of North American sports.

In September 2013, after the Pirates finally secured their first winning season in twenty years, Dayn Perry of CBS Sports, wrote an online essay entitled, "Regrets, I've Had a Few: A Tour of the Pirates' 20-Year Drought." In his essay, he detailed the Pirates' astonishing ineptness during that span: "The Pirates would be a cumulative 422 games below the .500 mark, and they'd be outscored by their opponents by almost 2,000 runs. They'd finish in last place seven times (in what was then a six-team division, mind you) and churn through seven different managers, four GMs, three ownership groups and two ballparks."[11]

The streak of twenty consecutive losing seasons started on September 22, 1993, in front of a modest crowd of 10,031, when the Pirates suffered their eighty-second loss of the season in extra innings against the New York Mets. That the Pirates would field a losing team in 1993 became predictable when star pitcher Doug Drabek followed Bonds out of Pittsburgh by signing a four-year $19.5 million contract with the Houston Astros following the 1992 season. After losing his best player and his best pitcher, general manager Ted Simmons decided to begin rebuilding the Pirates in 1993 around his one remaining star, Andy Van Slyke.

Simmons traded away Gold Glove second baseman José Lind. He then released or discarded several veteran players to make room for promising rookies, like Al Martin, who would have the daunting task of replacing Bonds, and infielders Kevin Young and Carlos García. When Gold Glove catcher Mike LaValliere complained about management's cost-cutting tactics, Simmons criticized him for being overweight and out of shape and then released him just a week into the new season.[12]

Simmons' strategy of infusing the Pirates with youth and new talent was undermined by the early struggles of his trio of promising rookies. The team also lost the one veteran star that Simmons had counted on to bring stability to the team, when, on June 14, 1993, Van Slyke crashed into the wall chasing a fly ball and broke his collarbone. A few days later Simmons, a heavy smoker and likely suffering under the strain of the job, suffered a heart attack that forced him to step down. Plagued by inexperience and injuries on the playing field and uncertainty in the front office, the Pirates ended the 1993 season with a 75–87 record and a fifth-place finish.

While the Pirates began their streak of twenty consecutive losing seasons in 1993, the groundwork for disaster had been laid as early as 1988 with the death of Pittsburgh mayor Richard Caliguiri. The more generous lease terms for Three Rivers Stadium and other financial support from the city promised by Caliguiri never materialized after his death. In 1991 his successor Sophie Masloff thought that the best way to help the Pirates with their lease problems was to build a new ballpark, but the proposal went nowhere with city and state officials. Facing mounting debt, even as the team started to become successful on the field in the late 1980s and made the playoffs in the early 1990s, the Pittsburgh Associates ownership consortium had to borrow money from PNC and Mellon banks to keep the franchise afloat. Added to the problem was an ownership group, made up mostly of business executives, that, as Bruce Keidan wrote in his September 1996 "Playing for Keeps" article in the *Pittsburgh Post-Gazette*, "had one objective. To save the Pirates. They had no game plan beyond buying the team."[13]

Reacting to rising debt and escalating player salaries, the Pittsburgh Associates began cutting costs in scouting and player development, areas that were critical to establishing a secure future for the franchise. They also failed to sign their young stars, like Bonds and Bonilla, to long-term contracts while they were still under team control and years away from free agency. When Pirates management finally did get around to making offers to these two players, they made a series of bad decisions that ended up costing them both players. When Bonilla, in his last year before free agency, turned down a four-year contract because he wanted five years, Bonds said that if the Pirates made him the same offer, he would take it. Instead of signing Bonds and increasing their offer to Bonilla, the Pirates decided to sign Van Slyke to a long-term contract, further alienating Bonilla and Bonds and opening themselves up to accusations of racism.

As early as the end of the 1992 season, the members of the Pittsburgh Associates were looking for a way out of ownership debt, and they saw a glimmer of hope in late 1993 when newly elected mayor Tom Murphy promised to help ease the burden of the Three Rivers lease and provide additional financial help. The Pittsburgh Associates also hoped that a new collective bargaining agreement between major league players and owners would include a salary cap and revenue sharing. When, however, the players and owners remained at an impasse going into the 1994 season, frustrated Pirates ownership decided to put the team up for sale. Mayor Murphy agreed with the decision as long as the city could broker a deal with any potential buyer to keep the Pirates franchise in Pittsburgh.

As it turned out, the Pirates ownership could not have picked a worse time to put the franchise up for sale. On August 12, 1994, a little more than a hundred games into the season, the players union, after rejecting the league owners' demand for a salary cap as a condition for revenue sharing, went on strike. When neither side refused to budge, the owners did the unthinkable and canceled the rest of the season, including the playoffs and the World Series. The Pirates were able to host the All-Star Game before the players walked out, but the work stoppage was a disaster for a team that was struggling at 53–61 at the time of the strike.

Undaunted, Pirates ownership moved ahead with its plan to sell the franchise. Among the early leading candidates were the Pittsburgh Steelers' Rooney family and Larry Lucchino, a Pittsburgh native and former president of the Baltimore Orioles. Lucchino's investment group included former Pitt and NFL star quarterback Dan Marino. Rumors also circulated around Penguins owner Howard Baldwin and golfer Arnold Palmer, who laughingly said he would buy the Pirates if they would play their home games in Latrobe.[14]

The clear front-runner, however, was John Rigas, who had turned his family's small Greek restaurant in Coudersport, PA, into an impressive business conglomerate headed by Adelphia Cable. A deal with Rigas seemed a certainty until questions were raised about his willingness to provide the cash needed to buy out the current owners and deal with the franchise's outstanding debt. When, however, Rigas made a formal offer of $88 million—which was $4 million short of the price set for the franchise that included a cash buyout of $26 million and the assumption of $20 million in debt—the Pirates ownership and the city were eager to accept the deal.[15]

For a time it looked like there would be no 1995 baseball season in Pittsburgh, no matter what happened to the Pirates franchise. During the winter, the major league players and owners refused to budge from their separate positions. Even when President Bill Clinton urged the two sides to accept binding arbitration, the owners refused and, instead, announced the unilateral implementation of a salary cap. When the owners began signing replacement players for the start of the 1995 season, the union, just two days before the scheduled opening day, filed for an injunction with the National Labor Relations Board. The case went to federal court, where future Supreme Court justice Sonia Sotomay-

or ruled that the owners were violating federal labor law and ordered baseball to return to its expired collective bargaining agreement until the parties could reach a new agreement. Her decision effectively ended the strike, which had lasted 234 days, cost the owners $700 million, and alienated baseball fans, who saw the strike as a battle of millionaires against billionaires.

When Major League Baseball finally began its shortened 1995 season in late April, Mayor Murphy called a press conference on Opening Day to announce the deal with Rigas, who would be arriving later that day in Pittsburgh to sign the agreement, even though league executives had yet to give their blessing. MLB officials concluded that too much cash was flowing out of the franchise and not enough staying in. When they withheld approval until Rigas agreed to provide more cash, Rigas, even though he had the resources, thought the deal had become too risky and, by midsummer, he had withdrawn the offer.

When the cash issue became a deal-breaker for Rigas, the Pirates and the city hastily turned to a new candidate, Kevin McClatchy, whose only tie to Pittsburgh was that he had roomed and played sports with Dan Rooney Jr. in prep school at Trinity-Pawling in New York. The Sacramento-based McClatchy at the time was a thirty-two-year-old heir to a newspaper-publishing fortune. He claimed that he had read about the Pirates' pending sale in the *USA Today* after his unsuccessful effort to purchase the Oakland As. When he first visited Pittsburgh in February 1995, he did not make much of an impression on Mayor Murphy, but when McClatchy returned in late spring as the Rigas deal began to unravel, Murphy was desperate for an alternative buyer.[16]

McClatchy was charming and direct, but he was an outsider with little baseball experience beyond ownership of the minor-league Modesto As. He also raised suspicions that he wanted to move the team to Sacramento. After the Rigas fiasco, there were also doubts that McClatchy had the financial backing to make the purchase. Despite the skepticism, McClatchy set up headquarters in a Downtown Pittsburgh hotel and began a whirlwind of negotiations with the city over relief from the stadium lease. He also went about the precarious business of forming a financial coalition of general and limited partnerships that he hoped would include a few of the current Pirates owners. At the insistence of the MLB, McClatchy also had to reach an agreement that included a commitment from the city to build a new ballpark within five years.

As negotiations struggled past deadline after deadline, there was a growing sense that 1995 would be the Pirates' last season in Pittsburgh. The team was not helping matters on the playing field. While fans booed the players as they returned from the strike and threw dollar bills at them in frustration, the Pirates started the season poorly on their way to a final record of 58–86. As they prepared to play their last home game of the season and perhaps their last game in Pittsburgh, Leyland told reporters, "it's been a miserable year, a disastrous year. It's one of the toughest years I've had in 32 years in baseball."[17]

There was plenty of blame to go around, but Pittsburgh sportswriters focused their criticism on the lack of attendance at Pirates games. In the *Post-Gazette*, Gene Collier predicted, "10 years after the final game in Pittsburgh, the bottom line on the big game sheet is going to read only this: not enough people came to the games."[18] Noting the Pirates' last-place finish in attendance and the poor turnout for the last home game, Smizik wrote that the people of Pittsburgh have spoken, and "they do not care if there is a major league baseball team in Pittsburgh."[19] An angry Steve Blass defiantly said, "To me, it's impossible that the Pirates won't be here. Therefore it won't happen," but his fellow pitcher-turned-broadcaster Bob Walk decided, "just in case," to collect a "little dirt from the pitcher's mound, put in a jar and take it home. . . . if we're back next April, I'll bring the jar to the stadium and put the dirt back out there on the mound."[20]

Going into the offseason, the Pirates needed a miracle to stay in Pittsburgh for the 1996 season, and that is what McClatchy gave them. Just as Caliguiri had saved the Pirates in 1985 by forming a private-public partnership, McClatchy, despite all the doubts and criticism, saved the Pirates by convincing a coalition of local, regional, and national investors to support his effort to buy the team. The asking price for the franchise was around $85 million, including $60 million in debt obligations and a repayment of $25 million to buy out the current ownership. After reaching an agreement with Murphy on a $6.5 million lease enhancement at Three Rivers Stadium, he managed to convince several of the current owners to stay on, thereby cutting the cash buyout of $25 million in half. With the help of individuals like Paul Martha, a former player for the Steelers and current executive with the Penguins, McClatchy was able to form a financial team of three general partners, who invested $5 million apiece, and more than a dozen limited partners, including auto-racing-team-owner Chip Ganassi and Heinz CEO Tony O'Reilly, who committed up to $2 million dollars each. McClatchy, who put in $10 million of his own money, was to become the franchise's CEO and managing partner. With the help of U.S. Senator Arlen Specter, Major League Baseball approved the deal, though it still insisted that a new stadium be a part of the final agreement. On February 14, 1996, the city breathed a collective sigh of relief when the papers were signed to transfer ownership from the Pittsburgh Associates to McClatchy and his partnership. The Pirates, seemingly all but certain to be playing baseball in another city in 1996, would still be playing baseball in Pittsburgh come Opening Day.

If McClatchy thought that he would be given a honeymoon period by his new partners and Pittsburgh sportswriters or that the Pirates would suddenly transform from cellar-dwelling losers to World Series winners, he was badly mistaken. McClatchy also had early problems with two of the general partners. When they realized that they were not going have an active role in the management of the ballclub, Pittsburgh beer distributor Frank Fuhrer and Wilkes-Barre utilities executive Kenneth Pollock, withdrew their investment. Facing a partnership crisis just months after assuming ownership, McClatchy was ridiculed as a business lightweight. The *Post-Gazette*'s Keidan wrote, "You could put his business acumen in a thimble and have plenty of room left over for your thumb."[21]

Compounding matters, McClatchy discovered by midseason that the Pirates, who were playing poorly despite increasing payroll from $17 to $21 million, were going to lose around $8 million in 1996 rather than a projected $4 million. He ordered general manager Cam Bonifay, who had replaced Simmons, to start cutting payroll by trading off high salaried players for minor league prospects. To make matters worse, as the Pirates headed toward their second last-place finish in a row, Leyland informed McClatchy in late September that after eleven seasons as Pirates manager he wanted out. It was not an easy decision for Leyland, who went "back and forth" and talked to his many "close friends in Pittsburgh."[22] In the end, however, he decided that for the sake of his health and his career, it was time to move on from the city that he had grown to love.

Leyland, only fifty-one, still had four years and $4 million remaining on his contract, but he claimed that he had a handshake agreement with the previous owners that he could leave if the team ever decided on another rebuilding period. When McClatchy agreed to release Leyland from his contract, after telling him that the Pirates were beginning a youth movement and likely would not be competitive for the next few years, Leyland told reporters, "I just decided I didn't want to wait that long. I've been through rebuilding for four years and it's been tough. I just don't think I can go through another three years of it." A tearful Leyland bid goodbye to Pittsburgh fans at the Pirates' last home game. After saying he loved Pittsburgh "and it's always going to be my home," he signed a contract shortly thereafter to manage the Florida Marlins.[23] Under Leyland, the Marlins would win the World Series in 1997.

Pirates fans were devastated by the loss of Leyland, and many believed it was part of McClatchy's plan to weaken the franchise and eventually move it to Sacramento. A frustrated McClatchy responded, "If I wanted this thing to fail I could do it from California. I wouldn't be making 140 speaking engagements a year. By saying I'm going to move the club, they're essentially calling me a liar. It's tough to deal with that." McClatchy also pointed out that his own $10 million investment in the Pirates was no small financial risk, that he was not a huge corporation like Disney, which owned the Angels, or a mogul like Ted Turner, who owned the Braves, and that he would be "taking a big hit" if the franchise failed. As for his commitment to his ownership of the Pirates, "I live and breathe this stuff. And it's a dream at the same time." His challenge was to change what he perceived as a defeatist attitude born out of the city's economic decline. To do that, to "show the rest of the country that Pittsburgh is moving forward," he needed to convince the city to support his efforts to build a new ballpark.[24]

With Leyland gone, McClatchy needed a new manager and a miraculous turnaround in Pirates fortunes. To replace the seemingly irreplaceable Leyland, the Pirates turned to Gene Lamont, who had come to Pittsburgh in 1986 as one of Leyland's coaches and soon became his most trusted advisor. After the Pirates won their second consecutive division title in 1991, Lamont was hired as manager by the Chicago White Sox and went on to win the American League Manager of the Year Award in 1993. After his team struggled in 1995, he was fired by the White Sox at the end of the season and then quickly hired by the Pirates as the heir apparent to Leyland.

After finishing in last place in 1996 with a record of 73–89 and trading off Jay Bell, Jeff King, and Orlando Merced, the last of the stalwarts from the division champions of the early 1990s, the Pirates seemed doomed to sink deeper into baseball's lower depths. Early predictions going into spring training had them losing more than 100 games in 1997 and perhaps even challenging the modern franchise record of 112 games lost by the 1952 Pirates, arguably the worst team in modern Pirates history. They were also coming into the 1997 season with the lowest payroll in baseball. The entire team was making less than the $10 million the White Sox were paying out to home-run king Albert Belle.

No one expected the Pirates to be competitive, but they did have some talented young ballplayers, including Jason Kendall, a rookie sensation in 1996, and some promising young pitchers. When the Pirates started the 1997 season by playing .500 baseball, announcer Greg Brown, after an improbable come-from-behind win, dubbed the upstart Pirates the "Freak Show."[25] On the night of July 12, 1997, a sellout crowd of 44,119 turned out to watch the resurgent Pirates play the Houston Astros. On one of the most memorable nights in Pirates history, Francisco Córdova and Ricardo Rincón combined for an extra inning no-hitter. When pinch-hitter Mark Smith hit a three-run homer to win the game, the Pirates moved into a tie for first place with the Astros. After the game, McClatchy said, "It was the best game I ever saw. It was like something out of a movie."[26]

The Pirates were not able to keep pace with the Astros and finished the season with a 79–83 record; but it was good enough for a second-place finish, just five games out of first. During the offseason, GM Bonifay was named the National League Executive of the Year and *USA Today* gave the franchise the title of baseball's top organization. What was more important for McClatchy, who had been vilified the year before, was the hope that he now had the leverage he needed to secure financing for a new ballpark.

After the unexpected season of 1997, the Pirates had a dismal 1998 and finished in last place in their division with a record of 69–93. Though their next season was marred by a horrible ankle injury to Kendall, they bounced back in 1999 and had a chance to end their streak of consecutive losing seasons at six but were swept by the Mets in a three-game series finale and finished with a 78–83 record. In their first season of the new century, the Pirates fell back again, matching their 1998 season with a 69–93 record and extending their consecutive streak of losing seasons to eight.

While the Pirates were riding a roller coaster that always had a way of ending with a losing season, the real thrill ride was taking place off the field as Murphy and McClatchy tried to find a way to raise the $262 million needed to finance a new ballpark. Murphy likened the process to "riding the Jack Rabbit at Kennywood."[27] The first idea was the Regional Renaissance Initiative, a referendum proposed in March 1997 to increase sales tax by half a percent in eleven counties surrounding Pittsburgh, but it was soundly defeated by voters in November. Anticipating the defeat of the referendum, Murphy had another plan in place. Plan B, as it was called (or Scam B by its critics), won a narrow vote of support from the Regional Asset District board and tapped into an already existing one percent sales tax surcharge in Allegheny County to come up with the $143 million needed by the city for its share of the project.

The Pirates' share of $44 million received a boost when PNC Bank offered to pay $30 million for the naming rights of the new ballpark. When the Pirates made the announcement that the new ballpark would be called PNC Park, there was a flood of criticism from those who hoped it would be named in honor of Roberto Clemente. The remaining $75 million needed to fund the construction came from money pledged by Pennsylvania governor Tom Ridge, when the state legislature, in another close vote, approved a grant that included funding for baseball and football stadiums in Pittsburgh and Philadelphia.

With the funding finally in place, the Pirates worked out an agreement to build their new ballpark with HOK Sports of Kansas City, MO, a company that had already constructed Oriole Park at Camden Yards in Baltimore and Jacobs Field in Cleveland. Working with HOK's lead designer David Greusel, the Pirates selected a site on Pittsburgh's North Side near the Sixth Street Bridge to build a ballpark blending the traditional look of Forbes Field with the intimacy of Wrigley Field. The result was a design for a two-tiered ballpark with natural grass, a yellow limestone base, blue steel light towers, an asymmetrical shape, and a view of Downtown. When finished, it would win praise as the most beautiful ballpark in the major leagues.

On April 7, 1999, at a ceremony changing the name of the Sixth Street Bridge to the Roberto Clemente Bridge, the Pirates broke ground for the construction of PNC Park. No new major-league ballpark had been completed in less than twenty-seven months, but the twenty-three labor unions contracted to build the new ballpark agreed to a no-strike stipulation, and despite challenges to hiring procedures and occasional delays in steel deliveries, twenty-four months later, on April 9, 2001, Pirates fans were able to walk across the Clemente Bridge for the first Opening Day at PNC Park.

At the end of the 2000 season, the Pirates had fired Lamont as manager and replaced him, on October 23, with Lloyd McClendon. It was an odd choice for a team going through a rebuilding program. McClendon had been the Pirates' hitting instructor the past four seasons but had practically no managerial experience. He was, however, on the Pirates' division-winning teams in 1991 and 1992, and McClatchy and Bonifay liked his work ethic and energy. They also thought his "no-nonsense" approach to players was similar to that of his old manager Jim Leyland.

McClendon loved the idea of playing at PNC Park and thought it would give his young team a definite home-field advantage: "Our fans are going to be right on top of the action, and they're going to make it very tough for other teams to concentrate."[28] For the grand opening of the new ballpark, 36,954 fans showed up and cheered as McClatchy, wearing a Willie Stargell jersey in honor of the beloved "Pops," who had died just hours earlier, threw out the first pitch. Fans had little to cheer about during the game, however, as the Pirates lost, 8–2, to the Cincinnati Reds.

Fans continued to show up at PNC Park, and by season's end the Pirates had set an attendance record of 2,464,870. Sadly, no matter how hard the fans cheered, the Pirates kept losing games and finished the season with a 62–100 record. It was just the seventh time in club history that the Pirates finished with a hundred or more losses and the first time since the disastrous 1985 season. There was, however, one memorable game among the otherwise depressing string of losses. On September 17, 2001, the Pirates played and lost to the New York Mets. It was the first game back for the Pirates since Major League Baseball commissioner Bud Selig suspended play after the 9/11 tragedy. That night the Pirates wore caps with FDNY on them in honor of New York firefighters, while Pirates fans wore "I Love New York" buttons and contributed $88,598 in donations.[29]

In the middle of the 2001 season, with the team struggling at 19–41, the Pirates had fired GM Bonifay, whose five-year plan seemed to be going nowhere, and replaced him with the Miami Marlins' assistant GM

Dave Littlefield. Thanks to key trades by Littlefield for young talent and a few free agent acquisitions in the offseason, the Pirates started to show improvement in 2002 and, on June 22, 2002, became the fourth club in major league history to win nine thousand games. The season was marred before it even started, however, by Derek Bell, an ill-fated $9 million free agent signing by Bonifay for the 2001 season. After batting only .173 in 2001, Bell declared in spring training that he was going into "Operation Shutdown" when threatened with the loss of his starting outfield position in 2002.[30] The Pirates released Bell, but this did not prevent the team from finishing with their tenth consecutive losing season.

Toward the end of the 2002 season, after the Pirates defeated the Cubs, 13–3, McClendon gave his players a dozen bottles of champagne in celebration because they finished the season with ten more wins than the previous season. As his players sipped champagne from Gatorade cups, McClendon told them "the next time," after they won a championship, would be "for real."[31] He would have been better off, however, showing them the movie *Groundhog Day*, where actor Bill Murray plays a Pittsburgh weatherman who has to live the same day over and over again. After finishing with a record of 72–89 in 2002, the Pirates went 75–87 in 2003 and 72–89 in 2004. They were 55–81 when they fired McClendon in 2005. They finished at 67–95 under temporary manager Pete Mackanin for their thirteenth consecutive losing season.

After taking a chance on the inexperienced McClendon, the Pirates, on October 11, 2005, replaced him with former Dodgers manager Jim Tracy, who signed a three-year contract. Tracy had managed the Dodgers to four straight winning seasons, including a playoff appearance, but he parted ways with the Dodgers after the team struggled in 2005 and finished the season at 71–91. When Pittsburgh sportswriters pointed out that he was moving from a big market team with a national following to a small market team with little chance of success, Tracy said, "Challenges are something I like very, very much."[32]

He had no idea of the challenges he would face in the next two years. The Pirates hosted the 2006 All-Star Game at PNC Park, but despite Freddy Sánchez winning the NL batting championship and the excellent play of 2005 Rookie of the Year Jason Bay, the Pirates could do no better than duplicate the previous season's record of 67–95 for their fourteenth consecutive losing season. It was a challenging year for Tracy, but if he liked challenges, he would love what was about to happen to the Pirates in 2007.

Since McClatchy became the Pirates CEO and managing partner, one of his limited partners, G. Ogden Nutting, a West Virginia newspaper magnate, had been buying up the shares of other limited partners. By the end of the 2006 season, he held 25 percent of the franchise's shares, compared to 12 percent held by McClatchy. In January, the Nutting family became the majority owners, and Ogden's son Robert was appointed as chairman of the board and managing partner, reducing McClatchy's role to that of CEO. While McClatchy would continue to run the "day-to-day operations," Bob Nutting would be responsible for "strategic leadership."[33] Six months later, on June 7, 2007, as the Pirates headed toward their fifteenth consecutive losing season, just one short of a North American professional sports franchise record, McClatchy announced that he would be stepping down at the end of the 2007 season.

In his press conference, McClatchy blamed no one but himself for the Pirates' losing seasons: "It's been frustrating. And I take full accountability." As for his reason for stepping down, he told reporters, "John Madden once said you can take ten years in the frying pan. And then, you start to get burned out a little bit."[34] Whether burned out or pushed out, the departing McClatchy received praise from MLB commissioner Selig, who said, "Kevin McClatchy saved the Pittsburgh Pirates." Smizik reminded the city that McClatchy "was the driving force behind the building of PNC Park. If there is baseball in Pittsburgh for another 25 years, and there should be, the man most responsible for that is . . . McClatchy."[35]

In September, as the 2007 season wound down, Bob Nutting announced the appointment of Frank Coonelly, the MLB vice president and general counsel for labor relations, to replace McClatchy as the Pirates CEO and the firing of GM Littlefield, criticized for bad deals and poor draft picks. Littlefield's fate was sealed when he acquired pitcher Matt Morris from the Giants in midseason. For the cost-cutting Pirates, the deal was a fiasco. Morris, under a long-term contact and near the end of his career, had pitched badly for the Giants the last two seasons and was still owed $10 million for 2008. Morris went 3–4 with a 6.10 ERA for the Pirates in 2007. He went 0–4 with an ERA of 9.67 in 2008 before the team released him but still had to pay his full salary.

Coonelly named Neal Huntington, an assistant general manager with the Cleveland Indians, to replace Littlefield. In his first major decision, Huntington fired Tracy, even though the manager had another year on his contract, and hired John Russell, the former Pirates third base coach under McClendon. Though he had never managed in the major leagues, Russell had extensive experience as a minor league manager and a reputation as an outstanding tutor for young players.

The immediate reaction of fans and sportswriters to the new Nutting management team was deep suspicion. The *Post-Gazette*'s Smizik expressed the commonly held view that the Pirates, with a payroll of $43.4 million, twenty-eighth out of the thirty MLB franchises, were little more than a business investment for the Nutting family. Annual attendance had dropped by nearly a million fans since the opening of PNC Park, but this was enough to ensure the Nuttings, in the words of Smizik, "excessive profits."[36] When Huntington announced yet another rebuilding plan for the Pirates based on improvements in scouting and player development, fans translated the statement as the continuation of a policy of selling off the team's best players for minor league prospects to keep the payroll down and the profits up.

Faced with managing a team that finished with a 68–94 record in 2007 and that seemed likely to match the all-time sports team record of sixteen consecutive losing seasons held by the cross-state Phillies, Russell declared that Pittsburgh fans would see a more disciplined and better brand of baseball in 2008. For the first half of the season, the overachieving Pirates lived up to Russell's promise, but after Huntington traded away Bay and his high salary, the team swooned in August with a 7–21 record. On September 7, 2008, they lost their eighty-second game in San Francisco and clinched another losing season. They would finish with a record of 67–98, one game worse than in 2007, and tie the record for consecutive losing seasons.

There was little doubt in the minds of long-suffering Pittsburgh fans that they would be watching the once proud franchise of Honus Wagner, Pie Traynor, Roberto Clemente, Willie Stargell, and Bill Mazeroski humiliate itself in 2009 by breaking the all-time record for consecutive losing seasons. An awful May put the Pirates seven games under .500, and when they went 8–17 in July and 9–19 in August, it was no longer a matter of if, but when, they would set the record. On September 7, the Pirates lost their eighty-second game of the season, 4–2, to the

Chicago Cubs at PNC Park, guaranteeing them their seventeenth losing season in a row.

Not only had the Pirates set a new record in 2009 for consecutive losing seasons, they had barely escaped the further humiliation of losing a hundred games by finishing with a record of 62–99. To make matters even worse, they had traded away Jack Wilson and his $7 million salary and Sánchez, who was making $6 million, for mostly minor league prospects and marginal big league talents. While Huntington claimed that the Pirates were rebuilding the club's foundation, critics regarded the trades as nothing more than salary dumps.

In the midst of another awful season, there was, however, a reason for Pirates fans to hope that Huntington was right when Andrew McCutchen, a first-round draft pick in 2005, made his major league debut in June after Nate McLouth was traded away. An outstanding center fielder, McCutchen had a solid rookie season with twelve home runs, fifty-four RBIs, and a .286 average. He would be joined in 2010 by two other talented first-round draft picks, Pittsburgh native Neil Walker and Pedro Alvarez.

With its salary payroll reduced to $35 million and its team made up of either mediocre or promising but inexperienced players, the 2010 Pirates quickly spun into another losing spiral. They went 11–18 in May, 6–20 in June, 9–16 in July, and 8–21 in August. On August 20, 2010, they lost their eighty-second game to the Mets at PNC Park, on their way to a final record of 57–105, the worst since the Pirates starting playing a 162-game schedule in 1962. The 105 losses were also the most in franchise history since the 1952 Pirates lost 112 games. While extending their consecutive losing seasons record to eighteen, the Pirates managed to finish last in the National League in batting, pitching, and fielding, something not done since the 1965 Mets.

Although Russell had a year remaining on his contract, he was fired at the end of the season. The general opinion among unhappy Pirates fans and skeptical Pittsburgh sportswriters was that Russell had become a scapegoat for the Pirates' unwillingness to spend money to improve the franchise, a view seemingly supported by Huntington, when he stated that he did not blame Russell for the Pirates collapse but thought the team needed a change. Huntington, in defense of the organization, pointed out that McCutchen, Walker, and Alvarez were now on the major league roster and claimed that more talented players were soon to follow. As the dreary days of winter approached, all that Pirates fans could hope for was that the young players would live up to Huntington's claim and that he would find a new manager who could bring a winning season to Pittsburgh, a city that had been through two economic and cultural renaissances and desperately needed one for its baseball team.

CHAPTER TEN

HURDLE, MCCUTCHEN, AND THE END OF THE SLIDE

The 2011–2013 Seasons

When the Pirates' 2011 season began, there was little reason for optimism. After coming off their worst season in fifty-eight years, after amassing 299 losses in the prior three years, there was no reason to doubt in Pittsburgh that they were headed for a record-extending nineteenth consecutive losing season. In 2010 the Pirates had the highest ERA (5.00), the most errors (127), and the second worst batting average (.242) in baseball. With no real signs that the team would be improving any time soon, the biggest worry for fans, considering the team's past dealings, was whether management would be tempted to trade some of its promising young talent, including burgeoning star center fielder Andrew McCutchen, to help the team financially.

One hope for the upcoming season was the hiring of a new manager, Texas Rangers batting coach Clint Hurdle.[1] The fifty-three-year-old Hurdle had taken the Colorado Rockies to their first World Series just two years earlier. The Rockies suffered six losing seasons under Hurdle, but in 2007 the team won twenty-one of their final twenty-two regular-season games to make the playoffs as a wild card. They played their way past the Phillies and Diamondbacks to win the pennant but lost to the Red Sox in the World Series. After a losing season in 2008, Hurdle was fired a month into the 2009 campaign when the team began 18–28. He had only one winning season during his seven-plus years in Colorado, but that was one more than the Pirates had in two decades. Hurdle had a reputation for bringing a positive attitude to the game and for communicating and working well with young players. While John Russell also was known for his work with young talent, he was notorious for brooding in the dugout during games and refusing to argue bad calls or to defend his players. Hurdle was emotionally intense but also well known for his infectious optimism and sense of humor. His father described him as "happy-go-lucky."[2]

Upon his hiring, Hurdle was reminded of the team's financial restraint. He believed, however, that what was missing from the Pirates had nothing to do with money. He believed that attitude toward the game was as important as talent on the field, no matter what the payroll, and that the problem for the last two decades was the Pirates' lack of a winning attitude and their approach to the game. The Pirates had not played like a winning team since the early 1990s. When Hurdle said that he was "Proud to be a Pirate" upon his hiring, it was something fans had not heard for a long time. "Pride" was not a word the city associated with its baseball team. There was a T-shirt sold around town with the slogan "Pittsburgh: The City of Champions and the Pirates." For the city, the fans, and the team itself, the Pirates had become an embarrassment.

The one source of baseball pride in Pittsburgh was their ballpark. PNC Park had been voted the best major league ballpark that spring by both the *New York Times* and *ESPN* magazine. Unfortunately, baseball had become less of a draw in the park than the postgame fireworks and concerts or the fifth inning pierogi races that were often more competitive than the games. Despite his optimistic nature, even Hurdle was cautious about his approach to bringing winning baseball back to Pittsburgh. When asked how he would take on the daunting task of turning around the worst franchise in professional sports, Hurdle said, "It's like how do you eat an elephant? One bite at a time. We're going to fix one thing at a time."[3]

Hurdle had dealt with failure before. He was a first-round draft pick of the Kansas City Royals in 1975 and a *Sports Illustrated* cover boy in

March 1978, where he was labeled "This Year's Phenom." But in his ten-year career, he only twice played more than one hundred games in a season and hit only thirty-two total home runs. "I went from phenom to goat to erstwhile phenom to has-been to never-was," he said, looking back.[4] As a manager he had known some success, but his team was swept in the World Series, and he lost his job little more than a year later. In Pittsburgh, he also would have to overcome what had become known as the Sid Bream curse.

Despite Hurdle's promises for change, offseason moves by the Pirates' front office appeared to be business as usual. Their biggest acquisition was journeyman first baseman Lyle Overbay who, to Pirates fans, seemed overpaid at $5 million for one year. The Pirates followed the Overbay deal with mostly cost-conscious pick-ups of aging veterans, like former Braves bench player Matt Diaz. Hurdle may have been an optimist, but the Pirates had a familiar and depressing look about them to their frustrated fans.

Despite the usual gloom in Pittsburgh, 2011 opened with an unexpected bang. Second baseman and Pittsburgh native Neil Walker hit a grand slam against the Cubs at Wrigley Field that led the Pirates to an exciting Opening Day victory in what fans suspected might well be one of the few highlights of the season. Signs outside bars across the city sarcastically celebrated the first place Pirates "for a day."

Early in the season, however, the Pirates were playing above expectations, and on May 8, 2011, they stood at 17–17. They were struggling to score runs, but their pitching staff, led by free agent Kevin Correia and closer Joel Hanrahan, was keeping the Pirates in games. Although the ballclub had done little in the offseason to give their fans a reason to hope for a winning team, they hovered around .500 well into June. That was enough to stay competitive in the weak NL Central. On July 15, they moved into a tie for first place with a record of 48–43, and a few days later, on July 19, they were alone in first and seven games over .500 at 51–44. As the team kept winning, Hurdle's resurgent Pirates were celebrated not only in Pittsburgh but also by national sportswriters, as a team of destiny. ESPN dubbed the Pirates the new America's Team.[5] For Pittsburgh, it all seemed too good to be true—and as it turned out, it was too good to last.

The hope that the Pirates would finally shake the curse of "the Slide" began to fade one night in late July, and it happened appropriately in Atlanta. One night after their first appearance on national television in almost ten years (a game they won on ESPN's Monday Night Baseball), the Pirates were locked in a nineteen-inning marathon with the Braves, the same team that had sent the Pirates into an eighteen-year-and-counting losing streak. The game ended on a horrendous call at home plate by umpire Jerry Meals in which backup catcher Michael McKenry tagged a sliding Julio Lugo before he crossed home plate. When Meals called Lugo safe, Hurdle exploded out of the dugout and began screaming at Meals, who was trying to escape from the field. Interviewed after the game, even Braves players said they were baffled by the call. The next day Meals admitted that he had made a bad call and apologized.[6]

It was a painful loss and, worse yet, it sent the Pirates into a spiral in which they lost eleven of their next twelve games. While it was merely coincidence that it happened against the Braves, Pirates fans were convinced more than ever of the curse. Within two weeks, the Pirates went from first place to ten games out and well on their way to another losing season, their nineteenth in a row. They lost their eighty-second game on September 15 in Los Angeles against the Dodgers and ended the season eighteen games under .500 at 72–90.

Those who had been calling the Pirates America's Team were quick to jump ship once the Pirates collapsed in 2011, but fans in Pittsburgh thought they were seeing the first signs of real hope in nearly two decades. Attendance at PNC Park increased by over 300,000 in 2011 to 1,940,429, the highest total since the park opened in 2001 and the biggest jump in attendance in the park's history. In one season, Hurdle had brought excitement back to Pittsburgh baseball—if not yet the winning he had promised the city.

In the offseason, management showed its own confidence in the team by making a major trade with the Yankees for veteran pitcher A.J. Burnett. While Burnett had struggled in New York, general manager Neal Huntington was convinced that Burnett would return to form with a change of scenery.[7] Burnett's 5.15 ERA and 11–11 record in 2011 had fans booing in New York, but Huntington believed that Burnett would find Pirates fans more understanding and supportive. Huntington also felt that a strong veteran presence, like Burnett, would be of great help to the team's younger players in the clubhouse.

After flirting with but falling short of a winning season in 2011, "Finish" became Hurdle's mantra for 2012.[8] At spring training, the team handed out T-shirts with the "FINISH" slogan on the back. They also had maturing young talent, led by McCutchen, who had signed a six-year $51 million extension during the offseason, as well as exciting minor league prospects, like Starling Marté, waiting for an opportunity.

Things started badly in spring training, when Burnett bunted a ball in batting practice that deflected into his face, fracturing his right cheekbone and sidelining him for the first month of the season. But when Burnett finally made his debut in late April, he became the leader of the Pirates' pitching staff and a fan favorite. In a game against the Dodgers that August, Burnett felt that shortstop Hanley Ramírez, after hitting a home run, had mocked him by rounding the bases with his hands over his eyes like glasses. In Ramírez's next at-bat Burnett struck him out and then shouted, "Sit the fuck down."[9]

After a slow start, the Pirates surged in the first half of the season. By the All-Star break, they were in first place in the NL Central Division at 48–37. While Burnett and the starting pitching staff were solid, the bullpen, led by Hanrahan and newly acquired setup man Jason Grilli, was outstanding. Grilli was another Pirates reclamation project, a thirty-five-year-old right-hander who played under Hurdle in Colorado. Just a year earlier Grilli was recovering from knee surgery and pitching for the Lehigh Valley IronPigs, a Phillies AAA team.

The Pirates had talent in 2012, but they also had the Zoltan. After watching the movie "Dude, Where's My Car?," an inane stoner comedy, team members began to flash the "Z" hand signal used in the movie by the followers of Zoltan, a mysterious figure from outer space, when they got a hit. Walker explained to reporters, "This game is so difficult that when times are going good, you have to celebrate. When times are going bad, you have to forget about it and move on. It's a way for all of us to come together a little bit more and have fun with it."[10]

While the Pirates were beginning to have fun winning games, they were also getting stronger. When Marté finally made his major-league debut in July, he led off the game by lining the first pitch over the left-center wall at Minute Maid Park in Houston. He was the first Pirate to homer in his first major-league at-bat since Don Leppert in 1961.

The Pirates were two and a half games out of first place and sixteen games over .500 at 63–47 on August 8, 2012. Those in the media who followed them saw no warning sign of a collapse similar to 2011, but it happened again. The Pirates struggled against teams in their own division, and on September 14, after losing seven games in a row, they were only one game over .500 at 72–71. After a five-game losing streak that started the following week, they dropped to 74–77. On October 1, they lost their eighty-second game, to the ubiquitous Atlanta Braves, to guarantee their twentieth consecutive losing season.

The 2012 collapse, though slower than the one the year before, was just as devastating for Pirates fans, but the optimistic Hurdle still saw reasons for hope. The team had finished 2012 just four games shy of .500, a turnaround of twenty-two games in two years. Team leader Burnett was under contract for another year and the team's young talent was becoming more experienced and productive, especially McCutchen who finished third in MVP voting at the end of the year.

Reflecting this optimism, Pirates management did the unthinkable for a small-market team and outbid the New York Yankees for veteran catcher Russell Martin. Huntington believed that the Pirates were just one quality veteran player away from being a winning and contending team, and Martin's price tag of $17 million over two years, while steep by the Pirates' past standards, was worth the risk. Still, Martin was one of the biggest offseason free agent signings in Pirates history, and his salary would account for 11 percent of their entire payroll in 2013.

Martin was a former All-Star and, like Burnett, had experience in the postseason. Although his offensive production had been down the previous year with the Yankees (batting a lowly .211), Martin was an outstanding defensive catcher and, more important, he had a gift for helping young pitchers. Many free agents were reluctant to come to Pittsburgh because of the losing streak, but Martin was impressed with the city and felt that the Pirates were on the brink of winning. "I love Pittsburgh. The people are down to Earth. . . . This reminds me more of where I come from, as far as the working class. They grind it out."[11]

The Pirates' other notable signing during the offseason was free agent left-handed pitcher Francisco Liriano, who at one time looked like a staff ace for the Minnesota Twins. Because of his history of injuries, the Pirates were able to sign Liriano to a modest contract of $1 million. Pitching coach Ray Searage had restored Burnett's confidence, transformed Grilli into an All-Star hurler, and now faced the challenge of bringing Liriano back into top form.

At the beginning of spring training in 2013, Mike LaValliere, who was helping the team as an instructor, walked determinedly to home plate with a sledgehammer in one hand and an odd object in the other. The object was a three-figured bobblehead depicting the Sid Bream slide. The Braves had given the bobblehead away as a promotional gift to celebrate the twentieth anniversary of the 1992 NLCS-winning play, and Bream had sent one to LaValliere to thank him for giving permission to use his likeness. LaValliere placed the object on home plate and, with a swift swing of the sledgehammer, shattered the bobblehead into pieces.[12]

LaValliere may have hoped his act would put an end to the jinx of the infamous slide, but the beginning of the 2013 season was not encouraging. Hampered by injuries, the Pirates lost four of their first five games and then headed to the West Coast, where they had traditionally played some of their worst baseball. But they played well on the road trip, turned the season around, and by summer were one of the best teams in baseball.

After two seasons of promise and frustration under Hurdle, the club began to perfect his style of winning, by grinding out a few runs while shutting down teams with consistent pitching. The starting pitching staff was dominant and veterans Burnett and Liriano did some of their best work in years. By mid-July Liriano had an ERA of 2.00 and a record of 9–3. He would go on to win the National League Comeback Player of the Year Award. Under the tutelage of Burnett, young left-hander Jeff Locke went from barely making the starting rotation out of spring training to a surprising All-Star bid. In June, when the Pirates called up former number one overall draft pick, right-handed pitcher Gerrit Cole, he struck out the first batter he faced on three pitches and took a shutout into the seventh inning in an eventual 8–2 victory.

The success of the pitching staff was due in large part to the pitch calling and framing of Martin. Under his game management, the starting rotation went from thirteenth in the National League ERA rankings to second. Martin also contributed on offense with several game-winning hits. The Pirates were also getting a big boost on offense from Pedro Alvarez, who was maturing as a power hitter and led the National League in home runs at the All-Star break. No one, however, was more valuable than McCutchen. With his infectious personality and dynamic play, he was becoming the most popular player in Pittsburgh and attracting national attention. McCutchen was in his fifth year with the Pirates and had never disparaged the team or the city or set his sights on New York or Los Angeles. His father, Lorenzo, said, "He feels like he was predestined to be here. I think that it's important that you play where your heart is and I think his heart is in Pittsburgh."[13]

McCutchen was clearly the team leader, but the key to the Pirates' success in 2013 was a relief corps that became known as the Shark Tank. The bullpen was so dominant that the Pirates' record at midseason in close games was 40–2. The previous year's closer, Hanrahan, was traded to the Red Sox during the offseason in a controversial deal, but Grilli had stepped in and, by midseason, was a perfect 23-for-23 in saves. Mark Melancon, acquired in the Hanrahan trade after a disastrous season as Boston's closer, was just as effective as Grilli had been in a set-up role. Grilli and Melancon, along with Tony Watson, Justin Wilson, Jared Hughes, Bryan Morris, and Vin Mazzaro, were praised as "the best bullpen in baseball" by former Pirates manager Jim Leyland for the way they attacked opposing teams, like sharks sensing blood in the water.[14] At the suggestion of Grilli, management even agreed to install a tank with live sharks in the clubhouse, though with the understanding that he would not put his pitching hand in the tank.

By August the surging Pirates were twenty-five games over .500. Amid the mounting wins and *Sports Illustrated* covers, the players were inundated with questions about the twenty-year losing streak, as well as "the collapse" and "the swoon" that happened the prior two years. Most of the players, however, dismissed the idea of a curse. Grilli summed it up best, "We weren't a part of all those 20 years, a lot of us, we have nothing to do with that. But we have everything to do with fixing it."[15]

By September the Pirates were not only playing winning baseball for the first time in twenty years, they appeared to be headed to the playoffs. On the minds of every Pirates fan, however, was the eighty-second win. The city was in love with the Pirates, Jolly Roger flags were flying, PNC Park was repeatedly selling out, but until it was mathematically certain that the team would finish with a winning record, fans were not ready to relax and celebrate.

The last time the Pirates had a winning season, the Marlins, Diamondbacks, Rays, and Rockies did not even exist. Since then, each of these teams had been to a World Series. It took so long that Doug Drabek's and Andy Van Slyke's sons were playing major league baseball by the time Pittsburgh saw winning baseball again. When Bream slid into home plate that night in 1992, there were broken hearts all over

Pittsburgh. Twenty losing seasons later, there finally would be joy in Pittsburgh again for its baseball fans.

The Pirates got their eighty-first win against the Brewers on September 3 to ensure that they would not have a losing season. They then lost four in a row before at last claiming their first winning season since 1992—on September 10, 2013, with a victory against the Texas Rangers in Arlington. Rookie pitcher Cole finally brought Pirates fans that coveted eighty-second win, with an almost flawless game against Rangers' ace Yu Darvish. It was the kind of close, low-scoring game the Pirates had been winning all season. With the Pirates holding a thin 1–0 lead going into the top of the ninth, Melancon, filling in as closer for an injured Grilli, pitched a perfect ninth to ensure a winning season.

The twenty-year losing streak was over, but there were no champagne bottles popped in the clubhouse, no celebrating by the team, and no congratulatory address by Hurdle. The win had great significance for Pittsburgh, but not as much for Pirates players. Cole was only two years old when the Pirates lost Game 7 of the 1992 NLCS. Even Jay Bell, who had played in that game and was now the Pirates' hitting coach, played down the significance. "The ring is the goal . . . Getting over .500 is not the goal by any means."[16] It took Walker, who grew up in Pittsburgh, to put the win in perspective, "As a fan, as a growing-up fan . . . that number has some significance, yes. To the other 24 guys, I don't think it holds that much weight."[17]

With the losing streak officially over, the Pirates finished the 2013 season at 94–68, good for second place, three games behind the division-winning Cardinals, and a wild card spot in the playoffs. In three years, Hurdle had taken the worst team in baseball to the playoffs. Now he would need to get his Pirates ready to play a familiar playoff foe, the Cincinnati Reds, in the first postseason game in the history of PNC Park.

The assumption in the national media was that the Pirates had already accomplished their goal in 2013 when they finally ended their twenty-season losing streak. Most commentators predicted an early exit from the playoffs for an inexperienced Pirates team. They even wondered if Pirates fans would know what to do at a playoff game after so many years of losing. But Greg Brown, who was a Pirates broadcaster for all twenty losing seasons, remembered walking along an empty concourse at PNC Park just before the gates opened and sensing the excitement building as fans poured across the Clemente Bridge to attend the game.[18]

As the playoffs are structured, the Wild Card Game is a single-elimination playoff. Hurdle selected sixteen-game winner Liriano to pitch against Reds ace Johnny Cueto. Liriano was outstanding that night, pitching seven strong innings and giving up just one run, but Pirates fans made their own impact on the game in the second inning. One out after late-season acquisition Marlon Byrd brought the crowd to its feet with a home run that gave the Pirates a 1–0 lead, fans started chanting, "Cueto . . . Cueto . . . Cueto . . ." Visibly rattled, Cueto dropped the baseball and was met with a derisive roar from the crowd. On the very next pitch, Cueto gave up a 405-foot home run to Martin. The Pirates went on to win, 6–2.

After the Wild Card victory, the Pirates moved on to the National League Division Series to play the Cardinals. They took a 2–1 lead in a best-of-five series but lost the last two games and brought an end to one of the most exciting seasons in Pirates history. The Division Series was a disappointment, but instead of dreading next year, Pirates fans could now look forward to the beginning of a new baseball season.

As Barry Bonds drove past his old apartment in Coraopolis at the beginning of the 2014 season, he may well have had mixed emotions.[19] It was his first visit back to the city since his baseball career came to its controversial end following the 2007 season. He had given Pittsburgh some of the greatest baseball ever seen in the city, but many fans still thought he had deserted the team and the city. For many fans it was impossible to separate Bream's slide, Bonds's departure, and the twenty-year losing spiral that followed. In 2013, however the Pirates had finally broken the streak and moved beyond the feelings of heartbreak and betrayal.

Bonds was back in town to present the National League MVP award to McCutchen as part of the 2014 Opening Day festivities at PNC Park. The standing room only crowd of 39,833 at PNC that afternoon also saw the return of Leyland, who presented Hurdle with his Manager of the Year plaque. Earlier, Leyland and Bonds, who had managed to keep in touch over the years and become, in Leyland's words, "dear friends," sat side by side at a press conference.[20] Bonds looked around and remarked, "We had some good times here."[21]

At the pregame ceremonies, as he walked to home plate alongside McCutchen, Bonds appeared more nervous than he ever had been while wearing a Pirates uniform. Bonds's introduction triggered a few initial boos, but they eventually gave way to respectful and perhaps even forgiving applause. As Bonds looked over at McCutchen accepting the honor, it was a poignant moment. McCutchen now signified the promise and greatness that Bonds once held as a Pirate. His years in Pittsburgh were the stuff of Hall of Fame careers, and his Pirates teams, while falling short of greatness, had one of the most successful runs in franchise history. But the day was not about Bonds or about past disappointments. After finally ending twenty years of losing, the Pirates and their fans were looking beyond Bonds and into the future.

NOTES

CHAPTER ONE. THE DECLINE AND FALL OF THE PIRATES FAMILY

1. Nightingale, "The Pirate Problem."

2. Quoted in Feeney, "Bill Robinson's Tenth-Inning Homer Beats Sutter in Rain-Delayed Game."

3. Peterson, *Pops*, 208.

4. Clayton, "Parker Feeling Mighty Low after Assault with Battery."

5. Stargell and Bird, *Willie Stargell*, 241.

6. Quoted in Chass, "Baseball Players Go Out on Strike after Talks with Owners Fail."

7. Quoted in Donovan, "Stargell Act Tough One to Follow."

8. Quoted in Associated Press, "Parker Target of Battery Thrown from Stands."

9. Quoted in Chass, "Question in Pittsburgh." See also Nightingale, "The Pirate Problem."

10. Quoted in Nightingale, "The Pirate Problem."

11. Quoted in Lieb, *The Pittsburgh Pirates*, 46.

12. Graham, *Singing the City*, 9, 120.

13. Quoted in Smizik, "Buck Night Crowd Gives Hope for the Future."

14. All quoted in Chass, "Question in Pittsburgh."

15. Quoted in Chass, "Question in Pittsburgh."

16. Authors' telephone interview with Bob Walk, November 2014.

17. Skirboll, *The Pittsburgh Cocaine Seven*, 2.

18. Quoted in Skirboll, *The Pittsburgh Cocaine Seven*, 174.

19. Quoted in Skirboll, *The Pittsburgh Cocaine Seven*, 176.

20. Authors' telephone interview with Sam Reich, November 2014. Reich acted as Parker's defense attorney at the urging of his brother Tom Reich, Parker's agent.

21. Quoted in Skirboll, *The Pittsburgh Cocaine Seven*, 185.

22. Reich interview.

23. Skirboll, *The Pittsburgh Cocaine Seven*, 220.

24. Quoted in Kovacevic, "Chuck Tanner Manager Who Led Pirates' Family to 1979 Championship."

25. Nightingale, "The Pirate Problem."

26. Nightingale, "The Pirate Problem."

27. Quoted in Nightingale, "The Pirate Problem."

28. Quoted in Nightingale, "The Pirate Problem."

CHAPTER TWO. THE UNKNOWNS SYD THRIFT AND JIM LEYLAND

1. Boyer and Savageau, *Places Rated Almanac*, 70.

2. Quoted in Keidan, "Playing for Keeps."

3. Quoted in Keidan, "Playing for Keeps."

4. Keidan, "Playing for Keeps."

5. Keidan, "Playing for Keeps."

6. Quoted in Cook, "Thrift's Best Days Were with Pirates."

7. See Vanwyndarden, "A Man for All Seasons."

8. Smizik, "Why Thrift?"

9. Musick, "'El Syd' Embarks on Daring Adventure with Pirates."

10. Quoted in Zinsser, *Spring Training*, 44.

11. Authors' telephone interview with Jim Leyland, November 2014.

12. Leyland interview.

13. Leyland interview.

14. Leyland interview.

15. Quoted in Zinsser, *Spring Training*, 46.

16. Quoted in Fennessy, "Leyland Will Bring His Own Style to Bucs."

17. Quoted in Smizik, "Leyland Gets the Call from Pirates."

18. Collier, "It's a Dream Come True for Ex-Coach." See also Smizik, "Leyland Gets the Call from Pirates."

19. Will, "The Manager: Tony La Russa, on Edge," in Will, *Men at Work*, 7–76.

20. Holtzman, "Pirates Pluck Leyland."

21. Authors' telephone interview with Sid Bream, November 2014.

22. Quoted in Chass, "Question in Pittsburgh: Anybody Want a Team?"

23. Leyland, interview.

24. Quoted in Cook, "Leyland Lays It on the Line."

25. Quoted in Associated Press, "Bonds Sinks Phils in Ninth."

26. Feeney, "Pirates Must Make Some Tough Decisions."

27. Quoted in Hertzel, "Leyland Feeling at Home after Tough Rookie Year."

28. Leyland interview.

29. Authors' telephone interview with Doug Drabek, November 2014.

30. Authors' telephone interview with Mike LaValliere, November 2014.

31. Quoted in Associated Press, "Bucs."

32. *Pittsburgh Magazine*, January 1988.

33. Quoted in Meyer, "Bucs Retain Leyland, Thrift for Next Season."

34. Meyer, "Bucs Retain Leyland, Thrift for Next Season."

35. Keidan, "Bucs Could Lose Thrift over Contract Dispute."

36. Keidan, "Bucs Could Lose Thrift over Contract Dispute."

37. Keidan, "Bucs Could Lose Thrift over Contract Dispute."

38. Quoted in Meyer, "Sydnor W. 'Syd' Thrift Jr.: General Manager Who Resurrected the Pirates."

39. Quoted in Leonard, "DD Man of the Year Thrift Next Wants Two Million Fans."

40. Zinsser, *Spring Training*, 60 (also 58–68).

41. Authors' telephone interview with Darnell Coles, November 2014.

42. Will, *Men at Work*, 139.

43. Will, *Men at Work*, 140.

44. Will, *Men at Work*, 141.

45. Hertzel, "Second Banana."

46. Associated Press, "Leyland Asks Pirates for Raise."

47. Beaton, "Thrift Gone."

48. Smizik, "Thrift Made Some Mistakes, But Don't Sell His Salvage Job Short."

49. Quoted in Finoli and Ranier, *The Pittsburgh Pirates Encyclopedia*, 482.

CHAPTER THREE. LEYLAND AND BARRY BONDS LEAD THE WAY

1. Quoted in Collier, "Dodging Shadows."

2. Collier, "Dodging Shadows."

3. Authors' telephone interview with Gene Collier, November 2014.

4. Authors' email exchange with Mario Moccia.

5. Pearlman, *Love Me, Hate Me*, 54–55.

6. Pearlman, *Love Me, Hate Me*, 66.

7. Quoted in Pearlman, *Love Me, Hate Me*, 76.

8. Quoted in Collier, "Dodging Shadows."

9. Collier, "Dodging Shadows."

10. Quoted in Collier, "Dodging Shadows."

11. Quoted in Collier, "Dodging Shadows."

12. Quoted in Collier, "Bonds Has Potential."

13. Authors' telephone interview with Jeff Pearlman, November 2014.

14. Quoted in Collier, "Bonds Has Potential."

15. Quoted in Collier, "Bonds Has Potential."

16. Quoted in Collier, "Bonds Has Potential."

17. Perrotto, "Bonds, Bonilla."

18. Quoted in Perrotto, "Bonds, Bonilla."

19. Quoted in Hertzel, "Bonds Signs for $360,000."

20. Quoted in Robinson, "Bonds' Name Absent from Doughty's List."

21. Quoted in Meyer, "Padres Pick Dunne."

22. Quoted in Meyer, "Bonilla Says Arbitration Has Changed Him."

23. Quoted in Robinson, "Pirates May Lose Players to Free Agency."

24. Quoted in Associated Press, "Hard Feelings."

25. Quoted in Collier, "Bonilla Positions Himself to Say What's Right about Switch."

26. Unless otherwise noted, all quotes in the following twenty paragraphs come from Spotlight Presentation for the 1990 Season, produced and narrated by Rob King for Fox Sports Network/National Sports Programs, 2007.

27. Authors' telephone interview with Lanny Frattare, November 2014.

28. Quoted in Hertzel, "Pirates Show Off Best Stuff."

29. Despite their excellence, Bonds and Bonilla made the All-Star Game as reserves rather than starters. They were joined by Heaton as representatives of the Pirates. The starting outfielders were Andre Dawson of the Cubs and Lenny Dykstra and Kevin Mitchell of the Mets.

30. Quoted in Beaton, "Strawberry, Bonds Ready to Hop on Salary Escalator." See also Keidan, "Bonds Issuing Ultimatum for Pirates."

31. Authors' telephone interview with Zane Smith, November 2014.

32. "You Gotta Believe," at https://www.youtube.com/watch?v=8G9Q eSj1m1o/.

33. Authors' telephone interview with Bob Patterson, November 2014.

34. Authors' telephone interview with Steve Blass, November 2014.

35. Walk interview.

36. Walk interview.

37. Authors' telephone interview with Bob Kipper, November 2014.

38. Leyland interview.

39. Frattare interview.

CHAPTER FOUR. THE PIRATES TAKE ON THE NASTY BOYS

1. Pittsburgh Joe, "Can't Beat Pirates versus Reds."
2. Quoted in Solomon, "Healthy Pirates Boast Edge over Reds in NLCS."
3. Quoted in Solomon, "Pirates Rally, Win NL Opener."
4. Quoted in Solomon, "Pirates Rally, Win NL Opener."
5. Quoted in Solomon, "Pirates Rally, Win NL Opener."
6. Quoted in Solomon, "Reds' Win Kissed by the Sun."
7. Quoted in Solomon, "Reds' Win Kissed by the Sun."
8. Quoted in Solomon, "Reds' Win Kissed by the Sun."
9. Quoted in Perrotto, "First Playoff Game since '79 Draws 45,611, 13,000 Empty Seats."
10. Quoted in Perrotto, "Bucs Pay the Price."
11. Quoted in Perrotto, "Bucs Pay the Price."
12. Quoted in Prisuta, "After Three Games, Bucs' Big Guns Are Still Firing Blanks."
13. Quoted in Solomon, "Reds One Win from World Series, Relievers, Outfielders Stifle Pirates."
14. Quoted in Solomon, "Reds Gun Down the Pirates."
15. Quoted in Prisuta, "Larkin Wants to Keep Rijo, Dibble Quiet."
16. Quoted in Perrotto, "Last Chance, Season Rides on Drabek's Arm."
17. Quoted in Love, "The Stopper Does It Again."
18. Quoted in Perrotto, "Patterson, Bonilla Combine to Put Out Reds' Fire in Ninth."
19. Love, "The Stopper Does It Again."
20. Bell as told to Perrotto, "Confidence on Rise as Pirates Head to Cincinnati."
21. Quoted in Perrotto, "Bonds Questions Why King Sat Out Game."
22. Quoted in Plaschke, "Reds Advance to Series, with a Catch."
23. Quoted in Perrotto, "Braggs' Ninth Inning Catch"; Meade, "Thank You, Pirates."
24. Perrotto, "Braggs' Ninth Inning Catch."

CHAPTER FIVE. WINNING THE DIVISION, AFTER LOSING SID BREAM

1. Since the first award was given to Pittsburgh boxing legend Billy Conn for 1939, Pirates players and managers, beginning with pitcher Rip Sewell for 1943 and manager Frankie Frisch for 1944, had been honored more than

twenty times. Ralph Kiner, Dick Groat, Danny Murtaugh, Roberto Clemente, and Willie Stargell were recognized on more than one occasion, and in 1971 Murtaugh, Clemente, and Stargell shared the honor. Before Leyland, the most recent member of the Pirates family to be named Dapper Dan Sportsman of the Year, ironically, was the recently fired Syd Thrift, the Pirates' general manager who hired Leyland.

2. Quoted in Parascenzo, "Leyland's Man of Year Night."

3. Quoted in Associated Press, "Will Two Pirates Share MVP?"

4. Smizik, "Pirates Priority."

5. Smizik, "Pirates Priority."

6. Bream interview.

7. Leyland interview.

8. Quoted in Hertzel, "Bonds Demands Big Deal—Or Else."

9. Collier, "If Bonds Feels Insulted, What about the Pirates?"

10. Perrotto, "Trade Rumors Swirling around Bonds."

11. Less than a decade later Sosa and Mark McGwire would lead a steroid-enhanced assault on the single-season home-run record that would infuriate Bonds, who thought that they had stolen his rightful claim to being the best player in baseball. See Fainaru-Wada and Williams, *Game of Shadows*.

12. Quoted in Meyer, "The Silence of the MVP."

13. Quoted in "Bonds Says He Would Take Bonilla Offer."

14. Associated Press, "Leyland, Bonds Dispute."

15. Quoted in Hertzel, "Leyland, Virdon Exchange Angry Words with Bonds."

16. Authors' telephone interview with Don Slaught, November 2014.

17. Quoted in Associated Press, "Bonds, Leyland Have Showdown."

18. Quoted in Associated Press, "Bonds, Leyland Have Showdown."

19. Quoted in Associated Press, "Bonds, Leyland Have Showdown."

20. Quoted in Associated Press, "Latest On-Field Flareup by Bonds Draws Criticism from Teammates."

21. Quoted in Associated Press, "Latest On-Field Flareup."

22. Quoted in Robinson, "Leyland's Outburst Inspired All Managers."

23. Quoted in Robinson, "Leyland's Outburst Inspired All Managers."

24. Quoted in Robinson, "Leyland's Outburst Inspired All Managers."

25. Quoted in Smizik, "Seeing Pirates Bend for Others Hardens Bonilla."

26. Mehno, "An Unusual Outlook."

27. Smizik, "Give Him a Break, Don't Boo Bonds."

28. Authors' personal and telephone interview with Paul Meyer, November 2014.

29. Graham, "Let's Go Bucs," 121.

30. Quoted in Zinsser, *Spring Training*, 67–68.

31. McClendon had a fair major league career as a player. He played parts of eight seasons in the big leagues for three different teams. He hit thirty-five career home runs and never appeared in more than ninety-two games. But at the 1971 Little League World Series, he hit five home runs in five at-bats for his Gary, Indiana, team. See Tyler Kepner, "A Lasting Memory, a Remarkable Achievement."

32. Bream interview.

33. Bream interview.

34. Niedzielka, "Bonds Hasn't Changed."

35. Authors' telephone interview with Greg Brown, November 2014.

36. Quoted in Niedzielka, "Bonds Hasn't Changed."

37. Collier interview.

38. Collier, "Bonds Awesome, but Bonilla Number One Man."

39. Authors' telephone interview with John Wehner, November 2014.

40. Spotlight Presentation for the 1991 Season, produced and narrated by Rob King for Fox Sports Network/National Sports Programs, 2007.

41. Spotlight Presentation for the 1991 Season, produced and narrated by Rob King for Fox Sports Network/National Sports Programs, 2007.

42. Quoted in Hafner, "Pirates Win to Clinch NL East Title."

43. LaValliere interview.

CHAPTER SIX. TOO MUCH STEVE AVERY

1. Stevens, "Atlanta Braves," 36.

2. Spotlight Presentation for the 1991 Season, produced and narrated by Rob King for Fox Sports Network/National Sports Programs, 2007.

3. Slaught interview.

4. Walk interview.

5. Zane Smith interview.

6. Big TMLB, CBS Broadcast, Game 2, October 10, 1991 NLCS on You-Tube.

7. Quoted in Ritter, *The Glory of Their Times*, 27.

8. Bonds, "Incorrect Reporting Puts Unwanted Tint on Post-Season."

9. Quoted in Bagnato, "Pirates Rally to Beat Braves in Game 4."

10. Araton, "Tomlin Quietly Keeps Mets' Bats Silent."

11. Plaschke, "Drabek Not Quite Ready Yet."

12. Leyland interview.

13. Spotlight Presentation for the 1991 Season, produced and narrated by Rob King for Fox Sports Network/National Sports Programs, 2007.

14. Quoted in Verdi, "Pirates Weakened by Averyitis."

15. Spotlight Presentation for the 1991 Season, produced and narrated by Rob King for Fox Sports Network/National Sports Programs, 2007.

16. Spotlight Presentation for the 1991 Season, produced and narrated by Rob King for Fox Sports Network/National Sports Programs, 2007.

17. Leyland interview.

CHAPTER SEVEN. BARRY BONDS'S LAST HURRAH

1. Quoted in Sexton, "Mets Sign Bonilla for $29 Million, Making Him Richest in Baseball."

2. Frattare interview.

3. Collier interview.

4. Authors' telephone interview with Greg Brown, November 2014.

5. Quoted in Hertzel, "Bonds Signs Best One of All."

6. Quoted in Hertzel, "Bonds Signs Best One of All."

7. Walk interview.

8. Quoted in Associated Press, "Bonds Intends to Test Free Agent Market."

9. Authors' telephone interview with Bill Landrum, November 2014.

10. Quoted in Hertzel, "Feeling Left Out."

11. Quoted in Hertzel, "Feeling Left Out."

12. Frattare interview.

13. Quoted in Meyer, "Batting Fourth Fine with Bonds."

14. Bodley, "No Bonilla Proves to Be No Problem for Pirates, Bonds."

15. Quoted in Bodley, "No Bonilla Proves to Be No Problem for Pirates, Bonds."

16. Rushin, "Bonds Away," 22–23.

17. Pearlman, *Love Me, Hate Me*, 122–23.

18. Quoted in Robinson, "Bonds."

19. Quoted in Pearlman, *Love Me, Hate Me*, 122–23. For more on the complex history of race in Pittsburgh, see Trotter and Day, *Race and Renaissance*.

20. Coles interview.

21. Quoted in Pearlman, *Love Me, Hate Me*, 94.

22. Quoted in Robinson, "Bonds."

23. Authors' telephone interview with Paul Wagner, November 2014.

24. Quoted in Wakefield, *Knuckler*, 62–63.

25. Quoted in Sexton, "Pirates Are Hanging by Wakefield's Fingertips."

26. Spotlight Presentation for the 1992 Season, produced and narrated by Rob King for Fox Sports Network/National Sports Programs, 2007.

27. Perrotto, "Closing the Deal."

28. Quoted in Perrotto, "Closing the Deal."

29. Quoted in Newhan, "Simmons Misses the Newspapers."

CHAPTER EIGHT. SID BREAM'S SLIDE INTO HISTORY

1. Page 2, ESPN, *The World Series 100th Anniversary*, 2003.

2. Spotlight Presentation for the 1992 Season, produced and narrated by Rob King for Fox Sports Network/National Sports Programs, 2007.

3. Newhan, "Smoltz Shows He's Right Choice."

4. Smith interview.

5. Blass interview.

6. Quoted in Edes, "Smoltz Has Bucs in His Pocket."

7. Quoted in Edes, "Smoltz Has Bucs in His Pocket."

8. Quoted in Plaschke, "Pirates Jackson Recalls Hard Times."

9. Quoted in Kent, "Braves Batter Pirates into Bind."

10. Quoted in Kent, "Braves Batter Pirates into Bind."

11. Quoted in Kent, "Braves Batter Pirates into Bind."

12. Quoted in Kent, "Pirates Finally Win a Sellout after Seventeen Games."

13. Quoted in Sexton, "Pirates Are Hanging by Wakefield's Fingertips."

14. Quoted in Reaves, "Pirates Rookie Stops Braves."

15. Quoted in Reaves, "Pirates Rookie Stops Braves."

16. Quoted in Reaves, "Pirates Rookie Stops Braves."

17. Quoted in Sexton, "Van Slyke Makes a Point with His Bat."

18. Quoted in Nightengale, "It Seems the Pirates Have Double Faulted."

19. Quoted in Kent, "Pirates Finally Win a Sellout after Seventeen Games."

20. See Pearlman, *Love Me, Hate Me*, 130, for a description of this scene within the context of the Van Halen song "Right Now"—a Pittsburgh slogan throughout the season.

21. Quoted in Fitzpatrick, "Atlanta Takes 3–1 Series Lead."

22. Quoted in Sexton, "Invincibility of Avery Unravels in First Inning."

23. Pearlman, *Love Me, Hate Me*, 131.

24. Quoted in Reaves, "Bonds, Walk Give Pirates New Life."

25. Quoted in Sexton, "Invincibility of Avery Unravels in First Inning."

26. Quoted in Chass, "Bonds Resurfaces to Propel Pirates."

27. Quoted in Holtzman, "Leyland Defends Wakefield Going the Distance."

28. Quoted in Maske, "Pirates Pound Braves, 13–4, Send NLCS to Seventh Game."

29. Spotlight Presentation for the 1992 Season, produced and narrated by Rob King for Fox Sports Network/National Sports Programs, 2007.

30. Quoted in Fitzpatrick, "Pirates Blast Braves."

31. Spotlight Presentation for the 1992 Season, produced and narrated by Rob King for Fox Sports Network/National Sports Programs, 2007.

32. Walk interview.

33. LaValliere interview.

34. Spotlight Presentation for the 1992 Season, produced and narrated by Rob King for Fox Sports Network/National Sports Programs, 2007.

35. Meyer interview.

36. Spotlight Presentation for the 1992 Season, produced and narrated by Rob King for Fox Sports Network/National Sports Programs, 2007.

37. Pearlman, *Love Me, Hate Me*, 134.

38. Walk interview.

39. Blass interview.

40. Meyer interview.

41. Wehner interview.

42. Walk interview.

43. Spotlight Presentation for the 1992 Season, produced and narrated by Rob King for Fox Sports Network/National Sports Programs, 2007.

44. Frattare interview.

45. Spotlight Presentation for the 1992 Season, produced and narrated by Rob King for Fox Sports Network/National Sports Programs, 2007.

46. Leyland interview.

CHAPTER NINE. THE PIRATES SLIDE INTO HISTORY

1. See "World Series Ticket Rush Swamps Pirate Officials," 137–39.

2. Regalado, *Viva Baseball!*, 150.

3. Smizik, "Bonds Gets Head Start on Clemente's Greatness."

4. Smizik, "Bonds Gets Head Start on Clemente's Greatness."

5. Smizik, "Bonds Gets Head Start on Clemente's Greatness."

6. See Fainaru-Wada and Williams, *Game of Shadows*. In his first appearance on the Hall of Fame ballot in 2013, Bonds received 36.2 percent of the vote, far short of the required 75 percent. In 2017, he received 53.8 percent.

7. Quoted in Pearlman, *Love Me, Hate Me*, 142.

8. Smizik, "Unpopular Fact."

9. Meyer, "Bonds Gets Some Jeers."

10. Quoted in Meyer, "Bonds Gets Some Jeers."

11. Perry, "Regrets, I've Had a Few."

12. LaValliere interview.

13. Keidan, "Playing for Keeps."

14. Keidan, "Playing for Keeps."

15. Keidan, "Playing for Keeps."

16. Keidan, "Playing for Keeps."

17. Quoted in Meyer, "Manager Laments Plight of Team, Fans."

18. Collier, "McClatchy's Late Bid Must Include Big Bucks."

19. Smizik, "The Pirates May Return, but Fans Must Come Back."

20. Quoted in Meyer, "Saying Goodbye Would Be Hard."

21. See Rendleman and Ruck, "The Education of Kevin McClatchy."

22. Leyland interview.

23. Quoted in Perrotto, "Leyland Bids Farewell to Pittsburgh."

24. Quoted in Rendleman and Ruck, "The Education of Kevin McClatchy."

25. Brown interview.

26. Quoted in Graham, "Let's Go Bucs."

27. Quoted in Dvorchak, "The Political Struggle over Financing PNC Park Went into Extra Innings."

28. Quoted in Lachimia, "PNC Park Becomes a Reality," 21.

29. Dvorchak, "It's Hard to Cheer."

30. Perry, "Regrets, I've Had a Few."

31. Quoted in Dvorchak, "Pirates Have Much to Celebrate after 13–3 Win."

32. Quoted in Robinson, "Pirates Hire Ex-Dodger Skipper Tracy as New Manager."

33. Smizik, "Nutting Makes Himself Visible at Long Last."

34. Quoted in "Outgoing CEO McClatchy Hailed for Keeping Pirates in Town."

35. Smizik, "Remember McClatchy as Man Who Saved Pirates."

36. Smizik, "It's the Same Old, Same Old." For a more recent commentary, see Smizik, "About That Pirates' Payroll."

CHAPTER TEN. HURDLE, MCCUTCHEN, AND THE END OF THE SLIDE

1. Menendez, "Turning Frowns Upside Down," 113–14.

2. Quoted in Menendez, "Turning Frowns Upside Down."

3. Quoted in Menendez, "Turning Frowns Upside Down."

4. Quoted in Cook: "Once a Draft Bust, Clint Hurdle Has Been Pivotal as Pirates Manager."

5. Karabell, "Who Should Be America's Team?"

6. Sanserino, "MLB Admits Error in Tuesday's Pirates-Braves Game."

7. Brink, "Trade for Burnett Becomes Official."

8. Gallo, "Pirates Look to Finish What They Start in 2012."

9. "A.J. Burnett Tells Hanley Ramirez to Sit the Fuck Down," YouTube, August 11, 2012.

10. Quoted in Majors, "Dude, What's the 'Z'? Pirates Explain."

11. Quoted in Cook, "Finding a Home."

12. LaValliere interview.

13. Quoted in McCullough, "Center Fielder Andrew McCutchen Is Now the Face of the Pirates."

14. Quoted in Cook, "It's Time to Embrace Pirates' Pitching."

15. Quoted in Reiter, "Love Is in the Air," 41.

16. Quoted in Brink: "Losers No More."

17. Quoted in Brink, "Losers No More."

18. Brown interview.

19. Menendez, "Bonds' Healing Begins with MVP Presentation."

20. Leyland interview.

21. Quoted in Biertempfel, "Bonds Makes Nice with Pirates."

SELECTED BIBLIOGRAPHY

Araton, Harvey. "Tomlin Quietly Keeps Mets' Bats Silent." *New York Times*, August 7, 1991.

Associated Press. "Bonds Intends to Test Free Agent Market." March 6, 1992.

Associated Press. "Bonds, Leyland Have Showdown." March 5, 1991.

Associated Press. "Bonds Sinks Phils in Ninth." *Gettysburg (PA) Times*, September 24, 1986.

Associated Press. "Bucs: Bonds Is Key." *Greensburg (PA) Tribune Review*, March 1, 1987.

Associated Press. "Hard Feelings: Pirates Refusal to Negotiate Left Many Players Unhappy." *Washington (PA) Observer-Reporter*, March 23, 1990.

Associated Press. "Latest On-Field Flareup by Bonds Draws Criticism from Teammates." March 7, 1991.

Associated Press. "Leyland Asks Pirates for Raise." September 21, 1988.

Associated Press. "Leyland, Bonds Dispute." *New York Times*, March 5, 1991.

Associated Press. "Parker Target of Battery Thrown from Stands." *New London (CT) Day*, September 12, 1983.

Associated Press. "Will Two Pirates Share MVP?" August 24, 1990.

Bagnato, Andrew. "Pirates Rally to Beat Braves in Game 4." *Chicago Tribune*, October 14, 1991.

Baseball: The Biographical Encyclopedia. New York: Total/Sports Illustrated, 2000.

The Baseball Encyclopedia. 9th ed. New York: Macmillan, 1993.

The Baseball Timeline. New York: DK, 2001.

Beaton, Rod. "Strawberry, Bonds Ready to Hop on Salary Escalator." *USA Today*, July 11, 1990.

Beaton, Rod. "Thrift Gone: Will Bucs Stop Here?" *USA Today*, March 7, 1989.

Bell, Jay (as told to John Perrotto). "Confidence on Rise as Pirates Head to Cincinnati." *Beaver County (PA) Times*, October 11, 1990.

Biertempfel, Rob. "Bonds Makes Nice with Pirates, Fans at PNC Park Season Opener." *Pittsburgh Tribune Review*, March 31, 2014.

Blass, Steve, with Erik Sherman. *A Pirate for Life*. Chicago: Triumph Books, 2012.

Bodley, Hal. "No Bonilla Proves to Be No Problem for Pirates, Bonds." *USA Today*, April 13, 1992.

Bonds, Barry. "Incorrect Reporting Puts Unwanted Tint on Post-Season." *Pittsburgh Press*, October 11, 1991.

"Bonds Says He Would Take Bonilla Offer." *Pittsburgh Press*, March 29, 1991.

Boyer, Rick, and David Savageau. *Places Rated Almanac: Your Guide to Finding the Best Places to Live in America*. 2nd ed. Chicago: Rand McNally, 1985.

Brink, Bill. "Losers No More, with Victory in Milwaukee, Pirates End Two Decades of Futility." *Pittsburgh Post-Gazette*, September 4, 2013.

Brink, Bill. "Trade for Burnett Becomes Official." *Pittsburgh Post-Gazette*, February 2, 2012.

Chass, Murray. "Baseball Players Go Out on Strike after Talks with Owners Fail." *New York Times*, June 12, 1981.

Chass, Murray. "Bonds Resurfaces to Propel Pirates." *New York Times*, October 12, 1992.

Chass, Murray. "Question in Pittsburgh: Anybody Want a Team?" *New York Times*, July 7, 1985.

Clayton, John. "Parker Feeling Mighty Low after Assault with Battery." *Pittsburgh Press*, July 21, 1980.

Collier, Gene. "Barry Bonds, Dodging Shadows, Chasing Dreams." *Pittsburgh Press*, Sunday magazine, June 20, 1987.

Collier, Gene. "Bonds Awesome, but Bonilla Number One Man." *Pittsburgh Post-Gazette*, August 13, 1991.

Collier, Gene. "Bonds Has Potential to Excite and Exasperate." *Pittsburgh Press*, June 13, 1989.

Collier, Gene. "Bonilla Positions Himself to Say What's Right about Switch." *Pittsburgh Press*, January 23, 1990.

Collier, Gene. "If Bonds Feels Insulted, What about the Pirates?" *Pittsburgh Post-Gazette*, January 31, 1991.

Collier, Gene. "It's a Dream Come True for Ex-Coach." *Pittsburgh Press*, November 21, 1985.

Collier, Gene. "McClatchy's Late Bid Must Include Big Bucks." September 20, 1995.

Cook, Everett. "Finding a Home." *Pittsburgh Post-Gazette*, August 6, 2013.

Cook, Ron. "The Eighties: A Terrible Time of Trial and Error." *Pittsburgh Post-Gazette*, September 29, 2000.

Cook, Ron. "It's Time to Embrace Pirates' Pitching." *Pittsburgh Post-Gazette*, July 12, 2013.

Cook, Ron. "Leyland Lays It on the Line: 'We Stunk.'" *Pittsburgh Press*, June 30, 1986.

Cook, Ron. "Once a Draft Bust, Clint Hurdle Has Been Pivotal as Pirates Manager." *Pittsburgh Post-Gazette*, June 9, 2015.

Cook, Ron. "Thrift's Best Days Were with Pirates." *Pittsburgh Post-Gazette*, May 5, 2004.

Crasnick, Jerry. "When Pittsburgh Last Won." Available at ESPN.com: Baseball, August 31, 2013.

Curry, Jack. "Jealousy Led Bonds to Steroids, Authors Say." *New York Times*, March 8, 2006.

Donovan, Dan. "Stargell Act Tough One to Follow." *Pittsburgh Press*, September 7, 1982.

Dvorchak, Robert. "It's Hard to Cheer." *Pittsburgh Post-Gazette*, September 18, 2001.

Dvorchak, Robert. "Pirates Have Much to Celebrate after 13–3 Win." *Pittsburgh Post-Gazette*, September 28, 2002.

Dvorchak, Robert. "The Political Struggle over Financing PNC Park Went into Extra Innings." *Pittsburgh Post-Gazette*, April 15, 2001.

Edes, Gordon. "Smoltz Has Bucs in His Pocket." *Orlando Sun-Sentinel*, October 7, 1992.

Fainaru-Wada, Mark, and Lance Williams. *Game of Shadows: Barry Bonds, BALCO, and the Steroids Scandal that Rocked Professional Sports.* New York: Gotham, 2006.

Feeney, Charley. "Bill Robinson's Tenth-Inning Homer Beats Sutter in Rain Delayed Game." *Pittsburgh Post-Gazette*, April 15, 1980.

Feeney, Charley. "Leyland to Return Next Year; Thrift Sets Sights on '88." *Pittsburgh Post-Gazette*, August 26, 1986.

Feeney, Charley. "Pirates Must Make Some Tough Decisions." *Pittsburgh Post-Gazette*, August 22, 1986.

Feeney, Charley. "Thrift Due to Be Pirates GM." *Pittsburgh Post-Gazette*, October 8, 1985.

Fennessy, Dave. "Leyland Will Bring His Own Style to Bucs." *McKeesport (PA) Daily News*, November 21, 1985.

Finoli, David, and Bill Ranier, eds. *The Pittsburgh Pirates Encyclopedia.* Champaign: Sports Publishing, 2003.

Fitzpatrick, Frank. "Atlanta Takes 3–1 Series Lead." *Philadelphia Inquirer,* October 11, 1992.

Fitzpatrick, Frank. "Pirates Blast Braves." *Philadelphia Daily News,* October 14, 1992.

Gallo, D.J. "Pirates Look to Finish What They Start in 2012." Associated Press story, April 6, 2012.

Graham, Laurie. "Let's Go Bucs: Home, Family, and the Pittsburgh Pirates." In *Pittsburgh Sports: Stories from the Steel City,* edited by Randy Roberts. Pittsburgh: University of Pittsburgh Press, 2000.

Graham, Laurie. *Singing the City: The Bonds of Home in an Industrial Landscape.* Pittsburgh: University of Pittsburgh Press, 1998.

Hafner, Dan. "Pirates Win to Clinch NL East Title." *Los Angeles Times,* September 23, 1991.

Hertzel, Bob. "Bonds Demands Big Deal—Or Else." *Pittsburgh Press,* January 31, 1991.

Hertzel, Bob. "Bonds Signs Best One of All." *Pittsburgh Press,* February 2, 1992.

Hertzel, Bob. "Bonds Signs for $360,000." *Pittsburgh Press,* March 12, 1989.

Hertzel, Bob. "Feeling Left Out, Leyland Confronts His Bosses." *Pittsburgh Press,* March 21, 1992.

Hertzel, Bob. "Leyland Feeling at Home after Tough Rookie Year." *Pittsburgh Press,* December 10, 1986.

Hertzel, Bob. "Leyland: I Have a Long Way to Go." Front page. *Pittsburgh Press,* May 31, 1990.

Hertzel, Bob. "Leyland, Virdon Exchange Angry Words with Bonds." *Pittsburgh Press,* March 4, 1991.

Hertzel, Bob. "Pirates Show Off Best Stuff." *Pittsburgh Press,* July 6, 1990.

Hertzel, Bob. "Second Banana: That's the Way Leyland Likes It." *Pittsburgh Press,* April 4, 1988.

Holtzman, Jerome. "Leyland Defends Wakefield Going the Distance." *Chicago Tribune,* October 14, 1992.

Holtzman, Jerome. "Pirates Pluck Leyland." *Chicago Tribune,* November 21, 1985.

Karabell, Eric. "Who Should Be America's Team?" ESPN.com, August 9, 2011.

Keidan, Bruce. "Bonds Issuing Ultimatum for Pirates." *Pittsburgh Post-Gazette,* July 10, 1990.

Keidan, Bruce. "Bucs Could Lose Thrift over Contract Dispute." *Pittsburgh Post-Gazette*, October 21, 1987.

Keidan, Bruce. "Playing for Keeps." *Pittsburgh Post-Gazette*, September, 1, 1996.

Kent, Milton. "Braves Batter Pirates into Bind." *Baltimore Sun*, October 8, 1992.

Kent, Milton. "Pirates Finally Win a Sellout after Seventeen Games." *Baltimore Sun*, October 10, 1992.

Kepner, Tyler. "A Lasting Memory, a Remarkable Achievement." *New York Times*, August 27, 2011.

Kovacevic, Dejan. "Chuck Tanner Manager Who Led Pirates' Family to 1979 Championship." *Pittsburgh Post-Gazette*, February 12, 2011.

Lachimia, Jim. "PNC Park Becomes a Reality." *Pittsburgh Pirates 2001 Official Team Yearbook*. Elmont, NY: University Sports Publications, 2001.

Ladsin, William. "Barry Bonds: 'I'm the Best Newspaper Seller in Baseball.'" *Sport*, March 1992.

Leonard, Vince. "DD Man of the Year Thrift Next Wants Two Million Fans." *Pittsburgh Post-Gazette*, February 15, 1988.

Lieb, Frederick. *The Pittsburgh Pirates*. New York: G. P. Putnam, 1947.

Lorant, Stefan. *Pittsburgh: The Story of an American City*. Lenox, MA: Authors Edition, 1975.

Love, Steve. "The Stopper Does It Again." *Beaver County (PA) Times*, October 11, 1990.

Lubove, Roy. *Twentieth-Century Pittsburgh, Volume 1: Government, Business, and Environmental Change*. Pittsburgh: University of Pittsburgh Press, 1994.

Lubove, Roy. *Twentieth-Century Pittsburgh, Volume 2: The Post-Steel Era*. Pittsburgh: University of Pittsburgh Press, 1996.

Majors, Dan. "Dude, What's the 'Z'? Pirates Explain." *Pittsburgh Post-Gazette*, July 4, 2012.

Maske, Mark. "Pirates Pound Braves, 13–4, Send NLCS to Seventh Game." *Washington Post*, October 14, 1992.

McCollister, John. *The Bucs: The Story of the Pittsburgh Pirates*. Kansas City, MO: Addax, 1998.

McCollough, J. Brady. "Center Fielder Andrew McCutchen Is Now the Face of the Pirates." *Pittsburgh Post-Gazette*, March 31, 2013.

McCollough, J. Brady. "The Slide: The Moment That Begat a Legacy of Losing for the Pirates." *Pittsburgh Post-Gazette*, April 2, 2012.

Meade, Jeanne. "Thank You, Pirates." *Beaver County (PA) Times*, October 13, 1990.

Mehno, John. "An Unusual Outlook: The World through the Eyes of Andy Van Slyke." *Pirates Official 1991 Magazine and Scorecard.* Chicago: Sherman Media Company, 1991.

Menendez, Jenn. "Bonds' Healing Begins with MVP Presentation." *Pittsburgh Post-Gazette,* March 31, 2014.

Menendez, Jenn. "Turning Frowns Upside Down." In *Revival by the River: The Resurgence of the Pittsburgh Pirates.* Chicago: Triumph Books, 2013.

Meyer, Paul. "Batting Fourth Fine with Bonds." *Pittsburgh Post-Gazette,* February 2, 1992.

Meyer, Paul. "Bonds Gets Some Jeers, but Many Cheer Former Pirate." *Pittsburgh Post-Gazette,* May 2, 2001.

Meyer, Paul. "Bonilla Says Arbitration Has Changed Him." *Pittsburgh Post-Gazette,* February 10, 1990.

Meyer, Paul. "Bucs Retain Leyland, Thrift for Next Season." *Pittsburgh Post-Gazette,* October 2, 1987.

Meyer, Paul. "Manager Laments Plight of Team, Fans." *Pittsburgh Post-Gazette,* September 21, 1995.

Meyer, Paul. "Padres Pick Dunne." *Pittsburgh Post-Gazette,* December 5, 1989.

Meyer, Paul. "Saying Goodbye Would Be Hard." *Pittsburgh Post-Gazette,* September 21, 1995.

Meyer, Paul. "The Silence of the MVP." *Pittsburgh Post-Gazette,* February 26, 1991.

Meyer, Paul. "Sydnor W. 'Syd' Thrift Jr.: General Manager Who Resurrected the Pirates." *Pittsburgh Post-Gazette,* September 20, 2006.

Musick, Phil. "'El Syd' Embarks on Daring Adventure with Pirates." *Pittsburgh Press,* October 8, 1985.

Musick, Phil. "'El Syd' Embarks on Daring Adventure with Pirates." *Pittsburgh Press,* November 8, 1985.

Newhan, Ross. "Simmons Misses the Newspapers." *Los Angeles Times,* October 9, 1992.

Newhan, Ross. "Smoltz Shows He's Right Choice." *Los Angeles Times,* October 7, 1992.

Niedzielka, Amy. "Bonds Hasn't Changed, but His Image Undergoes Facelift." *Pittsburgh Post-Gazette,* August 12, 1991.

Nightengale, Bob. "It Seems the Pirates Have Double Faulted." *Los Angeles Times,* October 8, 1992.

Nightingale, David. "The Pirate Problem." *Sporting News,* September 9, 1985.

Osbourne, Bob. "Festive, for a While." *Pittsburgh Post-Gazette,* April 15, 1980.

"Outgoing CEO McClatchy Hailed for Keeping Pirates in Town." *Sports Business Daily*, July 8, 2007.

Parascenzo, Marino. "Leyland's Man of Year Night: Part Roast, but Pure Tribute." *Pittsburgh Post-Gazette*, February 11, 1991.

Pearlman, Jeff. *Love Me, Hate Me: Barry Bonds and the Making of an Antihero*. New York: HarperCollins, 2006.

Perrotto, John. "Bonds, Bonilla: Baby Boomers Bosom Buddies." *Beaver County (PA) Times*, May 22, 1988.

Perrotto, John. "Bonds Questions Why King Sat Out Game." *Beaver County (PA) Times*, October 11, 1990.

Perrotto, John. "Braggs' Ninth Inning Catch Helps Seal Pirates Fate." *Beaver County (PA) Times*, October 13, 1990.

Perrotto, John. "Bucs Pay the Price for Smith's Mistakes in Losing Game 3." *Beaver County (PA) Times*, October 9, 1990.

Perrotto, John. "Closing the Deal: Stan Belinda Established Himself out of the Pirate Bullpen." *Official 1992 Pittsburgh Pirates Magazine and Scorecard*. Pittsburgh: Pittsburgh Associates, 1992.

Perrotto, John. "First Playoff Game since '79 Draws 45,611, 13,000 Empty Seats." *Beaver County (PA) Times*, October 9, 1990.

Perrotto, John. "Last Chance, Season Rides on Drabek's Arm." *Beaver County (PA) Times*, October 10, 1990.

Perrotto, John. "Leyland Bids Farewell to Pittsburgh." *Beaver Valley (PA) Times*, September 18, 1996.

Perrotto, John. "Patterson, Bonilla Combine to Put Out Reds' Fire in Ninth." *Beaver County (PA) Times*, October 11, 1990.

Perrotto, John. "Trade Rumors Swirling around Bonds." *Beaver Valley (PA) Times*, February 10, 1991.

Perry, Dayn. "Regrets, I've Had a Few: A Tour of the Pirates' Twenty-Year Drought." cbssports.com, September 9, 2013.

Peterson, Richard, ed. *The Pirates Reader*. Pittsburgh: University of Pittsburgh Press, 2003.

Peterson, Richard. *Pops: The Willie Stargell Story*. Chicago: Triumph Books, 2013.

Pittsburgh Joe [pseud.]. "Can't Beat Pirates versus Reds." ESPN.com, updated May 26, 2005.

Pittsburgh Post-Gazette. *Revival by the River: The Resurgence of the Pittsburgh Pirates*. Chicago: Triumph Books, 2013.

Plaschke, Bill. "Drabek Not Quite Ready Yet." *Los Angeles Times*, October 14, 1991.

Plaschke, Bill. "Pirates' Jackson Recalls Hard Times." *Los Angeles Times*, October 7, 1992.

Plaschke, Bill. "Reds Advance to Series, with a Catch." *Los Angeles Times*, October 13, 1990.

Pomerantz, Gary. "The City of Chumps." *New York Post*, July 1, 1985.

Prisuta, Mike. "After Three Games, Bucs' Big Guns Are Still Firing Blanks." *Beaver County (PA) Times*, October 9, 1990.

Prisuta, Mike. "Larkin Wants to Keep Rijo, Dibble Quiet." *Beaver County (PA) Times*, October 10, 1990.

Reaves, Joey. "Bonds, Walk Give Pirates New Life." *Chicago Tribune*, October 12, 1992.

Reaves, Joey. "Pirates Rookie Stops Braves." *Chicago Tribune*, October 10, 1992.

Regalado, Samuel O. *Viva Baseball! Latin American Players and Their Special Hunger.* Urbana: University of Illinois Press, 1998.

Reiter, Ben. "Love Is in the Air: The Play-Off Bound Pirates and Their Sharknado Bullpen." *Sports Illustrated*, July 22, 2013.

Rendleman, Sam, and Rob Ruck. "The Education of Kevin McClatchy." *Pittsburgh Magazine*, April 1997.

Ritter, Lawrence S. *The Glory of Their Times.* New York: William Morrow, 1984.

Roberts, Randy, ed. *Pittsburgh Sports: Stories from the Steel City.* Pittsburgh: University of Pittsburgh Press, 2000.

Robinson, Alan. "Bonds' Name Absent from Doughty's List." Associated Press, December 5, 1988.

Robinson, Alan. "Bonds: Reaction to Bonilla Shows Racism." Associated Press, June 9, 1992.

Robinson, Alan. "Leyland's Outburst Inspired All Managers." Associated Press, March 7, 1991.

Robinson, Alan. "Pirates Hire Ex-Dodger Skipper Tracy as New Manager." Associated Press, October 11, 2005.

Robinson, Alan. "Pirates May Lose Players to Free Agency." *Gettysburg (PA) Times*, March 23, 1990.

Rushin, Steve. "Bonds Away: Bonds Powers the Pirates to Baseball's Fastest Start." *Sports Illustrated*, May 4, 1992.

Sanserino, Michael. "MLB Admits Error in Tuesday's Pirates-Braves Game." *Pittsburgh Post-Gazette*, July 28, 2011.

Sexton, Joe. "Invincibility of Avery Unravels in First Inning." *New York Times*, October 12, 1992.

Sexton, Joe. "Mets Sign Bonilla for $29 Million, Making Him Richest in Baseball." *New York Times*, December 3, 1991.

Sexton, Joe. "Pirates Are Hanging by Wakefield's Fingertips." *New York Times*, October 9, 1992.

Sexton, Joe. "Van Slyke Makes a Point with His Bat." *New York Times*, October 10, 1992.

Skirboll, Aaron. *The Pittsburgh Cocaine Seven: How a Ragtag Group of Fans Took the Fall for Major League Baseball.* Chicago: Chicago Review Press, 2010.

Smizik, Bob. "About That Pirates' Payroll." *Pittsburgh Post-Gazette*, October 22, 2014.

Smizik, Bob. "Bonds Gets Head Start on Clemente's Greatness." *Pittsburgh Post-Gazette*, April 14, 1992.

Smizik, Bob. "Buck Night Crowd Gives Hope for the Future." *Pittsburgh Press*, April 18, 1985.

Smizik, Bob. "Give Him a Break, Don't Boo Bonds." *Pittsburgh Post-Gazette*, April 7, 1991.

Smizik, Bob. "It's the Same Old, Same Old." *Pittsburgh Post-Gazette*, September 26, 2007.

Smizik, Bob. "Leyland Gets the Call from Pirates." *Pittsburgh Press*, November 21, 1985.

Smizik, Bob. "Nutting Makes Himself Visible at Long Last." *Pittsburgh Post-Gazette*, January 13, 2007.

Smizik, Bob. "The Pirates May Return, but Fans Must Come Back." *Pittsburgh Post-Gazette*, September 21, 1995.

Smizik, Bob. "Pirates' Priority: Keeping Leyland Happy." *Pittsburgh Post-Gazette*, September 9, 1990.

Smizik, Bob. "Remember McClatchy as Man Who Saved Pirates." *Pittsburgh Post-Gazette*, July 6, 2007.

Smizik, Bob. "Seeing Pirates Bend for Others Hardens Bonilla." *Pittsburgh Press*, April 1, 1991.

Smizik, Bob. "Thrift Made Some Mistakes, But Don't Sell His Salvage Job Short." *Pittsburgh Press*, May 26, 1989.

Smizik, Bob. "Unpopular Fact: Bonds Best Pirate." *Pittsburgh Post-Gazette*, May 2, 2001.

Smizik, Bob. "Why Thrift?" *Pittsburgh Press*, November 8, 1985.

Solomon, Alan. "Healthy Pirates Boast Edge over Reds in NLCS." *Chicago Tribune*, October 4, 1990.

Solomon, Alan. "Pirates Rally, Win NL Opener." *Chicago Tribune*, October 5, 1990.

Solomon, Alan. "Reds Gun Down the Pirates." *Chicago Tribune*, October 10, 1990.

Solomon, Alan. "Reds One Win from World Series, Relievers, Outfielders Stifle Pirates." *Chicago Tribune*, October 10, 1990.

Solomon, Alan. "Reds' Win Kissed by the Sun." *Chicago Tribune*, October 6, 1990.

The Sports Encyclopedia: Baseball. Edited by David Neft et al. New York: Grosset and Dunlap, 1974.

Stargell, Willie, and Tom Bird. *Willie Stargell: An Autobiography*. New York: Harper, 1984.

Stevens, David. "Atlanta Braves." *Encyclopedia of Major League Baseball Clubs Volume I The National League*, edited by Steven A. Riess. Westport, CT: Greenwood Press, 2006.

Trotter, Joe L., and Jared N. Day. *Race and Renaissance: African Americans in Pittsburgh since World War II*. Pittsburgh: University of Pittsburgh Press, 2010.

Vanwyndarden, Bruce. "A Man for All Seasons." *Pittsburgh Magazine*, April 1988.

Verdi, Bob. "Leyland Quickly Gives Avery His Due." *Chicago Tribune*, October 17, 1991.

Verdi, Bob. "Pirates Weakened by Averyitis." *Chicago Tribune*, October 17, 1991.

Wakefield, Tim, with Tony Massarotti. *Knuckler: My Life with Baseball's Most Confounding Pitch*. New York: Houghton Mifflin, 2011.

Will, George F. *Men at Work: The Craft of Baseball*. New York: Harper, 1990.

"World Series Ticket Rush Swamps Pirate Officials." In *The Pirates Reader*, ed. Richard Peterson. Pittsburgh: University of Pittsburgh Press, 2003.

Zinsser, William. *Spring Training*. New York: Harper Row, 1989.

INTERVIEWS (NOTES IN POSSESSION OF THE AUTHORS)

Blass, Steve. Authors' telephone interview, November 2014.

Bream, Sid. Authors' telephone interview, November 2014.

Brown, Greg. Authors' telephone interview, November 2014.

Coles, Darnell. Authors' telephone interview, November 2014.

Collier, Gene. Authors' telephone interview, November 2014.

Drabek, Doug. Authors' telephone interview, November 2014.

Frattare, Lanny. Authors' telephone interview, November 2014.

Kipper, Bob. Authors' telephone interview, November 2014.

Landrum, Bill. Authors' telephone interview, November 2014.

LaValliere, Mike. Authors' telephone interview, November 2014.

Leyland, Jim. Authors' telephone interview, November 2014.

Meyer, Paul. Authors' personal and telephone interview, November 2014.

Patterson, Bob. Authors' telephone interview, November 2014.

Pearlman, Jeff. Authors' telephone interview, November 2014.

Reich, Sam. Authors' telephone interview, November 2014.

Slaught, Don. Authors' telephone interview, November 2014.

Smith, Zane. Authors' telephone interview, November 2014.

Wagner, Paul. Authors' telephone interview, November 2014.

Walk, Bob. Authors' telephone interview, November 2014.

Wehner, John. Authors' telephone interview, November 2014.

OTHER SOURCES

Baseball Almanac, Inc. *Baseball Almanac.* Online at www.baseball-almanac .com/.

Historical Society of Western Pennsylvania documentaries for 1990, 1991, 1992 Pirate seasons. Produced and narrated by Rob King. Housed in the Heinz History Center.

Page 2, ESPN. *The World Series 100th Anniversary,* 2003.

Pittsburgh Pirates. *Pittsburgh Pirates 1988 Media Guide.*

Pittsburgh Pirates. *Pittsburgh Pirates 1992 Media Guide.*

Pittsburgh Pirates. *Pittsburgh Pirates 2007 Media Guide.*

Pittsburgh Pirates. *Pittsburgh Pirates 1991 Official Yearbook.*

Society for American Baseball Research. *SABR Baseball Biography Project.* Online at www.sabr.org/bioproject/.

Sports Reference LLC. *Baseball-Reference.* Online at www.baseball-reference .com/.

INDEX